Road to the Isles

Also by Derek Cooper

Skye

Hebridean Connection

Snail Eggs and Samphire

Road to the Isles

Travellers in the Hebrides 1770–1914

DEREK COOPER

MACMILLAN

First published 1979 by Routledge & Kegan Paul Ltd

This edition published 2002 by Macmillan
an imprint of Pan Macmillan Ltd
Pan Macmillan, 20 New Wharf Road, London N1 9RR
Basingstoke and Oxford
Associated companies throughout the world
www.panmacmillan.com

ISBN 0 333 90100 2

1 3 5 7 9 8 6 4 2

A CIP catalogue record for this book is available from
the British Library.

Typeset by SetSystems Ltd, Saffron Walden, Essex
Printed and bound in Great Britain by
Mackays of Chatham plc, Chatham, Kent

Contents

ONE: 1770–1790
9

A ruinous distillation prevales ~ *A few dozen of fish-hooks would have made them happy* ~ *Tales founded on impudence and nurtured by folly* ~ *A man of a most dreadful appearance* ~ *The pleasure of going where nobody goes* ~ *Their chaussure is economical for they wear neither shoes nor stockings* ~ *The seas seemed to be in perpetual convulsions* ~ *Macleod is at present in India* ~ *A good country and very improveable*

TWO: 1790–1810
31

A messy roof supported by tremendous pillars ~ *The West India fleet arrived in full view* ~ *A short walk sobered us completely* ~ *Thus blest in primal innocence they live* ~ *A compound of rotten fish, filth of all sorts and stinking sea-fowl* ~ *The door was split in pieces* ~ *They pass the long winter nights in great mirth and glee* ~ *Small clouds flew with amazing velocity* ~ *Spirits, wine and fruit in great abundance* ~ *Their chief is their world*

Contents

Contents

Contents

Acknowledgements

This has been a work of digging and delving and my labours have been lightened by many people who have drawn my attention to manuscripts or privately printed works which I would otherwise not have seen. I owe an especial thanks to Donald Hope, FLA, the Merton Borough Librarian, and his assistants, in particular Linda Davis and Linda Pegler, who quarried on my behalf to great purpose. I am also grateful to Margaret Gillies, librarian in Portree, who showed me the unpublished manuscript of *A Childhood in Skye*, and its author, Isobel Macdonald, who has kindly allowed me to quote from it. Similarly I am indebted to Mary Jean St Clair for the extracts from the so far unpublished diary of her grandmother, Alice Liddell.

And as always a very deep thank you to my wife Janet without whom this book would neither have been started nor finished.

DEREK COOPER

Portree, Isle of Skye

The Travellers

Sir Joseph Banks

Thomas Pennant

Moses Griffiths

Dr Samuel Johnson

Dr John Walker

Barthélémy Faujus de Saint Fond

William Thornton

John Knox

Abram

Dr Thomas Garnett

Bishop Uno von Troil

John Stoddart

Henry Brougham

Martin Martin, Gent.

Dr John Leyden

James Hogg

Rev. James Hall

John Spencer-Stanhope

John Macculloch

Sir Walter Scott

Lord Cockburn

William Daniell, RA

Dr James Johnson

Rev. Charles Lesingham Smith

Professor David James Forbes

A. P. Abraham

Sheriff Alexander Nicolson

Lawrence and Charles Pilkington

Joseph Mitchell

Lachlan Maclean

Allan Fullarton

Charles R. Baird

Catherine Sinclair

Sir Archibald Geikie

Rev. Thomas Grierson

Robert Carruthers

Sir Thomas Dick Lauder

James Wilson

Hugh Miller

Robert Somers

Queen Victoria

Rev. George Hely Hutchinson
('Sixty One')

John Colquhoun

Richard Ayton	Sir Randal Roberts
John Keats	Lady Macaskill
Felix Mendelssohn	Thomas Brassey
L. A. Necker de Saussure	Osgood Hanbury Mackenzie
Lord Teignmouth	Charles Bond
Beriah Botfield	Charles Richard Weld
George and Peter Anderson	Walter Cooper Dendy
J. M. W. Turner, RA	Alexander Smith
William Wordsworth	Robert Buchanan
William Macgillivray	W. Anderson Smith
R. Angus Smith	Frances Murray
John Inglis ('The Governor')	Charles Fraser-Macintosh
J. Ewing Ritchie	Hector Rose Mackenzie
John T. Reid	Robert Connell
T. Sidney Cooper, RA	Joseph and Elizabeth
Tina Brooke	Robins Pennell
Bell Munro	W. Scott Dalgliesh
Alice Liddell	Margaret Ismay
W. Bromley-Davenport	D. W. Logie
Alexander Shand	Norman Heathcote
Malcolm Ferguson	Ada Goodrich Freer
Captain J. T. Newall	F. G. Rea
Charles Peel	D. T. Holmes
'Nauticus'	Clifton Johnson
Constance Gordon Cumming	Lady Macdonald of the Isles

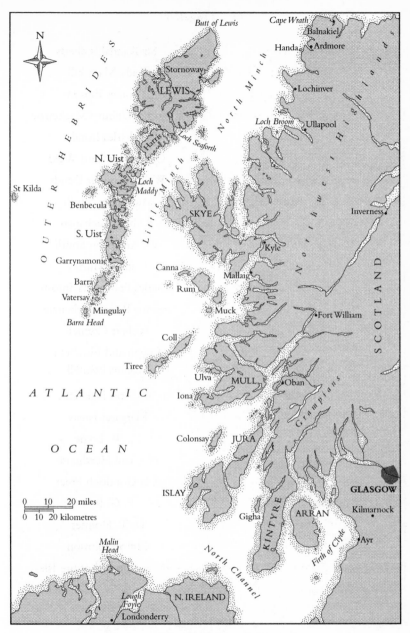

**Map 1   The Western Seaboard –
Cape Wrath to the Mull of Kintyre**

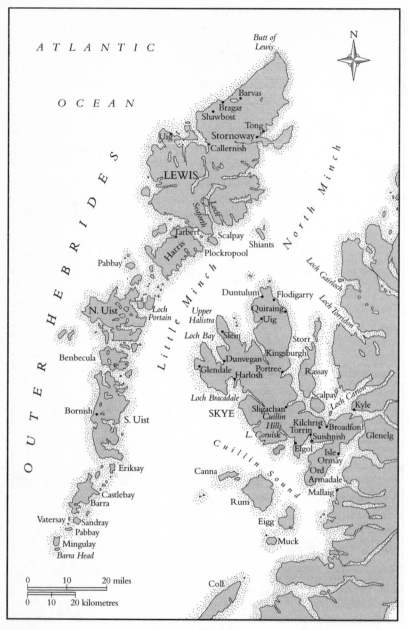

Map 2 The Hebrides

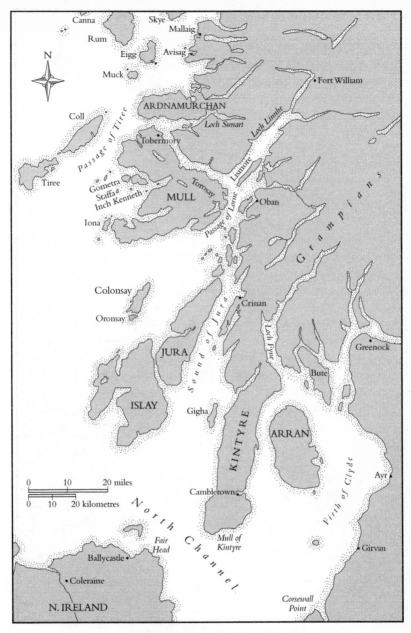

N

Canna
Skye
Rum
Mallaig
Eigg
Avisag
Muck

ARDNAMURCHAN
Fort William

Coll
Loch Sunart
Tobermory
Loch Linnhe

Tiree

Gometra
Staffa
Inch Kenneth
Torosay
MULL
Lismore
Oban

Iona
Passage of Lorne

Grampians

Colonsay
Crinan

Oronsay
Greenock

Sound of Jura
JURA
Loch Fyne
Bute

ISLAY
Gigha
KINTYRE
ARRAN

0   10   20 miles
0   10   20 kilometres
Ayr

North Channel
Cambletown
Firth of Clyde

Fair
Head
Mull of
Kintyre
Ballycastle
Girvan

• Coleraine

N. IRELAND
Corsewall
Point

Passage of Tiree

Map 3   Ardnamurchan and the Southern Isles

Introduction

In 1768 Captain James Cook set sail in the *Endeavour* for the South Seas. He was accompanied by the naturalist Sir Joseph Banks; the main business of their voyage was to make an observation of the transit of Venus for the Royal Society. It would be another four years before Banks, on his way to Iceland, would land on Staffa and make the first measurements of that remarkable island. Banks had circumnavigated the world and yet lying undiscovered a few miles off the coast of Scotland was a unique marvel of nature.

'Compared to this,' Banks wrote, 'what are the cathedrals or the palaces built by men! Mere models or playthings, imitations as diminutive as his works will always be when compared to those of nature. Where now is the boast of the architect! Regularity, the only part in which he fancied himself to exceed his mistress, Nature, is here found in her possession, and here it has been for ages undescribed.'

When Samuel Johnson finally made his celebrated journey to the Hebrides he, too, realized that he was bound for a part of the world which few outsiders had ever penetrated. 'To the southern inhabitants of Scotland,' he said, 'the state of the mountains and the islands is equally known with that of Borneo and Sumatra: of both they have only heard a little, and guess the rest.'

The Hebrides still remained largely unvisited by the new breed of eighteenth-century travellers and explorers – men of liberal education and scientific curiosity. I have chosen to begin this book in the 1770s because up to then very little had indeed been written about the Western Islands. The two most authoritative source books (one compiled by Dean Monro in 1549 and the other by Martin Martin in 1695) contained a great deal

1

of hearsay and disputable information which was copied and not infrequently misquoted by later writers.

When Boswell and Johnson looked around for a reliable guide to the Hebrides, Martin's book was the most recent – but that was rather like taking an eighty-year-old Baedeker to Paris today. No wonder that Boswell pronounced it to be 'a very imperfect performance'.

For many years to come journeying to the Islands was to remain a daunting and intrepid adventure; not something one undertook without special preparations. Stornoway was not only as far from London as Stavanger, Copenhagen or Prague, but was almost equally alien. John Keats, arriving in the west of Scotland in 1818, was able to report quite truthfully to his brother in Hampstead that he was 'for the first time in a country where a foreign language is spoken'.

When travellers wrote pejoratively of 'the natives' they accurately described the enormous gulf that existed between themselves and the Hebridean islanders with their half-Norse, half-Celtic ancestry, their Gaelic culture and language, and a social system quite unlike any other in Europe.

The visitors were almost without exception well-educated, well-fed and well-shod; the visited were soon to be faced with tribulations almost Biblical in their severity. The lean years of the nineteenth century were to seem unending, with famine and destitution recurring as frequently as influenza.

The old clan system, a kind of Celtic *Cosa Nostra*, had withered under the frosty Act of 1747 which, in the post-Culloden reprisals, disarmed the clans, proscribed Highland dress and abolished the feudal power of the chiefs. The chiefs themselves became absentee landlords; their agents, the estate factors, doubled and trebled rents, and the land which had once been tilled was put to sheep.

For a large part of the eighteenth century the burning of seaweed to produce potash had brought an artificial prosperity to the islands. Although much of the profit went into the pockets of the lairds and those few chiefs who still possessed land, there was plenty of work and the population rapidly increased. With the failure of this kelp industry the landowners faced ruin. Estates changed hands and rack-renting forced more and more families to abandon their homes.

It was as if, having created so much beauty and grandeur, God felt that this archipelago of Edens must also be afflicted with more than its fair share of misery. The succession of bad winters, the failure of the potato crop, the departure of the herring from the sea lochs – all these difficulties could have been surmounted. What eventually became intolerable was the deliberate attempt in many islands to clear the people from the land. By an unrelenting process of harassment, ground which had once produced food and supported families was turned into more profitable sporting estates. Any activity which hindered the natural increase of game or the pleasures of the chase was prohibited and the islanders, deprived of even the most minimal rights and privileges, found that their last and only freedom lay in leaving.

Nowhere in Britain in the mid-nineteenth century were people more oppressed or more cruelly treated. The spread of pauperism throughout the Hebrides, the devastation of the land and the ousting of the people was motivated by greed and condoned by a Kafka-esque social order in which the laird was also the magistrate. To hint at injustice was to risk summary eviction.

The transportation of entire communities to the inhospitable shores of eastern Canada continued well into mid-Victorian times, but surprisingly few people either noticed it or indeed were disturbed by it. The English have always had a great capacity for concerning themselves with injustices anywhere but on their own doorstep.

In the year that the liberal drawing-rooms of London were scandalized by Harriet Beecher Stowe's *Uncle Tom's Cabin* and its revelations of iniquities in the Deep South of America, Colonel Gordon of Cluny was forcibly depopulating his estates in South Uist and Barra.

'The duplicity and art which was used,' wrote an eye-witness, 'in order to entrap the unwary natives, is worthy of the craft and cunning of an old slave-trader. Were you to see the racing and chasing of policemen, constables and ground officers, pursuing the outlawed natives, you would think, only for their colour, that you had been, by some miracle, transported to the banks of the Gambia, on the slave coast of Africa.'

It was an era in which Palmerston could send gunboats to the Piraeus to protect a solitary Levantine but when it came to the needs of people nearer home the principles of *civis Romanus sum* remained uninvoked. If there was little sympathy with the victims of land-mongering in the Hebrides, it must be remembered that the rich regarded poverty as a self-inflicted disability. Those who insisted on remaining where they were not wanted, despite the offer of assisted passages and generous grants of land in the colonies, deserved what they got. No one was to blame except their stubborn selves.

Few travellers who came to the Hebrides questioned the system which had produced such extremes of affluence and poverty. The house guests at the castles of Armadale, Dunvegan, Kinloch and Amhuinnsuidhe had probably no idea of the squalor and hardship which were the common lot. Even when unrest did eventually break out, it was assumed that the simple-minded islanders were being misled by political agitators. The all too visible poverty was ascribed to fecklessness and a congenital indolence.

Gradually over the years emigration, like a pernicious anaemia, slowly drained the life away. On the million acres of the Inner Hebrides there are today only 15,000 people; on the 700,000 acres of the Outer Hebrides just 30,000. In all those Western Isles all that is left is a population half the size of the seaside town of Hove and, as in Hove, the elderly outnumber the young.

I'm never sure whether it's imagination or something less easily explained, but there are times in some emptied glen when I can almost feel the physical presence of the dispossessed.

And even if you can't feel the past then you can see signs of it all around you: the tumbled stones of the old black houses, the overgrown peat banks, the lazy-beds on the rocky hillsides where potatoes and corn were coaxed out of the thin soil, the cart tracks over the moors, the remains of ruined mills and steadings.

There are themes which recur throughout the period this book covers. The weather, of course, is always to the fore: the rain that could keep a party housebound for days or rot crops in the ground, the winds that blew your ship to unwanted destinations, the storms that prevented you from taking to the sea at all. There is a constant preoccupation with finding somewhere clean and dry to sleep and something reasonable to eat, an irritation with midge bites and missed boats, an exasperation at the obtuseness of those who cannot or will not understand simple requests in English.

But most remarkable of all is the way in which these remote and often inaccessible islands have exercised so magnetic an attraction on so many travellers – a fascination quite out of proportion to their size and quite unrivalled anywhere else in Europe.

Perhaps it's something to do with the quality of the light, the movement of cloud and sea. And perhaps it's something more than that; an alchemy which defies analysis. I have tried to avoid too many descriptions of scenery because the scenery is all still there, gloriously unchanged. I have gone for the itch of bedbugs not the grandeur of the glens and bens, remembering all the time that this is not necessarily how the Hebrides were, but only how travellers thought they were. I doubt that any of them saw more than a fraction of what was really going on. Out of a perverse courtesy they were all too often given only the answers they expected to receive.

And sometimes they were unintentionally confused. There is, in the recollections of the elderly, a tendency to skip generations and mix fact and myth so that one can often be hearing about totally different periods of time in the same sentence. Talking to an old man once he told me how 'they' had burned all the trees down on a certain island. From his earlier remarks I thought he meant Cumberland's soldiers. A few seconds later it emerged that he was referring to the Vikings.

There is no doubt that much of the topography of the Hebrides is uncannily timeless. In a landscape dominated by ancient dolmens and standing stones, Iron Age duns and brochs and the ruins of medieval castles, it is not they which constitute an anachronism – it's the breeze-block council houses and prefab bungalows of our time which seem an alien and imper-manent affront to the past.

In the last two centuries the islands have really changed very little. I was reminded of this a few months ago when I walked down the overgrown drive of a house that had been allowed to fall into decay on a Hebridean island. In the stables an elegant gig had crumbled where it stood and collapsed among the spokes of its own wheels. The rooms of the house contained strangely disparate relics. A 1703 edition of Martin Martin, a copy of the 1884 Napier Commission's report, a pile of *Morning Posts* dating from 1912, puffins stuffed by Victorian taxidermists, epaulettes in a rusty japanned box, several ullaged flagons of Deidesheimer hock of the 1865 vintage, ruined bamboo steamer chairs, oleographs and oil stoves.

I had never, outside an antique shop, stood amid such an emotive assemblage of bygones and random rubbish. There was a stillness outside; only the truffle odour of dry rot and decay within. Under a toppled sofa lay a broken moustache cup, a leather case of cut-throat razors, an empty tin of Carnation milk. The eye darted back and forth from one century to another. Here an Augustan portrait of a sometime beauty with curled ringlets, there a couple of wire-wickered seltzer syphons. Stag's heads, rifles, patent devices for trapping mice, a wind-up gramophone, all lay hotch-potch on the plaster-sprinkled floors. It was a still-life which marshalled up the past with vivid precision.

But if you feel the past is growing before your eyes in the pages that follow, have a care. There has always been a mischievous and entirely understandable refusal among Hebrideans to be intimidated by visitors, however pompously they present themselves: there is a repertoire of anecdotes in which the patronizing tourist is confused, misled or subtly put down.

A friend of mine who has travelled widely round the world, and indeed when he is not in his native Skye is to be found wintering in the Mediterranean, was weeding his sister's garden in Portree a few summers ago when a couple of visitors stopped to pass the time of day with him. Grey-haired and wearing old gardening clothes, he straightened and gave them a welcoming smile, the very picture of a dignified old crofter.

'A beautiful day,' said the husband, carefully enunciating his words in the patient manner of one addressing the mentally defective.

'Very nice, chust,' my friend replied, swiftly sizing up the situation.

'You like gardening?' asked the wife brightly.

'Well I do, chust, and that's a fact!'

'Isn't that nice,' the wife said, and then to her husband, 'Ask him if he ever gets off the island.'

'Do you ever leave the island?'

My friend nodded theatrically to indicate that he had understood the question and then appeared to rack his enfeebled brain. 'Well now,' he said, 'I did stretch down to the ferry at Kyleakin once. It was very interesting to see all the strange peoples there, chust!'

'Very good,' said the husband. 'Quite a little adventure. Well done!'

When my friend recounted the incident he said he thought it had given them great pleasure to meet an idiot. 'It must have made them feel their trip to the Hebrides hadn't been in vain!'

So. Tread warily from now on; for these pages may well be mined with the irreverent and subversive humour that is part of every Hebridean's survival kit.

ONE: 1770–1790

'ATTEMPT TO STEER FOR the island of *Ilay*, but in vain.' The year is 1772, the traveller Thomas Pennant, and like many another after him he is at the mercy of the wind and the tide. It is only twenty-six years since the Jacobite uprising and the defeat of Prince Charles Edward Stuart at Culloden. In a few days' time Pennant will be lodged in the very bed that the Prince, Cumberland's troops at his heels, used at Kingsburgh House in Skye. The following year Dr Johnson will occupy the famous bed. The tourist rush is starting.

Already emigration which is to reach its peak in the following century has begun, and the reasons are painfully apparent. As Pennant's boat edges its way into the Small Isles of Jura they see another boat filled with women and children cross over from Jura 'to collect their daily wretched fare, limpets and perriwinkles'.

In a good summer there was usually enough barley and oats to feed the people but all too often the grain was converted into whisky which was both a currency and a consolation to high and low. In Islay where the traditions of whisky-making were being illicitly laid Pennant noted that 'a ruinous distillation prevales', so much so that the people were drinking more of their barley than they ate, much preferring a dram to a bannock.

Throughout his account of the Hebrides Pennant is careful to distinguish between the lairds and tacksmen,* who entertained him and the natives. When describing the physical

---

* Tacksman – a man who leases a large 'tack' or piece of land and then sublets it in small farms.

attributes of the ordinary people he wrote as clinically as William Marsden was to do ten years later when he visited Sumatra.

Here is Marsden on Sumatran women: 'Chastity prevails more perhaps among these than any other people. Adultery is punishable by fine; but the crime is rare.'

Here is Pennant on the women of Jura: 'They are very prolific and very often bear twins; . . . there is now living a woman of eighty who can run down a sheep.' In the age of Rousseau people welcomed information about the noble savage whether she dwelt in Sumatra or the Hebrides.

In Islay Pennant notes that at half-past one on the morning of 4 July he can read the small print of a newspaper with no difficulty and in Jura encounters 'epidemical dropsies and cancers' which he puts down to the natural effects of bad food.

He visits Oronsay, Colonsay and Iona, and then in Canna is impressed by the apparent prosperity of the island:

> verdant and covered with hundreds of cattle: both sides gave a full idea of plenty, for the verdure was mixed with very little rock, and scarcely any heath: but a short conversation with the natives soon dispelled this agreeable error: they were at this very time in such want that numbers for a long time had neither bread nor meal for their poor babes: fish and milk was their whole subsistence at this time: the first was a precarious relief for, besides the uncertainty of success, to add to their distress their stock of fish-hooks was almost exhausted; and to ours, that it was not in our power to supply them. The ribbons, and other trifles I had brought would have been insults to people in distress. I lamented that my money had been so uselessly laid out; for a few dozens of fish-hooks or a few pecks of meal would have made them happy.

Sickness, Pennant was told, seldom visited Canna, except for smallpox, which came upon them every twenty years or so. In matters of religion, eighteenth-century Canna resembled twentieth-century Fair Isle. On Fair Isle the people, lacking a resident minister, worship one Sunday in the Church of Scotland kirk and the following Sunday in the Methodist chapel. Both the minister and the 'popish Priest' of Canna lived on Eigg.

> I admire [said Pennant] the moderation of their congregations who attend the preaching of either indifferently as they happen to arrive. As the Scotch are economists in religion, I would recommend to them the practice of one of the little Swiss mixed cantons who, through mere frugality, kept but one divine; a moderate honest fellow who steering clear of controversial points, held forth to the Calvinist flock on one part of the day, and to his Catholic on the other. He lived long among them much respected, and died lamented.

Here for the first time Pennant encountered practitioners of Second Sight. There was a Molly Maclean who had the power of foreseeing events through a well-scraped blade bone of mutton:

> Some time ago she took up one and pronounced that five graves were soon to be opened; one for a grown person: the other four for children; one of which was to be of her own kind: and so it fell out. I must not omit a most convenient species of second sight, possessed by a gentleman of a neighbouring isle, who foresees all visitors, so has time to prepare accordingly: but enough of these tales, founded on impudence and nurtured by folly.

And so to Skye which, says Pennant, 'has not in it a single town or village. But what is a greater wonder, there is not a town from *Campbelton* in the Firth of *Clyde* to *Thurso* at the end of *Cathness*, a tract of above two hundred miles.'

Pennant stays with the celebrated Mackinnon of Coirechatachan, visits Talisker, rows across Loch Bracadale, examines the dun at Struan, and delivers a panegyric on the virtues of

Macleod of Dunvegan: 'he feels for the distresses of his people, and insensible of his own, with uncommon disinterestedness has relieved his tenants from their oppressive rents; and has received instead of the trash of gold, the treasure of warm affection and unfeigned prayer.'

For persons of substance like Pennant, and Boswell and Johnson who were to follow so shortly in his footsteps, a progress round the islands was accomplished within an all-embracing chain of hospitality. Departing from Skye at Duntulm, Pennant took leave of several gentlemen, 'who according to the worthy custom of these islands, convoyed us from place to place, and never left us till they had delivered us over to the next hospitable roof, or seen us safely embarked.'

Sheep had not arrived yet in the islands except for a few kept for domestic use; the main business was in the raising of cattle, but husbandry was haphazard: 'There is certainly much ill management in the direction of farms: a tacksman of fifty pounds a year often keeps twenty servants; the laziest of creatures, for not one will do the least thing that does not belong to his department.'

Pennant's first tour of the mainland of Scotland was published in 1771. It is not unlikely that the appearance of this book and the news that Pennant was about to bring out a book on his Hebridean travels encouraged Samuel Johnson to set off on his own Highland jaunt.

It was in May 1763 that Boswell was introduced to his life's work. 'A man', he recorded in his Journal, 'of a most dreadful appearance. He is a very big man, is troubled with sore eyes, the palsy and the King's Evil.* He is very slovenly in his dress and speaks with a most uncouth voice.'

Hardly a cheery companion to take on an arduous journey over rough tracks and even rougher seas. But from that first

---

* Scrofula, once thought to be curable by the royal touch. The last monarch to practise the superstition was Queen Anne who touched Johnson in 1712, to no avail.

meeting Boswell nurtured the hope of bearing his idol off to Edinburgh and thence to the western seaboard. His plans matured and Johnson arrived in the Scottish capital in mid-August 1773. During the next four days Boswell brought most of his friends and acquaintances to pay court to Johnson, but the one man in town who could have given them a great deal of help was not known to Boswell.

Dr John Walker, Professor of Natural History at Edinburgh University, had, from 1760 onwards, made a series of journeys to the Hebrides, two of them lasting from May until late December. In the course of the years, Walker claimed, flinging both modesty and grammar to the wind, 'a greater extent of these distant parts of the kingdom was surveyed, than what had probably ever been traversed by any former traveller'.

Unfortunately none of Walker's observations on his journeys had been published and Boswell was quite accurate in describing Martin Martin's account of the Hebrides as 'the only book upon the subject'. Walker's posthumous *Economical History of the Hebrides* is discursive on manure, tillage and the remedies for trembles, cling, breakshaw and scab, but it can hardly be described as riveting. I acquired a copy some ten years ago and when I came to look at it again a few days back I found, to my embarrassment, many of the pages still uncut.

But had the travellers spent an hour with Walker he could have told them that leaving their trip so late in the year was going to make progress from island to island extremely difficult and at times impossible. He could have told them too that they would be journeying back in time to a style of life uncorrupted by modern improvements:

> Knowing nothing better, they are easily pleased. The spades, ploughs, harrows and sledges, of the most feeble and imperfect kinds, with all their harnessing, are made by the farmer and his servants; as also the boats with all their tackle. The boat has a Highland plaid for a sail; the running rigging is made of leather thongs and willow twigs; and a

large stone and a heather rope serve for an anchor and cable; and all this, among a people of much natural ingenuity and perseverance: there is no fulling mill nor bleachfield; no tanner, maltster or dyer; all the yarn is dyed, and all the cloth fulled or bleached by the women on the farm: the grain for malt is steeped in sacks in the river; and the hides are tanned, and the shoes made at home.

Had Johnson and Boswell heard all this at first-hand from Dr Walker they might have been better prepared for the inadequacies and the discomfort they were occasionally to find, but they set off in good heart and a fortnight later reached the shores of Skye at Armadale where they were received by Sir Alexander and Lady Macdonald in what Boswell thought was a rather poor house for a chief. They had, he claimed, 'an illdressed dinner.' Both Johnson and Boswell were fond of their bellies and Boswell was even fonder of his booze; he tended to judge a table by the prodigality of the liquor. Sir Alexander rather let him down: 'I alone drank port wine. No claret appeared. We had indeed mountain* and Frontignac† and Scotch porter. But except what I did myself, there was no hospitable convivial intercourse, no ringing of glasses.'

On the following day Boswell attacked Sir Alexander for the meanness of his appearance and his failure to provide his wife with a maid. The meal still rankled:

> In short, I gave him a volley. He was thrown into a violent passion; said he could not bear it; called in my lady and complained to her, at the same time defending himself with considerable plausibility. Had he been a man of more mind, he and I must have had a quarrell for life. But I knew he would soon come to himself. We had moor-fowl for supper tonight, which comforted me.

---

* Wine made in the hills to the north and east of Malaga.
† A sweet wine made from muscat grapes in the Frontignan region of Languedoc.

On Sunday Boswell walked with his host to the factor's house where the party drank a couple of bowls of punch. It was dark by the time they got back: 'I drank freely of punch by way of being social, and after supper I drank freely of port by way of keeping off a *taedium vitae*. Altogether, I had too much.' He also had another row with Sir Alexander. It was a boisterous start to their Hebridean holiday.

From Armadale they moved to the house of Mackinnon of Coirechatachan. Here there were books, clean beds, and above all good food:

> We had for supper a large dish of minced beef collops, a large dish of fricassee of fowl, I believe a dish called fried chicken or something like it, a dish of ham or tongue, some excellent haddocks, some herrings, a large bowl of rich milk, frothed, as good a bread-pudding as I ever tasted, full of raisins and lemon or orange peel, and sillabubs made with port wine and in sillabub glasses. There was a good table-cloth with napkins; china, silver spoons, porter if we chose it, and a large bowl of very good punch.

At Raasay House, where they repaired after a few days, the hospitality was, if anything, even warmer: 'our reception', wrote Johnson, 'exceeded our expectations. We found nothing but civility, elegance and plenty. After the usual refreshments and the usual conversation, the evening came upon us.'

What usual refreshments? What usual conversations? Johnson was an exasperatingly reticent reporter of the trivial. You have to turn to Boswell for the answers. From him you get an instant action replay; the smell of the food and drink in Raasay House on the night of 8 September 1773:

> We found here coffee and tea in genteel order upon the table, as it was past six when we arrived: diet loaf, marmalade of oranges, currant jelly; some elegantly bound books on a large table, in short all the marks of improved life. We had a dram of excellent brandy, according to the Highland custom, filled round. They call it a *scalck*. On a sideboard

was served up directly, for us who had come off the sea, mutton chops and tarts, with porter, claret, mountain and punch. Then we took coffee and tea. In a little, a fiddler appeared and a little ball began.

There was a picnic on top of Duncaan of cold mutton, bread and cheese, brandy and punch, and then from Raasay they rowed back to Skye, dined at the inn in Portree, and moved on to meet the celebrated Flora Macdonald at Kingsburgh:

She was a little woman, of a mild and genteel appearance, mighty soft and well-bred. To see Mr Samuel Johnson salute Miss Flora Macdonald was a wonderful romantic scene to me. We had as genteel a supper as one would wish to see, in particular an excellent roasted turkey, porter to drink at table, and after supper claret and punch. But what I admired was the perfect ease with which everything went on. My *facility of manners*, as Adam Smith said of me, had fine play.

And then it was on to Dunvegan and so comfortable a reception that Johnson insisted on staying for eight days. From there they moved to Ullinish and Talisker, experiencing yet more kindness which was eclipsed by the final hospitality at Coirechatachan where Boswell, sharing bowl after bowl of punch with old 'Corry', finally fell fuddled into bed at five in the morning.

It was October by now and the winter gales were beginning. They set off from Armadale for Mull in a twelve-ton sailing vessel but as the weather worsened they had to abandon their plan and run for shelter on Coll. Here they stayed for ten days until the gale blew itself out and they were able to make for Tobermory. 'Well, sir,' said Boswell, 'this is the fourth of the Hebrides that we have been on.'

'Nay,' replied Johnson, 'we cannot boast of the number we have seen. We thought we should see many more. We thought of sailing about easily from island to island; and so we should, had we come at a better season; but we, being wise men, thought it should be summer all the year round where we were. However, sir, we have seen enough to give us a pretty good notion of the system of insular life.'

Both men were frequently discountenanced by the minimal concern shown for the niceties of life even in the finest houses. They stayed with Dr Maclean, who had written the history of his clan, and Dr Johnson was so impressed by the elegance that he cried to Boswell: 'You're not observing. This is the prettiest room we have seen since we came to the Highlands.' But when Boswell went up to bed, Joseph, his manservant, drew his attention to the sheets:

> I looked at them and was shocked at their dirtiness. I threw off only my boots and coat and waistcoat and put on my greatcoat as a night-gown, and so lay down. The mixture of brandy punch at the inn and rum punch here, joined with the comfortless bed, made me rest very poorly.

And there were frequent solecisms. Boswell had been shocked at Coirechatachan by the behaviour of Mr Macpherson, the minister:

> After I was in bed, the minister came up to go to his. The maid stood by and took his clothes and laid them carefully on a chair piece by piece, not excepting his breeches, before throwing off which he made water, while she was just at his back.

Johnson also had his surprises. On their way from Mull to Iona they spent a night on Ulva, and after a liberal supper were conducted to their bed chamber. 'I found an elegant bed of Indian cotton,' recorded Johnson, 'spread with fine sheets. The accommodation was flattering; I undressed myself, and felt my feet in the mire. The bed stood upon the bare earth, which a long course of rain had softened to a puddle.'

There were some strange meals too. On Inchkenneth they spent a night with a former military man, Sir Allan Maclean:

Sir Allan had made an apology at dinner that he had neither red wine nor biscuits, but that he expected both. Luckily the boat arrived with them this very afternoon. We had a couple of bottles of port and hard biscuits at night, after some roasted potatoes, which is Sir Allan's simple fare by way of supper.

At length, after nearly seven weeks in the Hebrides, they set foot on the holy isle of Iona. As Boswell put it:

the seeing of Mr Samuel Johnson at Icolmkill was what I had often imaged as a very venerable scene. A landscape or view of any kind is defective, in my opinion, without some human figures to give it animation. What an addition was it to Icolmkill to have the Rambler upon the spot! After we landed I shook hands with him cordially.

Johnson pottered about and took some measurements. The party slept in a barn and there was a noticeable contrast between what had been and what was. An 'illustrious island,' as Johnson put it, 'which was once the luminary of the Caledonian regions, whence savage clans and roving barbarians derived the benefits of knowledge and the blessings of religion.' And now?

The inhabitants are remarkably gross, and remarkably neglected: I know not if they are visited by any minister. The island, which was once the metropolis of learning and piety, has now no school for education, nor temple for worship; only two inhabitants that can speak English, and not one that can write or read.

While Boswell's account of their journey is gossipy and dedicated in the main to recounting the quips and quiddities of his scrofulous companion, Johnson produced a self-conscious public record of the impressions made on a Great Man by a wild place.

They didn't always see the same things. Johnson reckoned he'd seen worse weather off the coast of Sussex than ever he

saw in the Hebrides: 'I never saw very high billows.' Which is
strange because on the passage from Skye to Coll, Boswell
stood in great fear of his life. 'I saw tonight', he wrote, 'what
I never saw before, a prodigious sea with immense billows
coming upon a vessel, so as that it seemed hardly possible to
escape. There was something grandly horrible in the sight.'

While Boswell was praying fervently to God and weighing
up Dr Ogden's doctrine on the efficacy of intercession with
his own feeling that the petitions of an individual had little
influence with the Divinity, the sage of Bolt Court was lying
'in philosophic tranquillity with a greyhound at his back
keeping him warm'.

In a letter to his great friend Mrs Thrale, Johnson dismissed
the storm as 'a violent gust'. He was a traveller of considerable
resilience. Despite his cold and deafness at Dunvegan, his
nocturnal flatulence in Coll, his chronic weakness in the knees
and his constitutional melancholy he relished the adventure and
the almost royal reception which he was accorded in the
Hebrides:

> The hospitality of this remote region is like that of the
> golden age. We have found ourselves treated at every
> house as if we came to confer a benefit. Company is, I
> think, considered as a supply of pleasure and a relief of that
> tediousness of life which is felt in every place elegant or
> rude. I have no reason to complain of my reception, yet I
> long to be again at home. My eye is, I am afraid, not fully
> recovered, my ears are not mended, my nerves seem to
> grow weaker, and I have been otherwise not as well as I
> sometimes am, but think myself lately better. This Climate
> perhaps is not within my degrees of healthy latitude.

It had been a marathon journey. As he lay at Armadale on
6 September 1773, Johnson informed Mrs Thrale that he was
saluting her from the verge of European life: 'I have now the
pleasure of going where nobody goes, and of seeing what
nobody sees.' A year later Johnson's account of his monumental

journey was ready for the printers – it preceded Boswell's by ten years. Before publication, Dr William Hunter, who had an entrée to the royal presence, agreed to present a copy to George III. 'You must not tell anybody but Mr Thrale,' wrote Johnson to Mrs Thrale, 'that the King fell to reading the book as soon as he got it, when anything struck him, he read aloud to the Queen, and the Queen would not stay to get the King's book, but borrowed Dr Hunter's.'

Charlotte Sophia must have been easily pleased, for Johnson frequently fudged over his inadequate knowledge of the islanders with empty truisms: 'Their method of life,' he observed, 'neither secures them perpetual health nor exposes them to any particular diseases.'

And he was not long enough in the islands to speak of much with accuracy. 'From the autumnal to the vernal equinox,' he claimed, 'a dry day is hardly known, except when the showers are suspended by a tempest.' A patent nonsense; some of the dryest and sunniest weather in the islands occurs in the depths of winter.

Gaelic, which 200 years later is enjoying a healthy renaissance, he dismissed as 'the rude speech of a barbarous people who had few thoughts to express, and were content, as they conceived grossly, to be grossly understood'. Second Sight, on the other hand, appeared to pierce his rational armour:

> Mr Boswell's frankness and gaiety made everybody communicative and we heard many tales of these airy shows, with more or less evidence and distinctness . . . where we are unable to decide by antecedent reason, we must be content to yield to the force of testimony.

Where Pennant laughed at the tales of foreknowledge, Johnson took them with great seriousness:

> A gentleman told me that when he had once gone far from his own island, one of his labouring servants predicted his return, and described the livery of his attendant, which he

had never worn at home; and which had been, without any previous design, occasionally given him.

When the book was published a fortnight after it had received the royal seal of approval, it fossilized polite society's view of the Hebrides for a whole generation. But it was Sir Joseph Banks, not Samuel Johnson, who was instrumental in attracting the first eminent foreign visitor to the Hebrides.

Barthélémy Faujus de Saint Fond was born into a wealthy family in Montélimar in 1741. He studied law but forsook it for the more congenial pleasures of natural history; zoologist, botanist, mineralogist, he was excited by Sir Joseph Banks's account of the columnar cliffs and caves of Staffa which Pennant had published in his *Tour in Scotland*. Faujus set off for Staffa in 1784 and his first call on landing in England was on Banks, who, as President of the Royal Society and the inheritor of a considerable fortune, kept open house for all who cultivated the sciences.

Faujus pursued an inquisitive and rewarding journey north to Edinburgh and thence west to Oban where he engaged an open boat to take him to Mull. The weather late in the year, was not of the best, but fortunately for Faujus he was able to visit Staffa in almost perfect conditions and once there, 'I ceased not to view, to review, and to study this superb monument of nature, which in regard to its form bears so strong a resemblance to a work of art, though art can certainly claim no share in it'.

His companion on the expedition to Staffa was the American naturalist, William Thornton, who had studied in Edinburgh and Paris. Both men worked hard all day. They took measurements, made sketches and collected lavas, zoolites and other stones. At nine o'clock in the evening they were back on Mull where they had been offered hospitality by Mr Maclean of Torloisk, to whom the Duke of Argyll had given Faujus a letter of introduction.

Like Pennant, Boswell and Johnson before him, Faujus was

greatly impressed with island hospitality. On their arrival his party had been 'instantly overwhelmed with civilities, kindnesses and delicate attentions which made all our troubles disappear. Everyone was so prepossessing and so affable that from that moment we regarded ourselves as in our own family. How attractive is this country politeness, seasoned with the expressions and gestures of the most delicate feeling.'

And Faujus was not the first to note the strange juxtaposition of elegance set in wild and windswept landscapes; cultivated conversation within, the howling of the gale without. Maclean, a man of birth and fortune, was anchored at Torloisk not because he knew no better but out of preference. He had built himself what Faujus described as a 'commodious habitation in the modern style, without parade, but in which great neatness and quiet simplicity everywhere prevail'. But the Frenchman was intrigued by a nearby dry-stone cottage with its turf and heather roof. Why, he asked, did Maclean allow this hovel to remain? 'It was there,' Maclean told him, 'that I was born. That is the ancient habitation of my fathers; and I feel an inexpressible regard for this modest site, which reminds me of their virtues and frugal life.'

Life at Torloisk was far from frugal. Maclean's daughter played with accomplishment upon the harpsichord and there were several attractive ladies from Edinburgh in residence. The domestics were in Hebridean dress and the women had long flowing hair which they allowed to fall freely on their shoulders:

> Their chaussure is economical; for they wear neither shoes nor stockings; and in spite of the length of the winter, and the incessant wetness of the climate, though they go with their feet bare, and their heads uncovered, they yet have very fine teeth.

Faujus noted three different kinds of bread at Maclean's table:

The first which is a luxury for the country, is sea-biscuit, which vessels from Glasgow sometimes leave in passing. The second is made of oatmeal, kneaded without leaven and then spread with a rolling pin into round cakes about a foot in diameter and the twelfth part of an inch thick. These cakes are baked, or rather dried, on a thin plate of iron hung over the fire. This is the principal bread of such as are in easy circumstances.

The third kind of bread, preferred at breakfast and tea, was made of unleavened barley. Breakfast was taken at ten in the morning and on hearing the bell the quality made their way to the parlour where in front of a peat and coal fire was a table laid with slices of smoked beef, cheese of the country and English cheese on mahogany trays, fresh eggs, salted herrings, butter, milk and cream, currant jelly, blaeberry jam, tea, coffee and Jamaica rum. There was too, something which Faujus presumably had not encountered before: 'A sort of pap of oatmeal and water. In eating this thick pap, each spoonful is plunged alternately into cream which is always alongside.'* There was also another dish new to Faujus; egg yolks beaten with sugar, rum and milk. 'This singular mixture is drunk cold and without having been cooked. Such is the style in which Mr Maclean's breakfast-table was served every morning, while we were at his house.'

Dinner was taken at four o'clock in the afternoon and all the food was brought to the tables at once, rather like a meal in a Chinese restaurant in London. Faujus noted one of these meals in his journal. Surely it couldn't have been the daily fare of the Macleans? If so they must have kept one of the best tables in the Hebrides:

> A large dish of Scottish soup, composed of broth of beef, mutton and sometimes fowl, mixed with a little fine oatmeal flour, onions, parsley and plenty of pease.

---

* Thus a Frenchman encountering porridge for the first time.

Instead of slices of bread, as in France, slices of mutton
    and the giblets of fowls float about in this soup.
Black pudding made with bullock's blood and barley soup,
    seasoned with plenty of pepper and ginger.
Slices of beef, broiled; excellent.
Roasted mutton of the best quality.
Potatoes done in the juice.
Sometimes heath-cocks, wood-cocks or water-fowl.
Cucumbers and ginger pickled with vinegar.
Milk prepared in a variety of ways.
Cream with Madeira wine.
Pudding made of barley-meal, cream and currants and
    cooked in dripping.

Mrs Maclean served the guests and was also responsible for
giving the first toast. On the sideboard were three large glasses,
one for beer, another for wine and the third for water. These
were passed communally from lip to lip and the glass was
wiped in between with a linen cloth.

After dinner the shining mahogany tables were covered
with decanters filled with port, sherry, Madeira and large bowls
of punch. 'Small glasses are then distributed in profusion to
every one.' After many toasts the ladies withdrew to order tea.

They were absent but a short time and returned in about
half an hour after. The servants then brought in coffee,
slices of buttered bread, butter, milk and tea. Music,
conversation, reading the news, though somewhat old by
the time they reach this, and walking when the weather
permits, fill up the rest of the day which is thus quickly
brought to a close. But what is perhaps a little unpleasant,
is that at ten o'clock one must again take one's seat at table
and share until mid-night in a supper of nearly the same
kind as the dinner, and in no less abundance. Such is the
life that is led in a country where there is not a road nor a
tree, where the mountains are covered only with heath,
where it rains for eight months of the year, and where the
sea, always in motion, seems to be in perpetual convulsions.

I am inclined to think that when a distinguished visitor descended on an island a special abundance was provided over and above the ordinary daily fare. John Knox, who embarked on an extensive tour of the western seaboard and the Hebridean islands two years after the visit of Faujus, also reported groaning tables and a wealth of food remarkable for so agriculturally barren an area. At breakfast he found

> a dram of whisky, gin, rum or brandy, plain or infused with berries that grow among the heath; French rolls, oat and barley bread; tea and coffee; honey in the comb, red and black-currant jellies; marmalade, conserves and excellent cream; fine-flavoured butter, fresh and salted; Cheshire and Highland cheese, the last very indifferent; a plateful of very fresh eggs; fresh and salted herrings broiled; ditto, haddocks and whitings, the skin being taken off; cold round of venison, beef and mutton hams. Besides these articles, which are commonly placed on the table at once, there are generally cold beef and moor-fowl to those who chose to call for them. After breakfast the men amuse themselves with the gun, fishing, sailing, till evening; when they dine, which meal serves with some families for supper.

Although Hebrideans have never prosecuted their fishings with any zeal, they have always resented the invasion of fishermen from foreign parts. In the sixteenth century, for instance, the herring shoals of Loch Broom attracted boats from England, France, Flanders and other parts of Scotland. The Dutch, instructed by Scots who had settled in the Low Countries, became the most skilful poachers of all. So persistent were their attentions that in the reign of James V they were given a gentle reprimand – a number of them were apprehended and decapitated. A barrelful of their heads was despatched to Holland with cards bearing their names affixed to their foreheads.

By the seventeenth century the Dutch had ousted the French and Spaniards as the chief fishers round Lewis. Charles

I established outposts of the Company of the General Fishery of Great Britain and Ireland in Lewis but the Civil War disorganized the scheme and it was eventually abandoned in 1690.

It was to help the people of the west coast feed themselves and to provide a reserve of seafaring men for the navy that the British Fisheries Society, established in 1786, set up fishing stations in places like Ullapool, Stein on Skye, Tobermory on Mull and in the Long Island. The inducements should have been attractive – each family was given a house and a small croft – but the lack of salt for preserving the fish and its high price when available inhibited enthusiasm.

The research for the project was undertaken by John Knox, who believed that if only the herring could be exploited the resulting commerce would employ thousands of the indigent. He pointed out that there was some 400 miles of coast in the north 'not furnished with a town, harbour, or place where a ship in distress can be supplied with an anchor, cable or sail. From a coast so ill provided in whatever relates to navigation, the royal navy cannot be furnished with the necessary supplies of seamen and carpenters, when called for, by the emergencies of the state.'

At the time he wrote the only town in the Western Isles was Stornoway and the idea of establishing 'free towns', as they were called, seemed imperative.

To this end Knox journeyed all round the Hebrides and along the west coast observing the movement of the herring shoals, and he finally recommended twenty-nine sites for the establishment of fishing villages. He was not particularly impressed with Dunvegan in Skye as a potential fishing headquarters:

Macleod is at present in India where his valour has raised him to the rank of major-general; but his return is sincerely wished for, by all ranks and descriptions of people on his estate. In the meantime, the house is inhabited by major Alexander Macleod and his lady, a daughter of the celebrated Flora Macdonald, who protected the young Pretender through all his hair-breadth escapes, during six months, after the battle of Culloden, when wandering among the wilds of the Highlands, where he found safety, though known to hundreds of people whose fidelity resisted the temptation of 30,000.L. offered to those who should secure him.

Being here upon a Sunday, our company became, after church time, very numerous, and was composed chiefly of gentlemen who had been in the army. My object was to push the subscription which I endeavoured to represent as a very becoming supplement to the service of the day, in which the company readily acquiesced among whom was the clergyman, who, though his income is only 40L per annum, bestowed his mite with great good will.

I could not however see the propriety of selecting this place as a station for a town, in preference to other places that I viewed, particularly Brackadale. Neither could I perceive any particular inducement for making Dunvegan the chief residence of the family of Macleod, excepting the strength which it afforded to the Danes, and afterwards to the chiefs of the Macleods, who are supposed to be the descendants of the Danish vice-roys.

The country is barren and almost unimprovable, the people are few in number; and this part of the bay is out of the track of shipping and seldom frequented by the herring shoals. Some gentlemen in company, who were of the same opinion with myself, mentioned Loch Bay, as greatly superior to Dunvegan.

I had proposed to sail for the Long Island, by a packet that goes from Dunvegan once every fortnight; but as the vessel happened to be on the other side, I set out for Loch Bay . . .

Our company now dispersed; and here I parted from my obliging conductor, Mr Macdonald of Portree. Macleod's factor, and other gentlemen supplied the place of those who returned home and we soon reached the house

of a venerable person aged ninety, who lives at the head of
Loch Bay. Here the scene changed from rugged moors and
difficult passes to a track of considerable fertility, both in
grain and pasturage, owing probably to limestone which is
found immediately upon the shore.

The people are all dabblers in the herring and white
fisheries, which they sell to a trader in the neighbourhood
in exchange for meal and necessaries; yet, such is their
poverty, that they are continually in arrears, both with the
trader and the factor, though their rents do not generally
exceed from sixteen to forty shillings.

The entrance into Loch Bay is sheltered by Elen Isa, a
verdant island, nearly one mile in length, and by some
lesser ones contiguous to it. Vessels may come in or go out
by either side of these islands, agreeably to the direction of
the winds. The head of the bay is the only proper harbour,
formed by the hand of nature; but there are other places
towards the entrance where small piers would make secure
harbours for boats, and coasting vessels with any wind.

The advantages of this coast are many and important.
A good country, and very improveable; abundance of
limestone; a numerous people already fishermen; waters,
harbours, and fish, on every side; lying in the track of
shipping which pass and repass through the outer channel
and having an easy communication, in moderate weather,
with the Long Island.

When the village of Stein was established at Loch Bay it
was easier for the inhabitants to communicate with the Long
Island, whose nearest point was twenty miles across the sea,
than with Portree on the east coast of Skye. Today a good road
connects Stein with Portree; by car the journey takes about
twenty-five minutes. In the eighteenth century there were no
roads on Skye at all; the 'carriages' of the lairds were open
boats and it was almost always quicker to take to the sea and
row or sail round the coast than walk across moorland and bog
to some distant part of the island.

Often the only track from a laird's house led down to the shore where his boat would lie at anchor; primitive roads would not begin to be made for another forty years. If you lacked a boat, as most people did, then there was no alternative but to walk. In 1854 the *Inverness Courier* reprinted a journal kept in the 1780s by an English servant called Abram. He came to Fort George in the employ of a Captain Macleod and his family. When the captain died in 1782 Abram remained with the widow and they went to live for a time with relatives at Arnisdale on the shores of Loch Hourn. From there they moved to Skye and Abram records the journeys he was forced to make to keep the family supplied with food:

I used to go for butter and cheese to a place called Boreland which was seventeen miles from our house, I once made this journey and back again the same day with 75 lbs. of butter and cheese on my back, but the creel blistered me severely. I have several times, when meal was to be sold at Dunvegan, brought a boll, of 160 lbs weight, home on my back, a distance of five miles. I often used to cross the mountains to Portree to buy tea and sugar, with any other articles I could get, and this journey would be betwixt thirty and forty miles for me. There are no bridges over the many rivulets in the island, and there was no other way of crossing but by fording them, yet though I was thus continually on my feet and out in everlasting rains, I cannot say that I ever had colds. The Highland gentry are fond of going about from place to place to visit one another, sometimes being a fortnight or three weeks from home; and when they return they perhaps carry along with them those they have been staying with. This they call hospitality, but it is only paying them in their own way by killing time together.

A stranger such as I was, and in a humble situation, need not go to the Highlands and Islands. If the Highland servant's master rides anywhere, the man must run after him on foot, be it ever so far; and when they come to the place they are going to, he may be for hours without getting anything to eat or drink, although he is melting with heat and wet with running through bogs and fording streams.

TWO: 1790–1810

WHAT WOULD YOU consider essential items of equipment for
a Hebridean journey today? A camera certainly, perhaps a set
of Ordnance Survey maps. At the end of the eighteenth century
the well-heeled traveller took along a copy of Pennant's *Tour*
and if he was bent on writing a book then he took as a
travelling companion a landscape artist.

When Dr Thomas Garnett set off on 9 July 1798 from
Glasgow on an extended tour round the Highlands he had
Pennant in his luggage and an artist in tow. Being a doctor of
medicine his progress through the remoter parts of the High-
lands and Islands was not unlike Livingstone's through Africa.
Wherever he halted the sick and maimed were instantly alerted.
On Mull while visiting the minister of Torosay he held his first
impromptu surgery:

> I had scarce been an hour at Mr Fraser's before I had above
> a dozen patients from the small village of Killeen who had
> in some way heard I was a physician and for whom I
> prescribed such simple remedies as I thought they were
> likely to procure. Mrs Fraser keeps a few medicines and
> with the help of Buchan administers to their distresses.

The highlight of any visit to Mull was of course an
expedition to Staffa. And as Faujus had found, the best place to
stay was with Mr Maclean, the hospitable laird of Torloisk.
Stormy weather kept Garnett and his companion housebound
there for two days but by 20 July the seas were tolerably calm
and a boat came over from Gometra to collect them:

> On going on board we witnessed another proof of Mrs
> Maclean's goodness, for we found wine for ourselves and

spirits for the boatmen with a plentiful supply of provisions for us all. We left Mull at about eleven o'clock and it being perfectly calm, our rowers were obliged to exercise their oars, and soon brought us through the sound of Gometra, or the narrow passage between Gometra and Ulva. As soon as we had passed this sound we saw Staffa about ten miles distant presenting nothing particularly striking in its appearance, seeming only at this distance an abrupt rock, flat at the top but whose sides descend perpendicularly into the ocean.

The day continued very fine but as a light breeze had sprung up, the sail was hoisted and we steered for the island. When we were at a distance of about three miles, we heard what we supposed to be the report of guns, which were repeated at regular intervals, perhaps every half minute; the sound appeared to come from no great distance, and as we supposed it to proceed from some vessels either firing guns of distress or engaged with each other, we were anxious to reach the island that we might have a view of them: but when we turned the northern point, we perceived the cause of these sounds. In the rock on the north side of Staffa was a cavity resembling an immense mortar and though there was not much wind, yet the waves which had been raised into mountains by the violence of the preceding tempest were still very high and broke with violence against the island. Whenever a wave came against this part of the rock by its irresistible force it condensed the air in the cavity, and more than half filled it with water; but when the force of the wave was exhausted, and its immense pressure removed, the spring of the condensed air forced out the water in the form of a fine white froth like smoke, accompanied with a report similar to the firing of cannon.

As we proceeded along the western coast of the island the basaltic pillars were very evident, though in many places irregular and reaching only half way down the rock which together with the pillars was of a dark colour inclining to black. In other places they proceeded from the water upwards and were abruptly terminated or broken. As we turned the southern point they became vastly more regular and the view of the side of the island was grand beyond conception: it appeared like the end of an immense cathedral, whose messy roof was supported by stupendous pillars, formed with all the regularity of art: at the bottom appeared the ends of broken pillars standing upright, and forming an extensive causeway. . . .

Proceeding still farther along the same side of the island, we had a view of Fingal's cave, one of the most magnificent sights the eye ever beheld. It appears like the inside of a cathedral of immense size, but superior to any work of art in grandeur and sublimity and equal to any in regularity.

Regularity is the only part in which art pretends to excel nature but here nature has shown, that when she pleases, she can set man at nought even in this respect, and make him sensible of his own littleness. Her works are in general distinguished by a grand sublimity, in which she disdains the similar position of parts, called by mankind regularity, but which in fact, may be another name for narrowness of conception, and poverty of idea; but here, in a playful mood, she had produced a regular piece of workmanship and on a scale so immense as to make all the temples built by the hand of man, hide their diminished heads.

It is difficult for a generation which has unleashed atomic power and walked on the moon to appreciate the awe and wonderment which overwhelmed early visitors to Staffa when they entered what was popularly believed to be the ancient palace of the father of Ossian. It was not only awesome and astonishing but a suitable subject for emphasizing the superiority of the hand of God over the puny hand of man. The Bishop of Linkoeping, Uno von Troil, who accompanied Sir Joseph Banks on his investigation of Staffa, had been moved to hyperbole by the scene:

How splendid do the porticoes of the ancients appear in our eyes, from the magnificence displayed in the descriptions we have received of them, and with what admiration do we look even on the colonnades of our modern edifices! But when we behold the cave of Fingal* it is no longer possible to make a comparison, and we are forced to acknowledge that this piece of architecture, executed by nature, far surpasses that of the colonnade of the Louvre, that of St. Peter at Rome, and even what remains to us of Palmyra and Paestum, and all that the genius, the taste, and the luxury of the Greeks could invent.

Although they may not have heard of Palmyra or Paestum, it wasn't long before everyone with a boat within five miles of Staffa realized that Fingal's new-found cave was going to be worth quite a few drams. John Stoddart, who arrived in Oban in 1799, found that the accepted price of a round trip to Staffa was fifteen shillings and two bottles of whisky. 'In these poor regions which are occasionally visited by wealthy travellers', Stoddart wrote, 'it is not surprising that the inhabitants should be on the watch to derive a profit from their presence.'

But, as he pointed out for the benefit of those who might come after, it was by no means unusual to have to wait a fortnight for fair weather and even if you did set sail it didn't mean that your boatmen had any intention of landing you on Staffa:

> Our excursion afforded us a proof of that respectful deference with which the people here, probably for interested motives, consult the inclinations of their wealthy visitors. In the narrow Sound of Ulva, the sea was heaved into huge, white, breaking surges, by a most violent gale, and we were driven along so rapidly, that had we struck on any of the bold pointed rocks, by which we were surrounded, we must have been instantly dashed to pieces.

* It was Banks who gave the cave the name that Mendelssohn later immortalized in music.

After a little experience of this dangerous navigation, finding that the more we advanced into the open sea, the more tremendous it appeared, I asked the only one of our boatmen who understood English, whether we could possibly get to Staffa. He answered 'assuredly not': and when pressed to know why they had taken us out on so fruitless an errand, he replied that it was merely in compliance with our wish to set sail.

On his second excursion Stoddart succeeded in landing on the island and he was as impressed as Sir Joseph Banks had been seven years earlier. Banks and von Troil had sailed on to Iceland after leaving Staffa, and it was an expedition to Iceland, facilitated by Banks, that brought the young Henry Brougham to the Hebrides in the late summer of 1799. Brougham was born in Edinburgh in 1778 and played many roles in his life: lawyer, parliamentarian, opponent of slavery, law reformer, minister of the Crown, educationalist and author. Few men of his time were more active or more touched with brilliance. The Iceland expedition had been organized by John Joseph Henry, a nephew of Lord Moira, but by the time they sailed the season was so advanced and the weather so unfavourable that they abandoned their ambitious plans to explore Iceland and settled for a more modest excursion round the north of Scotland. Before leaving they obtained with the help of Sir Joseph Banks a Government letter protecting them against press gangs. During the Napoleonic Wars naval ships had full power to impress any able-bodied men they came across, a liberty which could leave a privately owned ship crewless.

As they set sail from Greenock they were enlivened by a pleasant breeze and a memorable sight:

when turning a point the homeward bound West India fleet arrived in full view and sail. The setting sun showed us such a sight as I shall never forget; and whilst they passed us with a salute, slowly fired, I could not help thinking that if a romance-writer had wished to select circumstances for an outset of his piece, or indeed for any part of it, his fancy might have never conjured up such a collection of agreeable traits as conspired to illuminate our *debut* upon the sea.

Brougham, fit and twenty-one, observed the scene sitting aloft with a pint tumbler of claret in one hand and a sea biscuit in the other. In a letter to his kinsman Lord Robertson, young Brougham described the terrifying storm that subsequently blew them west and their arrival on the shores of Islay where after a botanical and mineralogical walk they cooked a live salmon in a pot alfresco, watched by the curious local inhabitants:

> You have no idea, sir, how good boiled salmon is. To acquire this three things are requisite – a stormy voyage, then a rustic entertainment without knives and forks and chiefly the utter and absolute and animated freshness of the fish. We concluded our meal, or rather *feast*, with some fine mutton and quaffed goblets of the delicious nectar of Bordeaux and Rhine – in other words, claret and old hock from our ship. A short walk up the country sobered us completely and we returned to the village to tea. At supper we had the heads of the town and (*inter alios*) a man who has written wisely against tea, and still more wisely against the Newtonian theory. It is amusing to find in this remote and barbarous corner a *carle* who holds Sir Isaac in utter contempt. The natives are a very simple and worthy set of men and the women either very handsome or intolerably ugly.

From Islay they sailed north and west and out into the Atlantic to the remotest inhabited islands of Britain; the isolated archipelago of St Kilda. Its history was first chronicled in detail by Martin Martin, tutor to the Macleods of Skye who held title to the three islands and three stacks which rise sheer out of the sea over a hundred miles from the mainland.

The inhabitants of St Kilda were always a national curiosity

and they remained an object of interest until their final evacuation in 1930. Writers, and more latterly journalists, tended to
treat them as being more exotic than they really were, rather
like freaks in a marooned circus. Indomitable they may have
been but certainly not daft and, considering their outlandish
location, they really were disappointingly normal.

But Martin Martin, having got to St Kilda in 1695 and
having landed, a feat which in those rough waters was often
impossible, was determined to get as much mileage out of the
natives as possible. The title-page of his book promised 'an
ACCOUNT of the very remarkable Inhabitants of that Place,
their Beauty and singular Chastity (Fornication and Adultery
being unknown among them); their Genius for Poetry, Music,
Dancing; their surprising Dexterity in climbing the Rocks and
Walls of their Houses; their Contempt of Gold and Silver as
below the Dignity of Human Nature . . .'

According to Martin Martin these were the lost children of
a Golden Age. William Collins, the precursor of the Romantic
poets who died with mind unhinged in 1759, celebrated their
innocence in his unfinished *Ode on the Popular Superstitions of
the Highlands*. Collins must have seen Martin's book and no
doubt believed in the pristine innocence of the islanders:

> But oh, o'er all, forget not Kilda's race,
> On whose bleak rocks, which brave the wasting tides,
> Fair Nature's daughter, Virtue yet abides.
> Go! – just as they, their blameless manners trace!
> Then to my ear transmit some gentle song,
> Of those whose lives are yet sincere and plain,
> Their bounded walks the rugged cliffs along,
> And all their prospect but the wintery main.
> With sparing temperance at the needful time
> They drain the scented spring, or, hunger prest,
> Along the Atlantic rock, undreading, climb,
> And of its eggs despoil the Solan's nest.
> Thus blest in primal innocence, they live
> Sufficed and happy with their frugal fare,

Which tasteful toil and hourly danger give.
Hard is their shallow soil, and bleak and bare;
Nor ever vernal bee was heard to murmur there!

It was a harmless conceit – that distance and isolation conferred a high degree of moral superiority. But the truth was that life on St Kilda was bleak and only made possible by the twice-yearly descent of the Macleod chamberlain who bought necessary supplies and removed the year's meagre tribute – wool, fulmar oil, cheese, barley, cloth and birds' feathers.

Inhabited from prehistoric times, St Kilda lay far from the shipping lanes and the only regular visit was from the Macleods. Even when the occasional sailing vessel, perhaps blown off course or seeking shelter, did anchor off the island of Hirta where the St Kildans dwelt, they regarded it as a dubious blessing; they welcomed the opportunity to barter but usually succumbed to what they called Boat-cough. Lacking immunity they were laid low by every germ brought ashore. Later, in the nineteenth century, when the SS *Dunara* began making regular summer tourist trips, the St Kildans were also laid low by cupidity; in the manner of Red Indians on reservations they even began charging to have their photographs taken.

But in 1799 they were so cut off from the outside world that when the yacht with Brougham and his party on board arrived off Hirta, the St Kildans fled into the interior fearing that they were about to be attacked by a French privateer. The captain ordered a boat to be lowered and the crew landed with some difficulty on a rocky part of the island. The yacht stood out to sea and waited for some sign of life.

The grandeur of the scenery was heightened by the fineness of the day, and still more by the idea that a single puff of wind might prove fatal to us, by raising the whole fury of the Western Ocean. At last came two boats, one belonging to the place and ours besides, but both manned by the *savages*. This alarmed us: we thought that our party must be lost or taken and the arms chest was instantly opened;

but the boats approaching we found the natives quite pacific, and several came on board – among others their priest, without whom nothing would induce them to venture near us.

When they went ashore they found the islanders in a blissful state of ignorance concerning the rest of the world:

they had heard of the war with France, but knew nothing of Lord Howe's victory, nor any subsequent event; yet the proprietor's tacksman goes there twice a year: but we were told that he carefully conceals every event from them if successful, in order to keep up their *alarms*, which, we found, he turns to good account. They live in as constant dread of invasion as if all the wealth of London and Liverpool were stored up in St Kilda.

Going ashore the party distributed tobacco and a dram, 'their two greatest prizes, though neither had been in the island for two and a half years.'

Brougham sat drinking tea and milk with the clergymen until nearly five in the morning when they sallied forth to inspect the island:

The view of this village is truly *unique*. Nothing in Captain Cook's voyages comes *half* so low. The natives are savage in due proportion; the air is infected by a stench almost insupportable – a compound of rotten fish, filth of all sorts and stinking sea-fowl.

A total want of curiosity, a stupid gaze of wonder, an excessive eagerness for spirits and tobacco, a laziness only to be conquered by the hope of the above-mentioned cordials, and a beastly degree of filth, the natural consequence of this render the St Kildian character truly savage.

From savage St Kilda the party sailed to Lewis where Brougham found Stornoway far more to his liking:

Every morning we shoot grouse, hares, snipe and deer till five o'clock, then eat the most luxurious dinners of game and fish, drinking claret, champagne, hermitage and hock: at night we are uniformly and universally *dead* [drunk]. Yesterday Campbell and I and two natives set in to it, and among four had twelve port-bottles: the natives and Bob being stowed away, I finished another bottle and a half of port with an old exciseman, major of the volunteers. This morning I went out and found all Stornoway in full tongue at my astonishing feat; went to the moors, walked it off, and killed a brace of hares at one discharge (keeping their skins for shoes) above a hundred yards off, and a grouse soon after still farther; and to-night we give a ball.

There is almost a touch of Baron Münchhausen about the young Brougham, astonishing Stornoway with his bottle-and-gunmanship. The following year a more serious and learned visitor descended on the islands. Like Banks and Faujus de Saint Fond, Dr John Leyden was one of those Baconian figures who took all knowledge unto their province. He was, by turns, poet, historian, geologist, archaeologist, orientalist, and insatiable traveller. A polymath equally at home in Barra or Borneo and a great friend of Walter Scott, Leyden left behind a manuscript which came to light at the end of the nineteenth century.

The journal, published with a series of letters to Scott and other literary friends in Edinburgh, is a dry document; scholarly Dr Leyden was for certain, but he lacked an enlivening eye. Like many another academic of the time, he was obsessed with the minutiae of his mineral surroundings: 'The basalt of Scour-egg and of the greater part of the strata in the island,' he observes of Eigg, 'is entirely different in appearance from that of Staffa and from the arrangement of its particles and colour, which is a deep vitreous black marked with red, may be compared to hematites.' Dull stuff. Even the rigours of Hebridean travel in those early days of voyaging are coolly underplayed:

From Iona we procured a boat to coast along the east shore of Mull, which we had not seen and to carry us to Oban.

Our boat was only a clumsy open coble rowed by four unskilled fishermen, with very awkward oars, over a space which none of them had traversed. But the most disagreeable circumstance was that there was no room to lie and hardly any to sit or stand. We coasted along the low shore of Ross, the rocks of which consist almost entirely of red and grey granite and porphyry. Finding that our boat by some mistake had not been sufficiently victualled – as we had now the appearance of continuing all night at sea – we hove-to near Carsaig Bay and landed amid a strange cluster of rock where we found a hut and procured some goats' milk and goats' milk cheese, but no bread. About seven o'clock in the morning we reached Oban in safety, having experienced no real dangers, though we encountered numerous possible ones.

Walter Scott must have been kept almost as busy reading letters as he was writing historical novels. There seems to have been a general conspiracy at the beginning of the nineteenth century to tell him things. John Leyden's journal and letters to Scott were followed in 1803 by still more letters from the Highlands and Islands, this time from James Hogg, the self-educated 'Ettrick Shepherd'. On 27 May he dressed himself in black, put a spare shirt and two neck-cloths in his pocket, took a staff in his hand, flung a plaid over his shoulders and left Ettrick on foot 'with a view to traversing the West Highlands at least as far as the Isle of Skye'.

He arrived in Stornoway in mid-June and was favourably impressed not only by the almost complete absence of night in those northerly latitudes but by the elegant houses and their genteel inhabitants. But the gentility was, he found, not universal:

Although the island is not noted for riots, I had no very favourable specimen of their absolute command over their passions. On the very first night of my arrival a desperate affray took place in the room adjoining to that in which I slept. Several respectable men, the collector and one of the bailiffs were engaged in it. It was fought with great spirit and monstrous vociferation. Desperate wounds were given and received, the door was split in pieces and twice some of the party entered my chamber.

Hogg, being extremely tired, contrived to sleep through most of the minor skirmishes but not of course the big set-pieces:

A ship's captain in particular wrought terrible devastation. He ran foul of the table, although considerably to the windward, which he rendered a perfect wreck, sending all its precious cargo of crystal, china etc., to the bottom and attacking his opponents with such fury and resolution that he soon laid most of them sprawling on the deck. Some of the combatants being next day confined to their beds, summonses were issued and a prosecution commenced but the parties being very nearly connected a treaty was set on foot and the preliminaries signed before I left Stornoway.

At that time Stornoway, the largest port in the Hebrides, lacked many of the amenities which would have been found in mainland towns. There was no brewery, no bakery, no barber, but at the leading inn Hogg found that the landlord, 'a silly despicable man', was 'privileged in having an excellent wife'. To eat they were given 'very good wheaten loaves, seldom beef or mutton but abundance and variety of fish, fowls and eggs. I expected my bill to run high but I was charged no more than sixpence for each meal.'

On the voyage back to the mainland the vessel was becalmed at night half way across the Minch in sight of Skye:

The light of the moon at length prevailed. She hovered above the Shiant Isles and shed a stream of light on the glassy surface of the sea in the form of a tall crescent of such lustre that it dazzled the sight. The whole scene tended to inspire the mind with serenity and awe.

Hogg, as befitted his status as a Practising Poet, wrote some verses of which a little would perhaps be more than enough:

> While viewing this scene with amazement and wonder
> I see Thee in yonder moon's watery gleam.
> Thy voice I have heard from the cloud burst in thunder
> Now hear it from wild fowls which over me scream.

Hogg went back to the Hebrides the following summer with two companions. They walked, often lashed by rain, to Loch Crinan where they took passage on a small English-built sloop bound for Skye with what Hogg described as a 'valuable cargo of luxuries'. As they made their way to Tobermory the weather worsened. At ten in the morning they anchored in the bay and went ashore but fierce rain forced them to spend most of their time within doors. There were members of the crew, particularly an old sailor called Hugh, who thought they would be better off riding at anchor in the shelter of the harbour until the weather improved, but the master, anxious to get on, gave the order to sail.

Hogg gave Scott a graphic account of the physical endurance that a sailing ship's crew needed to weather a storm, particularly when rounding Ardnamurchan Point. They had already tacked to the windward of it when 'the sea growing prodigiously heavy and the wind continuing to increase the sailors were affrighted and though ten or twelve miles advanced, turned and run again for Tobermory.'

The gale was blowing offshore now and the struggle to bring the ship into port nearly proved disastrous:

> They now made a strong effort to weather the straits, putting her about almost every three minutes; all hands assisted in hauling in the sheet; and after a struggle of nearly two hours, they succeeded in working her through and expected at the next stretch to gain the harbour. There being ten in all on board and the deck rather throng, I had stepped below to prevent confusion; but my two companions assisted with all their might, not without imminent

danger to their persons, for the boom overthrew Mr. John every time it was dragged in, and very nearly turned him overboard, he not having experience how to manage himself. I was at length alarmed by an unusual noise and bustle above, but still kept tenaciously by my berth in the cabin until I heard Mr M'Alister cry out in great agitation, O! Lord we will go in a thousand pieces! – my God! my God! cried the old man at the helm. What's the matter now, thought I; and setting my head out of the companion door saw every man rivetted to the spot awaiting his fate in silent horror.

The mainsail had been dashed into the sea and the sloop was driving straight on to the rocks. But Providence intervened and six or seven yards away from disaster the boat veered and stood out to the open sound:

> It was now wearing late, and I shall never forget the stormy appearance of that awful night: the sun, when about to sink into the waves beyond the isles of Barra, frowned upon us through a veil of pale vapour, and seemed swelled to three times his ordinary size. The atmosphere was all in a ferment, having a thin white scum settled steadfastly on its surface, over the face of which at short intervals, small clouds flew with amazing velocity.

There was worse to come; the rigging began to give way and as they ran for shelter into Loch Sunart the Lord vouchsafed Hogg the reverse of the previous year's idyllic nocturne off the Shiant Isles:

> The elements were in a tumult and seemed to be taking flame: the pale, vivid bolts bursting from the rolling clouds added horror to the scene, and to minds already nearly stupified: the sea seemed covered with sparkling fire, an appearance quite new to us, and which we had no conception of, though we were told it was common in great storms.

It took the travellers so long to reach Harris that no sooner were they in Rodel than it was time to leave. Hogg's companions, preoccupied with the wind and rain and the relentless heaving seas, became 'somewhat frenzied' or more often than not cast into a state of utter despair. They eventually reached the mainland at Arisaig and the worst stages of what Hogg described in italics as *the unfortunate journey* were over.

The expedition, Hogg assured Scott, was

> not productive of one good effect. We never in our way out walked an hour without being drenched to the skin and muddied to the knees: we never went on the sea though but for a few miles without encountering storms, accidents and dangers: nor ever, after leaving Greenock, proceeded one day by the route we intended but either lost our way by land or were thwarted by the winds and the sea.

Small wonder that Hogg believed the Lord had frowned upon his designs and, as he assured his patron, 'I am resolved never more to take another journey of such a nature.'

But the weather wasn't always so incommoding. The Rev. James Hall fared better. On 15 April 1803, having procured letters of recommendation to some of the best-informed men in the north of Scotland, he left Edinburgh on a tour which was to take him both to the Orkneys and the Hebrides. Just north of Aberdeen he fell in with a traveller on horseback with whom he had a long and stimulating conversation: 'He told me of a late lord who had kept a number of concubines, of whom fresh supplies were sent every year from London.'

No such spicy tales enlivened his Hebridean wanderings. It took him three days to sail from Lerwick to Stornoway where he noted that most of the houses, although imposing without, were bare within:

> Such is the fashion, or rather craze of the people that they choose to have a fine house even if they should have almost nothing to furnish it withal, and borrow money to

build it. Indeed, masons, slaters, carpenters, &c. flock, particularly in summer, to the Western Isles, where they often earn five shillings a day; and so neatly are the houses in general finished, particularly in the outside, that you would think all the inhabitants rich and opulent.

In Barra, where he went next, Hall found the people more enterprising in their diet than they are today. (When I last stayed in the Isle of Barra Hotel I was offered nothing that I could easily identify as being locally produced despite the fact that the beach where the plane lands is one of the most noted cockle strands in Europe.)

In two summers of very great scarcity, not less than from one hundred to two hundred horse-loads of cockles were taken off the sands at low water every day of the spring tides during the months of May, June, July and August.

Limpets, clams and cockles were boiled and the broth was thickened with oatmeal. A dish perhaps well worth reviving for today's visitors.

Hall commented on other aspects of the sea's bounty:

Ships from all quarters are not unfrequently driven into the bays and roads among the islands. From these, for a very little money, or in exchange for fish, potatoes or fresh meat, the inhabitants get spirits, wine and fruit in great abundance; so that it is astonishing with what elegance and luxury the gentlemen of even very small fortunes live.

Among the lairds in the Western Isles, Hall found a degree of comfort worth remarking:

The produce of the sea and of their own fields and mountains, with those foreign luxuries, furnish their tables nobly. In every house there is a piper or fiddler, or both. They pass the long winter nights in great mirth and glee.

But if you were born into the class destined to till the land there was little to be gleeful about. Hall likened the labouring people, the scallags, to virtual slaves: 'And praedial slaves they most completely are, with this exception, that they cannot either be sold, or transferred for hire from one master to another.'

The scallags were allowed to build themselves a hut with stones and turf and they were given a bit of ground:

> For the cultivation of this they are allowed one day in the week to themselves: the other five they must work for their master. These poor people are obliged to carry their instruments of husbandry or for cutting kelp on their backs, every Monday morning over mountains or to the rocky shores, often a space of six, seven or eight miles, and back again to their huts on Friday evening.

They lived on water gruel, barley cakes, sometimes kale and sometimes potatoes which they ate without any, or very little, salt.

Reading this very objective account of the hardships of the scallags, it's difficult to believe that Hall was on Barra in the year that Beethoven composed his Kreutzer Sonata:

> They are forced to provide themselves with the implements they use in working. Neither are they allowed bedding, clothes or firing. For firing they must prepare, on their own day, Saturday, some peat moss. Clothes must be provided by the wife from bits of wool picked up in the hills, or obtained by begging from the wives of the tenants and tacksmen, and from spinning a little flax, raised as well as barley and potatoes on the scallag's little possession or peculium.

Hall claimed that it was quite common for the tenants and sub-tenants to kick and beat the scallags:

> The miserable condition of these unfortunate men is quite hopeless: to seek relief from a change of masters is utterly impracticable. It is reckoned as unhandsome in any man to receive into his service the scallag of another, as it would

be in a Jamaica plantation to harbour another's runaway negro. The state of our negroes is paradise compared with that of the scallag.

It was a serfdom flourishing without hindrance at home only four years before the Act to abolish slave trading in the colonies received the royal assent. And flourishing alongside it was the old spirit of clanship and fealty to the chief which John Spencer-Stanhope was able to observe at close quarters in the summer of 1806. At the age of nineteen he was invited to accompany Archibald Macdonald, brother of the eighteenth Chief of Sleat, on an election tour of Inverness-shire.

Stanhope's mother tried to dissuade him from making the trip: 'I should much prefer a Welsh to a Scotch tour,' she wrote, 'but then I have not the smallest wish to visit the Northern Islanders. I have no desire to spy the nakedness of their land. Even in reading the famed tour of Dr Johnson, we acquire little knowledge – *only enough, in my opinion, to make us wish never to go there!*' As well visit the Hottentots!

Undeterred, Stanhope joined Archibald Macdonald and set off from Edinburgh full of enthusiasm.

We shall go first to Dupplin Castle, then to Blair, the Duke of Athole's. We shall then go to the coast and Staffa. The Laird of Staffa will then send his boat for us, and he will entrust us to the Lord of the Isles, Lord Macdonald, for he still retains that title though it was forfeited in the rebellion and given to the Prince of Wales.

The first part of the journey was leisurely and comparatively luxurious but the track west from Fort Augustus through Glen Shiel and on to Mam Ratagan was boggy and often flooded, suitable, as Stanhope said, only for goats. Descending into Glenelg on the landward side of Skye, the wind was so strong that Stanhope's pony could hardly make its way forward. Johnson had celebrated the horrors of the inn at Glenelg but according to Stanhope, thirty-three years later it was even worse:

There was nothing at all to eat, beds there were none, there was not even a chair! There was indeed a room which they offered *either to us or to our horses*! Wet, cold, weary and hungry as we were, we determined, in preference, to face the storm and cross over to Skye. We therefore left our servants to take care of the horses and persuaded some boatmen by the bribe of a large sum to take us over.

Perhaps Wales might have been a more comfortable option. As Stanhope wrote to his mother:

Talk not to me of bad roads! What can you know of travelling, who have not gone starving, frozen, sleepless, and supperless, in real danger of death by bog, torrent or exposure. Such is the journey to the Hebrides, and none but the hardy need undertake it.

But their travails were over. At Armadale Lord Macdonald came down to meet them at the almost identical spot where his father had greeted Boswell and Johnson three decades earlier.

Oh what luxury [wrote Stanhope] to find oneself once more in places of comfort! Here all is delightful; and our appetites are so keen that we eat everything which is put before us. A statue of hospitality should be placed upon this shore, holding out her hands to welcome strangers as they arrive. Here we seemed suddenly to have become the near relatives or intimate friends of every individual we saw, while I almost began to fancy we must have recently succeeded to the whole island, and were come to take possession!

Their host was in a few years' time to commission Gillespie Graham to build him an imposing Gothic castle which today stands unroofed. He was also, according to Stanhope, in the throes of stimulating commerce and industry. One of his schemes was to import six fishermen from Peterhead and put each in command of a boat manned by Skyemen to whom, Lord Macdonald hoped, they would impart their skills. A shop had been established and Lord Macdonald had set his mind against large-scale emigration:

> He was perfectly convinced that were he to buy lands in America and present them to the superfluity of his tenants his estate would be materially benefitted. But although he was a heavy sufferer by their living upon him, he could not endure the idea of his subjects wandering about the world, exiled and despairing, in search of some places where they might lay their heads.

That was one reason, perhaps, why the young Chief's tours through Skye were almost regal:

> We accompanied Lord Macdonald and his chamberlain on a royal tour over the island, and no king could command the homage, veneration and service which wherever he trod, was his undisputed right. Wherever he journeyed, he and his guests stopped where he chose, and no man dreamed of saying him nay. He sheltered sometimes in a great house, sometimes in a shanty. And where he went, all the clansmen were not only bound to receive him, but bound to follow him – to make one of the 'Chief's tail' as it was called, until he had a following of his clan, growing, ever growing and journeying round his Island Kingdom, all in the Macdonald Tartan! It was truly a sight which, once seen, lived in one's recollection for ever.

It was indeed a vanishing society in which Stanhope had moved, a world isolated from the mainstream of events:

> At this distance from what is generally known as the civilised world the politics of England are viewed as of small importance, partly owing to the impossibilities of obtaining information due to the differences of language and also to the difficulties of transit. Bonaparte might easily have effected a landing and England have been long under

the insulting dominion of a conqueror, before the knowledge of his departure from Paris could penetrate here: even
then it is doubtful if it would make much sensation! And
thus it is that the confined patriotism of the inhabitants
is bounded by the sea that foams against the rocks of
Skye; their chief is their world; his conduct affords them
their politics and his motions engross the attention of all
classes more than the proceedings of a Napoleon or a King
of England.

THREE: 1810–1830

No one in the nineteenth century wrote more about the Hebrides, nor in many ways more authoritatively, than John Macculloch, who was born in Guernsey in 1773. He qualified as a surgeon but like many men of his time was fascinated by the riddle of the Universe as revealed in rocks. He spent a part of every year between 1811 and 1821 in the Highlands but particularly in the Islands, and his geological work remained unchallenged for decades. He was not only knowledgeable but opinionated and some of the remarks he made in his *Description of the Western Islands* made him as unpopular in certain quarters as Dr Johnson. The celebrated Mackinnon of Coirechatachan furnished his friends with chamber pots which contained Macculloch's portrait *on the inside*.

In his major work, four octavo volumes cast in the form of encyclopaedic letters to his old friend Walter Scott, he ranges over the entire human condition in the Western Isles, sparing neither the follies of the inhabitants nor his own. Climbing the Scuirr of Eigg he and his companion, Neil Maclean, were drenched by a sudden storm and they made for what Macculloch remembered from a previous visit as the only inn on the island. The rest of the story is like something straight out of the pages of *She Stoops to Conquer.*

> In a few minutes we arrived at the door, pushed it forcibly open and bounced in. A venerable-looking old gentleman immediately came out of a side parlour where some other persons were collected round a table, before a blazing fire. I requested a fire in my bedroom that I might dry my clothes. The good innkeeper discovered that I had not

clothes to change and in a few minutes I was rigged out in a fresh suit; while Neil Maclean was smoking below at the kitchen fire, like an over-heated hay stack. I could not help thinking that this was the civilest innkeeper that I had ever seen in the Highlands and, as is the usage, asked for dinner. They had dined, he said, but would get me something; and he disappeared. I began however to doubt, when left alone, I found a chamber that had more accommodations and furniture and books than belong to Highland hostelleries. 'There cannot surely be two houses so much like each other and I cannot have taken the wrong one.' I looked out on all sides; there was no other house visible.

But Macculloch had indeed mistaken the laird's house for an inn. When apologies had been offered and accepted his host pressed hospitality on him and the party stayed for three days until the storm had blown itself out.

Macculloch was travelling round the islands at the dawn of the Steam Age when, as he described it, 'the essence of forty horses, or of a whole regiment of cavalry can be comprised in a kettle and distilled,' and he foresaw the day when his book would be thumbed by weavers and tobacconists 'all making their way with ease by the new-fangled steamers to North Rona and Barra Head'.

But for the moment the Hebrides were still a world apart, innocent of any sense of urgency. In the very south of the Outer Isles Macculloch had

> an opportunity of imagining how life is passed in a remote island, without society or neighbours and where people are born and die without ever troubling themselves to enquire whether the world contains any other countries than Vatersa and Barra. The amusement of the evening consisted in catching scallops for supper, milking the cows and chasing rabbits.

That evening Macculloch was promised a treat on the morrow: a boat to take him to explore the neighbouring islands:

I therefore went to bed full of hope. I had forgotten that I was in Highland land. Morning came, and six; but breakfast did not come till ten. Then came the cows to be milked and the calves to be admired. At length we arrived at the beach and then the Laird recollected that a few days before, his boat had been carried away by the tide and dashed to pieces; as he had forgotten to anchor or fasten her. But there was another boat on the island; we should probably find it; which we accordingly did.

But the oars had been floated away by the tide. Other oars were sent for but then there were no men,

our kind host having sent all his people to Barra. But there was an expedient ready for this also; and another messenger was despatched to borrow four of the islanders. The borrowed oars of one fisherman were at length fitted to the borrowed boat of another: but when the second messenger returned, all the islanders were absent making kelp.

The expedition was abandoned. As Macculloch remarked with some irony:

Need you wonder now how happily people can live in the Highlands, how easily they can find employment, even in such solitudes as this, and how little time can hang heavy on those hands that have found so many expedients for occupying it.

Time, said Macculloch, does not exist:

it is never present, but always past or to come. It is always too soon to do anything, until it is too late: and thus vanishes the period of weariness and labour and anxiety and expectation and disappointment which lies between the cradle and the grave.

Macculloch writes as if this timeless environment had performed an unconscious and involuntary leucotomy upon the natives. But he was quick to admit that their comparative inactivity made them excellent and unhurried hosts:

> In all the wilds I ever visited, I never yet entered the blackest hut without having what was to be given, the best place by the fire, the milk-tub, the oat-cake, the potatoes, the eggs if it was possible to persuade the hens to do such a deed, and a glass of whisky if it was to be found. All this too seems quite matter of right, not of favour.

Macculloch visited St Kilda as other travellers had done before him but he also landed on an oceanic island even less frequented, North Rona. It was more luck than accurate navigation that took him there. They set off in the revenue cutter from Cape Wrath and made for Rona but it wasn't where it should have been. They sailed further to the north-west, but still no sign of land. They hove-to for the night. 'It seemed not a little extraordinary', wrote Macculloch, 'that within a few miles of the continent of Britain, we had as much difficulty in finding two islands which must have been visible ten miles off, as if we had been exploring the seas of another hemisphere.'

North Rona at the beginning of the nineteenth century was still indicated notionally on the charts and there was scanty information available:

> among the Western Isles, they were spoken of as we speak of the islands of the South Seas. Nor could we discover aught of their history, except the general belief that they were inhabited by several families. The statistical writers had never heard of them and the manufacturers of longitudes and latitudes had tabulated them each according to his own fancy or belief.

During the night the tide had drifted them far to the northward and at dawn they saw Rona on the horizon:

> By mid-day we were abreast of Rona; and making an observation for its latitude, I found that it was about

thirteen miles to the north of the assigned place; an amusing illustration of the geographical pursuits of a nation which had explored half the seas of the globe, and was then engaged in hunting after northwest passages and Polar basins.

They landed with some difficulty and scaled a rocky cliff about fifty feet high:

The first objects we saw as we reached the surface of the cliff were a man and a boy who, with a dog, were busily employed in collecting and driving away a small flock of sheep. It was plain that they had taken us for pirates or Americans.

A friendly greeting in Gaelic from one of the cutter's crew arrested their flight. Macculloch was impressed by the isolation of the family on Rona: a man called Kenneth MacCagie, his wife, their three children and his aged mother:

It is the total seclusion of Rona from all the concerns of the world which confers on it that intense character of solitude with which it seemed to impress us all. No ship approaches in sight; seldom is land seen from it. Rona is forgotten, unknown, for ever fixed, immoveable in the dreary and waste ocean.

Once five families had lived on the island, but there was a boating tragedy and all the men had been drowned. The island was evacuated. Then MacCagie and his family came to tend fifty sheep. 'We understood that he had, for seven years, seen no human beings but ourselves and the people of his employer.'

There was a cow on the island brought from Lewis when in milk and replaced when it had run dry. From the milk of the sheep the family made cheese; they grew barley, oats and potatoes and caught saithe from the rocks. MacCagie was paid £2 a year and was bound by an indenture for eight years:

a superfluous precaution for a man who was already secured by a barrier as unsurmountable as the nine chains of Styx. The wife and mother looked as wretched and melancholy as Highland wives and mothers generally do; but MacCagie himself seemed a good humoured careless fellow, little concerned about to-morrow, and fully occupied in hunting his sheep about the island. Everything appeared wretched enough; a climate where winter never dies; a smoky subterranean cavern; rain and storm; a deaf octogenarian grandmother; the wife and children half naked; and to add to all this, solitude and a prison from which there was no escape.

Like all the early travellers, Macculloch wasn't at all concerned with sparing anyone's feelings. The Nicholsons who ran the inn at Kyle Rhea ferry received the full strength of his quill. Mounted on Roger, the pony lent him by a local worthy, he reached the narrows between Skye and Glenelg early in the morning.

'This is the ferry house?' he asked the good wife.

'Aye, aye, ye'll be wanting the ferry, nae doot?'

'To be sure; and you can give me some breakfast.'

'It's the sabbath.'

'I know that; but I suppose one may breakfast on the sabbath?'

'Aye, I'se warn ye. That's a bonny beast.'

'It's my Lord's pony.'

'Aye, I thought it was Roger; I thought I kenn'd his face. And where 'ill ye be gaun?'

'I am going to Eilan Reoch and I want some breakfast.'

'A weel, a weel, I dinna ken; Lassie! Tak the gentleman's horse.'

Mrs Nicholson, according to Macculloch, then washed her hands of him. It was twelve o'clock before she laid on the table, not the tea and eggs he asked for but a dirty wooden bowl of salt herrings and potatoes. 'It was impossible to eat salt herrings', Macculloch complained, 'after six hours walking and riding in a hot summer's day.'

He was charged two shillings for the meal and, unable to find the ferryman, went by small boat to the island he wanted to explore and returned on the following day for his horse. There was then a long and painful altercation with Mr Nicholson, who charged him six shillings for looking after Roger, and Mrs Nicholson, who accused him of stealing the horse from its owner. Macculloch got his own back two years later. When passing Kyle Rhea in a revenue cutter he related the story to the crew. They leapt ashore, dashed into the inn and reappeared with three casks of the Nicholsons' illicit whisky which they confiscated.

Should such a story have been told? Macculloch defends himself by pointing out that it was the early tourists in Wales who by writing about the 'fraud, negligence and incivility' of the inhabitants forced them to learn that honesty and civility were good policy. 'The very sight of a memorandum book', Macculloch wrote, 'is now sufficient to keep them in order.'

One of the slight social embarrassments Highland travellers faced in the eighteenth and early nineteenth centuries was the sudden startling of smugglers at work. The punitive duty on legally distilled whisky had made illicit distilling as much a part of the rural scene as haymaking.

Barley converted into *uisge beatha* was often the only currency available in the islands. Smugglers, the term used to describe both those who made whisky and those who dealt in it, abounded in every glen and some of the best malt was made in islands like Arran and Islay where distance and wild seas made the task of detection doubly difficult.

Macculloch, travelling by revenue cutter, often found himself a gratuitous spectator at some confiscation of contraband, or else taking a passive part in a skirmish with smugglers. Being a drinking as well as a thinking man, his sympathies lay perhaps more with the enterprising islanders than the excise men. Every now and again as the revenue cutter sailed among the islands they would see the tell-tale wisp of smoke on the shore which might be someone innocently burning kelp or less innocently distilling whisky. The stills were often sited on the seashore at the mouth of a burn where a hostile sail could be seen in sufficient time for the apparatus to be dismantled and spirited into the boggy interior. A smuggler might have to abandon the liquor but he could escape with the equipment and live to distil another day.

Macculloch has left a vivid portrait of a seizure on the island of Lismore in Loch Linnhe which probably took place at about the time of the Battle of Waterloo. He and his crew were sailing along the shores of Lismore when suddenly a gauger's predatory eye spied a whiff of smoke:

> Beneath a rock, close by the edge of the water was burning a bright and clear fire, near which sat an old man and a young girl, with two or three casks scattered about. An iron crook suspended on some rude poles supported a still and the worm passed into a tall cask into which fell a small stream from the summit of the rock behind. Two or three sturdy fellows were lounging about; while the alchemist in chief sat over the fire, in the attitude of Geber or Paracelsus waiting for the moment of projection. A rough shed erected under another rock seemed to contain some tubs and casks; nor could anything be more picturesque than this primitive laboratory or more romantic than the whole scene.

The excise men leapt ashore and the still was captured. Thanks to Macculloch's entreaties the rest of the gear was returned to the islanders. If a lone visitor was viewed with suspicion in the days before the 1823 Act of Parliament made legal distilling possible and profitable for the first time, it was only to be expected. When James Hogg returned to Tobermory for his second visit in 1804 he noted a great curiosity among the villagers:

Although I did not tarry above two hours at this place last year, I was surprised at being told by a native who went abroad with us, that the whole village knew me: that they wondered much what my business was there last year and much more when they saw me return this year . . . I rather think that the great number of excise-men on these coasts obliges the highlanders to keep a sharp look-out.

When Pennant made the first of his tours in Scotland in 1771 he was able to claim without exaggeration that the country was then 'almost as little known to its southern brethren as *Kamtschatka*'. He added, with some pride, that after his travels had been published the country became '*inondée with visitants*'. None was more famous than Dr Johnson.

But it was Walter Scott who opened the floodgates. To understand the way in which the Wizard of the North was able to fire the popular imagination and turn an unvisited area into a centre of pilgrimage overnight, one only has to look at the phenomenal success of *The Lady of the Lake*, which was published in May 1810.

Robert Cadell the Edinburgh publisher wrote:

The whole country rang with the praises of the poet – crowds set off to view the scenery of Loch Katrine, till then comparatively unknown; and as the book came out just before the season for excursions, every house and inn in that neighbourhood was crammed with a constant succession of visitors. It is a well-ascertained fact, that from the date of publication of *The Lady of the Lake*, the post-horse duty in Scotland rose in an extraordinary degree, and indeed it continued to do so regularly for a number of years, the author's succeeding works keeping up the enthusiasm for our scenery which he had thus originally created.

At two guineas each (more than a skilled craftsman could earn in a month), the first edition of 2,050 copies disappeared instantly; four more editions followed in the course of the year. As Lord Cockburn recorded in his diary in the spring of 1838:

The inn near the Trossachs could, perhaps, put up a dozen, or at the very most, two dozen of people; but last autumn I saw about one hundred apply for admittance, and after horrid altercations, entreaties and efforts, about fifty or sixty were compelled to huddle together all night. They were all of the upper rank, travelling mostly in private carriages, and by far the greater number strangers. But the pigs were as comfortably accommodated. I saw three or four English *gentlemen* spreading their own straw on the earthen floor of an outhouse with a sparred door, and no fire-place or furniture. And such things occur every day there, though the ground belongs partly to a duke and partly to an earl – Montrose and Willoughby. These are the countrymen of Sir Walter Scott. His genius immortalises the region. This attracts strangers, and this is their encouragement. Is there any part of the Continent where this could happen?

It was a fortuitous invitation from the Laird of Staffa which induced Scott to undertake his first journey west in 1810. In company with his family and a few friends the journey to Oban was leisurely. As his biographer put it:

He travelled slowly with his own horses, through Argyle-shire as far as Oban; but indeed, even where post-horses might have been had, this was the mode he always pre-ferred in these family excursions, for he delighted in the liberty it afforded him of alighting and lingering as often and as far as he chose; and, in truth, he often performed the far greater part of the day's journey on foot – examin-ing the map in the morning so as to make himself master of the bearings – and following his own fancy over some old disused riding track, or along the margin of a stream, while the carriage with its female occupants adhered to the proper road.

At Oban they took to the sea, among the party a detribal-ized Highland chieftain, the Mackinnon of Mackinnon:

a young gentleman born and bred in England, but never-the-less a Highland chief. It seems his father had acquired wealth, and this young man, who now visits the Highlands for the first time, is anxious to buy back some of the family property which was sold long since. Some twenty Mack-innons, who happened to live within hearing of our arrival (that is, I suppose within ten miles of Aros), came posting to see their young chief, who behaved with great kindness, and propriety and liberality.

As a Lowlander, Scott may have cherished romantic illusions about chieftainship but he also saw its less attractive side. This is how he described the laird of Staffa, who was a cadet of the Clanranald family and owner of several other islands and a large estate on Mull:

By dint of minute attention to this property, and particu-larly to the management of his kelp; he has at once trebled his income and doubled his population, while emigration is going on all round him. But he is very attentive to his people, who are distractedly fond of him, and he has them under such regulations as conduce both to his own benefit and their profit; and keeps a certain sort of rude state and hospitality in which they can take much pride. I am quite satisfied that nothing under the personal attention of the landlord himself will satisfy a Highland tenantry, and that the substitution of factors, which is now becoming general, is one great cause of emigration. This mode of life has, however, its evils; and I can see them in this excellent man. The habit of solitary power is dangerous even to the best regulated minds, and this ardent and enthusiastic young man has not escaped the prejudices incident to his situation.

Scott kept no journal of his few days on Mull, Staffa and Iona, the region which was to furnish him with the backdrops for his last lengthy poem, *The Lord of the Isles*. But five years later he was offered another opportunity to visit the islands, as a guest of the committee which was responsible for the lighthouses and beacons scattered round the northern coast of Scotland.

> We have [Scott wrote to a friend] a stout cutter, well fitted up and manned for the service by Government; and to make assurance doubly sure, the admiral has sent a sloop of war to cruise in the dangerous points of our tour, and sweep the sea of the Yankee privateers, which sometimes annoy our northern latitudes.

The party set sail from Leith on 29 July 1814 and disembarked at Greenock on 8 September. On the twenty-second day of the voyage, with Orkney and Shetland behind them, they rounded Cape Wrath and sailed south towards the isle of Harris where Robert Stevenson, the leader of the expedition, a remarkable man who had built his first lighthouse on the island of Little Cumbrae when he was only nineteen, went ashore to inspect the lighthouse on Eilean Glas off the island of Scalpay.

At Rodel they examined the church which had lately burnt down and came upon an excise officer who had a few days before seized a whisky still on a neighbouring island after a desperate resistance:

> Upon seeing our cutter, he mistook it, as has often happened to us, for an armed vessel belonging to the revenue, which the appearance and equipment of the yacht, and the number of men, make her resemble considerably. He was much disappointed when he found we had nothing to do with the tribute to Caesar, and begged us not to undeceive the natives, who were so much irritated against him that he found it necessary to wear a loaded pair of pistols in each pocket, which he showed to our Master, Wilson, to convince him of the perilous state in which he found himself while exercising so obnoxious a duty in the midst of a fierce-tempered people, and at many miles distance from any possible countenance or assistance.

Scott then made his much-quoted visit to Dunvegan Castle and after that the cutter sailed round what he described as the 'highly romantic' coast of Skye. Macleod had urged them to go to Loch Scavaig where they would find 'a fine romantic loch'. This was, of course, Coruisk or, as Scott recorded it, Corriskin. Taking to a small boat they landed just below the loch:

we found ourselves in a most extraordinary scene: we were surrounded by hills of the boldest and most precipitous character, and on the margin of a lake which seemed to have sustained the constant ravages of torrents from these rude neighbours. The shores consisted of huge layers of naked granite, here and there intermixed with bogs, and heaps of gravel and sand marking the course of torrents. Vegetation there was little or none, and the mountains rose so perpendicularly from the water's edge that Borrowdale is a jest to them. We proceeded about one mile and a half up this deep, dark, and solitary lake, which is about two miles long, half a mile broad, and, as we learned, of extreme depth. The vapour which enveloped the mountain ridges obliged us by assuming a thousand shapes, varying its veils in all sorts of forms, but sometimes clearing off altogether. It is true, it made us pay the penalty by some heavy and downright showers, from the frequency of which, a Highland boy, whom we brought from the farm, told us the lake was popularly called the Water Kettle. The proper name is Loch Corriskin, from the deep corrie or hollow in the mountains of Cuillin, which affords the basin for this wonderful sheet of water. It is as exquisite as a savage scene, as Loch Katrine is as a scene of stern beauty. After having penetrated so far as distinctly to observe the termination of the lake, under an immense mountain which rises abruptly from the head of the waters, we returned, and often stopped to admire the ravages which storms must have made in these recesses when all human witnesses were driven to places of more shelter and security.

Stones, or rather large massive fragments of rock of a composite kind, perfectly different from the granite barriers of the lake, lay upon the rocky beach in the strangest and most precarious situations, as if abandoned by the torrents which had borne them down from above; some lay loose and tottering upon the ledges of the natural rock, with so little security that the slightest push moved them, though their weight exceeded many tons. The opposite side of the lake seemed quite pathless, as a huge mountain, one of the detached ridges of the Cuillen, sinks in a profound and almost perpendicular precipice down to the water. On the left-hand side, which we traversed, rose a higher and equally inaccessible mountain, the top of which seemed to contain the crater of an exhausted volcano. I never saw a spot on which there was less appearance of vegetation of any kind; the eye rested on nothing but brown and naked crags, and the rocks on which we walked by the side of the loch were as bare as the pavement of Cheapside. There are one or two spots of islets in the loch which seem to bear juniper, or some such low bushy shrub.

It was this scene which Scott was to poeticize in *The Lord of the Isles*, a work which he himself described to a friend as 'Scottified up to the teeth'. It was not received kindly by either *The Edinburgh Review* or the *Quarterly Review* but it was due mainly to Scott's new-found enthusiasm for the Hebrides that the artist and aquatinter William Daniell spent so much time there when he was compiling sketches for his *A Voyage Round Great Britain*.

Until Daniell's visit the few drawings and engravings made in the Hebrides were designed to convey not beauty but information. Pennant took the Welsh draughtsman Moses Griffiths on his Scottish tour to provide a detailed record of geological formations, landscapes and relics of antiquity. The illustrations were as factual as diagrams in a textbook; they were not intended to be picturesque embellishments.

Indeed at that time the picturesque was considered to be

only that which had been adapted and improved by the hand of man. The uncouth dwellings of the Hebrides, the absence of trees and other signs of cultivation, rendered the area curious but certainly not attractive.

Johnson, far from being enraptured by the scenery, was offended by its ugliness. To him the bare peaks of the Cuillins were as inviting as a slagheap:

> An eye accustomed to flowery pastures and waving harvests is astonished and repelled by this wide extent of hopeless sterility. The appearance is that of matter incapable of form or usefulness, dismissed by Nature from her care and disinherited of her favours.

Defoe in Scotland in the 1720s thought the mountains were hideous; other visitors found them 'barbarous' and 'uncouth'. It was not until Scott clothed the Highlands with romantic and historical associations that the stern, the savage and the wild became an object of admiration. By the time Daniell began his journey in the summer of 1813, setting off from Land's End to circumnavigate the coastline of Britain, the sublime had become fashionable and the barren peaks of the Cuillins were a subject for inspiration and awe. Daniell's original idea was to execute the whole journey by boat, 'the better to examine every point and stone and cranny of the coast', but that proved so difficult that he and his friend Richard Ayton, who accompanied him as a text-writer, gave up the idea and their journey turned into a walking tour.

It took Daniell ten years to complete his project and he has left behind an extraordinarily accurate view of the Hebrides at the dawn of the Steam Age. His prints have graced the walls of island inns and hotels for years, and his mannered groups of shepherds draped before imposing ruins, kilted peasants cutting peats, sloops in full sail scudding past rugged promontories, are the only visual record we have of what the islands looked like to a romantic in the summer of 1815. The engravings on copper plates have an almost Grecian elegance and stripped from their bindings, when the rare volumes do come up for auction, they now command around £50 for a single print.

Three hundred and five of the beautifully engraved original plates are now in the possession of the Tate Gallery and in 1977 a special and final edition of Daniell's *Voyage* was issued, limited to 45 copies. Included in the work was Richard Ayton's 900-page text. Ayton had spent a great deal of his time in the East and made light of the discomforts of travelling in Skye:

> On the present, as well as on various other occasions in the course of this tour, there was a striking demonstration of the facility with which the human frame adapts itself to any change of circumstances and with very little preparation can be brought to endure without injury, the privation of most of these artificial conveniences which the refinements of civilised life have rendered almost indispensable. After a ten years' exposure to the burning climate of India, it might be considered a severe trial of the constitution to circumnavigate the island of Great Britain; but truth requires it to be avowed that, in accomplishing this most arduous part of the undertaking, an improvement rather than a loss of health was experienced.

Ayton's costive prose effectively choked any description of what actually happened on the trip. There is no mention of Daniell at any time actually taking a pencil in his hand – indeed no mention of the great engraver at all. Ayton unfortunately saw his function more as caption writer than Boswell to Daniell's Johnson.

John Keats has left a more vivid account of the difficulties that attended travel in the Hebrides. In 1818 he journeyed to Oban, mostly on foot, the last fifteen miles in soaking rain. He and his companion Charles Brown had hoped to find a boat to take them to Staffa, 'but the expense is 7 guineas and those rather extorted – Staffa you see is a fashionable place and therefore every one concerned with it either in this town or the Island are what you call up. 'Tis like paying sixpence for an apple at the playhouse – this irritated me, and Brown was not best pleased – we have therefore resolved to set northward for Fort William tomorrow morning.'

Just after writing those words one of the boatmen with whom Keats had been negotiating returned and a bargain was struck. He would take them across to Mull by way of Kerrera and then on to Iona and Staffa if the weather permitted. Like many visitors before him, Keats found that when it came to describing Staffa words almost failed him:

It can only be presented by a first rate drawing. One may compare the surface of the Island to a roof – this roof is supported by grand pillars of basalt standing together as thick as honeycombs. The finest thing is Fingal's Cave – it is entirely a hollowing out of Basalt Pillars. Suppose now the Giants who rebelled against Jove had taken a whole Mass of black Columns and bound them together like bunches of matches – and then with immense Axes had made a cavern in the body of these columns – of course the roof and floor must be composed of the broken ends of the Columns – such is Fingal's Cave except that the Sea has done the work of excavations and is continually dashing there – so that we walk along the sides of the cave on the pillars which are left as if for convenient Stairs – about the island you might seat an army of Men each on a pillar. For solemnity and grandeur it far surpasses the finest Cathedrall. At the extremity of the Cave there is a small perforation into another cave, at which the waters meeting and buffeting each other there is sometimes produced a report as of a cannon heard as far as Iona which must be 12 miles. As we approached in the boat there was such a fine swell of the sea that the pillars appeared rising immediately out of the crystal. But it is impossible to describe it.

Keats tried in fifty lines or so of verse to distil the spirit of this 'cathedral of the sea . . . where the waters never rest, where a fledgy sea-bird quire soars for ever', but he was not particularly pleased with his efforts. 'I am so sorry,' he wrote to his brother Tom, 'I am so indolent as to write such stuff as this – it can't be helped. I have a slight sore throat and think it best to stay a day or two at Oban.'

But Staffa had worked its magic:

> Not Aladdin magian
> Ever such a work began;
> Not the wizard of the Dee
> Ever such a dream could see;
> Not St John, in Patmos' Isle,
> In the passion of his toil,
> When he saw the churches seven,
> Golden aisl'd, built up in heaven,
> Gazed at such a rugged wonder.

But it wasn't Keats or Wordsworth or Tennyson who captured the popular romantic feeling for Staffa. That was left to a twenty-year-old German who came to the Hebrides in August 1829. When he wrote to his family, Felix Mendelssohn sent them not a description of Staffa but part of the score of his *Hebrides Overture*. 'In order to make you understand how extraordinarily the Hebrides affected me, the following came into my mind there –

the best that I have to tell you is described exactly in the above music.'

The music, emotionally charged, sentimental, was as impressionistic a projection of the Hebrides as anything produced by Turner's brush. For Necker de Saussure, a Swiss who spent a considerable amount of time in Scotland, Staffa and all the ancient geological formations of the Western Isles were a source not of artistic inspiration but scientific enquiry. An Honorary Professor of Mineralogy and Geology in the Academy of Geneva, he also became a member of the Wernerian Society in Edinburgh.

Necker de Saussure made two trips to the west coast, not solely to look at rocks. He regarded himself as an observer of the whole spectrum of Scotland, and was careful to style his first book when it appeared in 1821 as *Travels in Scotland; Descriptive of the State of Manners, Literature and Science*. His Hebridean journey began in Arran, whose illicit whisky at that time was considered to be 'the Burgundy of all the vintages'. He found the inhabitants occupied in agricultural labours, some sowing rye, others planting potatoes,

> the culture of which, admirably adapted to the soil, and to the climate of the country, is an invaluable resource for the poor insulated inhabitants. We frequently quitted the coast in order to go through the villages, built on tops of hills which bound it; the inhabitants, little accustomed to see strangers, took us for custom-house officers; thus we saw them flying before us, and shutting up, at our approach, all their huts in which they had established private distilleries of whiskey, which are prohibited by law.
>
> Arriving at the foot of the rocks, at a distance from all habitation, we stumbled by accident on the depot of all the contraband. In a small cavern, the entrance into which was covered with briars, were ranged thirty or forty casks of whiskey, destined to be transported during the night on board a vessel anchored at a little distance. Some very ancient iron lances were lying at the mouth of the grotto;

they were the arms used by the smugglers in case of attack. Raising our eyes, we perceived, on the top of the rocks a troop of men who, with eager looks, were attentively watching all our movements. These were the proprietors of the whiskey. We hastened to calm their uneasiness, by retiring without touching the depot; but no doubt these unfortunate people, seeing their enterprise discovered, expected their casks to be seized before the close of the day.

Necker must have departed with a strange picture of Arran, for after a twenty-one mile walk through drenching rain the inn his party eventually found soon became a scene of impromptu bacchanalia. Although 'harassed with fatigue', they summoned a celebrated piper to play for them:

We sent our guide to invite this Orpheus of the North to entertain us with the harmonious sounds of his *bag-pipe*; he soon brought in a tall and meagre figure who with his bagpipe under his arm placed himself in a corner of the room awaiting our signal. The order was given and blowing vigorously with his bagpipe, there issued sounds capable of deafening the most intrepid amateur of this wild instrument. Afterwards he successively played *pibrocks*, or warlike marches of the tribes; *laments* or complaints for the death of the chiefs and heroes; and lastly *reels* or Highland dances.

Those of the Inn recognizing the airs of the dance, flew to join in. The bagpipe made such a noise that it was impossible, not only to hear each other, but even to hear an unfortunate drunkard who burst open the door in order, notwithstanding all we could do, to join the party. This animated dance, the singular steps of our guide, the length-ened mien of the Piper seated gravely in a corner of the room, formed a most grotesque picture.

In those days there were no roads on Arran and conse-quently few visitors, which must have been a satisfactory state of affairs for the illicit distillers, harassed as they were by the gaugers. What the whisky tasted like Necker didn't record but it must have been fairly fiery:

I shall terminate my remarks on Arran by a short anecdote which will serve to depict the still wild spirit which prevails among the inhabitants. While we were on our tour, a tall well-made man of a robust appearance entered into conversation with our guides. 'Do you see that man', said one of them to us, 'he is the strongest man in the Island, and of a vigour that no one can resist; one day that he had been invited to a wedding, a dispute arose between two of the guests, and by degrees the others took part in it; they began to fight, and this man, who was generally of a mild character, endeavoured to restore peace, but seeing he could not succeed, he was seized by a movement of anger, and launching into the midst of us,' continued my guide with a tone of admiration and emphasis; 'he fought alone against all, *and killed half the wedding.*'

Necker was careful to point out in a foot-note that *kill* should not be taken in a literal sense, it merely meant that he laid them out. The Swiss geologist made a second and longer voyage to the Western Isles, to Mull, Eigg, Canna, Coll, Tiree, and Skye, but on occasion he was blown slightly off course. From Canna (this was in mid-September) he intended to go straight to Skye, but that was not to be:

Our sailors came at an early hour in the morning to inform us that the weather was fine, and the wind slight, but blowing towards Long Island. Curiosity to see this island, and the pleasure of traversing a country which no traveller had yet visited, made us forget the distance, the advanced state of the season, the uncertainty, and perhaps the danger of returning. We gave orders to get all ready, and immediately embarked. We coasted some time along the basaltic rocks of the south of Canna, then, after doubling that island, we steered towards the west, where we perceived the blue hills of South Uist, like a mist in the horizon. We were eleven hours at sea, and during this long but agreeable passage we saw nothing worthy of attention, with the exception of two or three vessels, in full sail, coming from Norway or the Baltic, and destined for the south. We arrived at sun-set on the banks of Long Island, which is an assemblage of different isles, Barra, Eriskay, South Uist, &c. all similar in appearance, and separated from each other by narrow arms of the sea. We now reached the small isle of Eriskay, a rock about a mile in diameter, on which are some houses and pasturage, where Mr Macdonald, of Boisdale, proprietor of a part of South Uist, breeds some cattle.

We there met the proprietor himself, for whom his brother, Mr Macdonald, of Staffa, had given me a letter; we met with the most friendly reception from him; he offered us places in his boat to repair with him to his abode at Kilbride-house, in the Isle of South Uist. He was at first, on seeing us at a distance astonished at the appearance of strangers in this district; before even knowing who we were, his reception was at once polite and hospitable. He conducted us to the shore, where his boat was waiting to convey us across the dangerous strait of Eriskay; but the beauty of the weather, the serenity of the sky, and the perfect calmness of the sea, removed all idea of danger.

We landed at Kilbride, a handsome country-seat, situate on the sea-coast, in the southern part of the Isle of Uist. Mr Macdonald now introduced us to his family; no words can describe the pleasure a traveller feels when, in the midst of these retired and wild countries, he finds himself, as if by enchantment, transported into the most amiable and elegant society, where he might imagine himself at the extremity of the world, and far from every vestige of civilization. These are contrasts which particularly strike the stranger who travels through the Hebrides. For upwards of six weeks the inmates of Kilbride-House had received no intelligence from the rest of the world; thus we had many public events to relate, of which, but for our accidental arrival, they would for a time have remained in ignorance. The want of communication with the mother-country, is, perhaps, the greatest inconvenience experienced by the resident proprietors, and in no place is this inconvenience more felt than in this portion of Long Island, where, for want of regular packet-boats, a person may be several months in succession without the arrival either of letters or friends. As a proof how far the inhabitants of the Hebrides are in arrear for news, we could not find, during the whole of our journey, a newspaper of a later date than that which appeared in Edinburgh, on the evening of my departure from that city.

The country surrounding Kilbride-House is perhaps one of the most barren and uninteresting to be met with; there are no trees, and hardly any verdure; scarcely any thing is to be seen but rocks and sands; yet, notwithstanding, thanks to the sea, we there enjoyed an interesting prospect. At the west, we saw the unbounded ocean, as no land rises between this island and the continent of America. At the south, the strait of Eriskay appears like a large river strewed with rocks and isles; beyond this rises the Isle of Barra, and several other small islands of sand, among which, that surmounted by the venerable ruins of the ancient Castle of Weavers, is particularly to be remarked. In fine, at a short distance from the house, we could see, at the east and at a distance, the Isle of Canna, and those of Rum and Sky, with their bold and picturesque mountains. Thus a residence in these wild places still presents to the lover of nature many sites capable of inspiring his rapture and admiration.

Up to the time of Necker's visit there were few explicit directions for the casual visitor to the Hebrides. *The Travellers Guide through Scotland and its Islands* first published in 1798 had by 1811 run into its fifth edition, but only twelve of its 570 pages were devoted to the islands of the west and although the inhabitants were described as being 'sober, hospitable and peaceable', there was no suggestion as to the best way to reach Skye or the Outer Isles.

In 1820 *Lumsden & Son's Steam-Boat Companion* or *Stranger's Guide to the Western Isles & Highlands* appeared to mark, as it were, the emergence of steam in western waters. Its references to the Hebrides were luke-warm and cautionary. He who goes that far west, the book appeared to be saying, goes largely alone:

> The Storr, a scene of indescribable ruggedness and magnificence which, though in some situations it would command the admiration of mankind, is here doomed to perpetual silence and desolation, the foot even of the native seldom disturbing the repose of nature.

Despite the advantages of steam navigation ('a journey may now be performed in a day which one hundred years ago would have been considered the business of a week and the boast of a life'), there were few people who saw a Hebridean jaunt as a relaxing holiday. It was still a region for the scientist and the serious-minded:

> Besides exhibiting innumerable scenes of sublimity, these mountainous regions contain inexhaustible subjects of natural history [reported the *Companion*]. The natives of these regions are hospitable, intelligent and polite. The gentlemen being distinguished for their urbanity, the ease of manners and the vivacity of their conversation. The mountains, minerals and scenery may be examined as if they were the exclusive property of the stranger.

There were other guidebooks on sale. The *Scottish Tourist*, published in 1825, was a rival to *An Account of the Pleasure Tours in Scotland*, which by June 1827 had already run into four editions. Interesting they certainly are, but there were discrepancies, which suggest that much of the information was based on hearsay and not on accurate observation.

In one book Skye was fifty-four miles long and thirty-five miles broad; in the other forty-five miles long and twenty-five miles broad. *Pleasure Tours* is the more fanciful of the two and much of it appears to have been written by an early victim of dyslexia. In Skye the traveller is advised to proceed from *Bradford* to *Sconce* and thence to *Sligekan*, *Straun*, *Stien* and *Repstaphen*, which might roughly be translated as Broadford, Sconser, Sligachan, Struan, Stein, and Staffin. Not so much a journey without maps as a journey obscured by metathesis.

The *Scottish Tourist* was the first guide to make extensive reference to 'steam-boat conveyances', but it gave the name neither of the owners nor the agents, just a general impression that there were certain unnamed boats driven by steam plying in western waters.

It was possible to take a steamboat from Glasgow to Oban, Tobermory and Staffa, another to Oban and Inverness and yet another on alternate Tuesdays to Stornoway. It was on one of these boats that the second Baron Teignmouth embarked in 1829. His objective, both serious and high-minded, was 'to survey the scenery and acquire information respecting the moral and social conditions of regions which he regarded with early and strong predilection'.

Much of the material appeared as a series of articles in the *Saturday Magazine*, the journal of the Society for Promoting Christian Knowledge. Although the party set off on their trip to Mull by steam-vessel they found that inland travel in the islands was still as difficult as it had been in the time of Johnson and Boswell: 'A lady living on the south-east side of the island,' Teignmouth noted on Mull, 'when she visits her distant friends is conveyed by eight Highlanders on a litter.'

Small wonder that the author came to the conclusion that if you had to hoof it from place to place then it was best to make a virtue of the necessity:

The traveller must be unencumbered by carriage, horse or vessel of his own; but depend on the opportunities of proceeding which he may chance to meet with, doubtless much facilitated by the hospitality and friendliness of the people and he must command leisure and patience sufficient to submit to the fatigue and privations to which he is occasionally exposed by the vexatious despotism of the elements.

Thus free in his power of locomotion and fortified in spirit, he may enjoy a gratification to which the tourist who rolls along the beaten track of continental travellers, transferred by the tyranny of his courier from the safe custody of one set of waiters and cicerones to another is utterly unacquainted.

There was no doubt that in those early days part of the pleasure of sailing among the islands lay in the workings of serendipity. Storm-tossed on the way to Rum, Teignmouth's boat, a cutter built in Coll from driftwood and the timbers of ship-wrecked vessels, was blown back to the Bay of Arisaig. But all was far from lost:

We soon espied a boat pushing forth gallantly towards us; and one of the rowers, evidently above the rank of a fisherman, invited us to come ashore, promising us hearty hospitality; and, on landing, we perceived, indistinctly, the form of a person wrapped in a Highland plaid, who acknowledged our approach by a slight inclination of the head, and led us through a ravine to a house about a mile distant, where we were introduced, dripping with wet, into a room, illuminated by a blazing fire, containing a large table covered with tea and divers viands, and surrounded by a family who welcomed us with genuine hospitality, as expected guests to bed and board. The sudden and unexpected transition from a stormy sea to comfort, good cheer, and cordial welcome, enabled us to realize, in some degree, the truth of Dr Johnson's observations on the origin of romantic feelings suggested by similar circumstances.

The proprietor had notice of our visit to the coast in

the morning, and, from the promontory above his house, traced our vessel till the necessity of its return became obvious; when he immediately made ready for our reception. He and his ancestors had occupied this house during 200 years. Wind-bound, we enjoyed his kindness during three tempestuous days.

On arriving at Armadale in Skye, hoping no doubt for a few days' hospitality from Lord Macdonald, they found themselves out of luck – the Lord was away:

It was necessary, therefore, to seek the Inn. A little girl trotted forward, and soon led me to a row of fishing-huts, imbedded in a hollow scooped out of the hill-side, one of which proved to be the Inn, containing two extremely small apartments: one the kitchen, without windows, its wall completely cased in soot, and apparently, as far as the eye could penetrate the dense atmosphere of smoke, crowded with inmates, whilst large quantities of fish and meat occupied the small interval between their heads and the ceiling, from which these stores depended. The other apartment was clean, and furnished with a bed; but as this was occupied by a young leddy, it was necessary that a bedding should be spread for me upon the floor. On my demurring to this arrangement, the young leddy disappeared, and the apartment was appropriated to the stranger. But never was a first ray of light more welcome than that which entered the single pane with which the chamber was furnished.

Teignmouth had other uncomfortable quarters on his journey round the coast. When he came in 1829 to visit Islay he took advantage of the steamship which ran from Tarbert to Islay, Mull and Skye. From there he sailed to Jura and Colonsay where he noted a social improvement which was being strongly resisted in the islands. Just as many people in the early twentieth century believed that furnishing council houses with baths would only encourage people to keep coal in them, so a

FOUR: 1830–1840

I SUPPOSE PART of the success of contemporary travel books lies in their skill in whetting your appetite to take off for distant parts. Such was not the object of George and Peter Anderson, who produced in 1834 the most complete guide to the Highlands and Islands yet available. George was General Secretary to the Northern Institution for the Promotion of Science and Literature, Peter was Secretary to the Inverness Society for the Education of the Poor in the Highlands.

Their guide warned potential tourists not to travel in parties of more than four because they would find it difficult to secure either accommodation or transport in large numbers. Take, they suggested, an umbrella, a pocket compass, a spyglass: 'forget not a few buttons, pins, thread, and needles and soap and shaving materials and a little medicine, chiefly laxative and sedative.'

Travellers were advised not to press for sheets on their beds because they would probably be damp: 'when obliged to sleep in a shepherd's or a labourer's cot, endeavour to get straw or *ferns* as your mattress and next to them *heather*.' It took sixteen hours to reach Inverness from Perth by coach and west of Inverness there were no regular coaches at all. Tourists were advised to hire a four-wheeled gig and not to expect too much from such inns as there were:

If much refinement and elegance is not to be seen, there is at least abundance of substantial commodities: no lack of black-faced mutton and poultry with the addition of salmon, and various other excellent fish on the sea coasts; and, indeed, scarcely a burn but affords a trout. The traveller may everywhere calculate on the luxuries of tea and sugar, and general loaf-bread or biscuits;- eggs and milk; with whisky etc., always in abundance.

And always in abundance was a kaleidoscope of unpredictable weather. The summer of 1831, a particularly tempestuous one, brought two of the most creative figures of the nineteenth century to the west, one a painter, one a poet.

J. M. W. Turner was fifty-six when he set off from London on 18 July to visit Walter Scott in his baronial mansion at Abbotsford near Melrose. Scott's publisher Robert Cadell was convinced that if Turner were to illustrate the collected edition of Scott's poems it would ensure its success. Turner was not particularly anxious to journey to Scotland, but when Cadell offered to pay his expenses he made up his mind to go. 'When I get as far as Loch Katrine', he wrote to Scott, 'I shall not like to turn back without Staffa, Mull and all. A steamboat is now established to the Western Isles, so I have heard lately, and therefore much of the difficulty becomes removed, but being wholly unacquainted with distance I will thank you to say what time will be absolutely wanting.'

After visiting Scott and executing the necessary sketches, Turner drove through the Trossachs to Glasgow, where he took the steamer to Kyleakin in Skye. From that visit came his atmospheric painting of Loch Coruisk wreathed in cloud and evanescent light. From Skye he made his way to Tobermory, where he joined the *Maid of Morvern* which was making a trip to Staffa and Iona. But a strong wind and a head sea prevented them from reaching Staffa until late in the day when there was no longer any time left to sail round Iona:

> After scrambling over the rocks on the lee side of the island, some got into Fingal's cave, others would not. It is not very pleasant or safe when the wave rolls right in. One hour was given to meet on the rock we landed on. When on board, the Captain declared it doubtful about Iona. Such a rainy and bad-looking night coming on, a vote was

proposed to the passengers: 'Iona at all hazards, or back to Tobermoray.' Majority against proceeding. To allay the displeased, the Captain promised to steam thrice round the island in the last trip. The sun getting towards the horizon, burst through the rain-cloud, angry, and for wind; and so it proved, for we were driven for shelter into Loch Ulver, and did not get back to Tobermoray before midnight.

The day yielded a vignette for *The Lord of the Isles* and an oil-painting of Staffa which was exhibited the following year. Just as Turner was returning to London, 'his health not improved by the excursion', William Wordsworth was paying his respects to Scott at Abbotsford and then moving west to Mull to stay with friends. His daughter Dora drove a small phaeton and the poet, then in his sixty-second year, walked alongside covering between fifteen and twenty miles a day. Nothing escaped his illuminating eye:

> The foliage was in its most beautiful state; and the weather, though we had five or six days of heavy rain, was upon the whole very favourable; for we had most beautiful appearances of floating vapours, rainbows and fragments of rainbows, weather-gales and sunbeams innumerable, so that I never saw Scotland under a more poetic aspect.

Where William Wordsworth saw rainbows, William Macgillivray saw only rust. Writing in the *Edinburgh Journal of Natural and Geographical Science* he warned visitors about the damp, so all-pervading that

> iron is covered with rust in a few days and finer articles of wooden furniture, brought from foreign parts, invariably swell and warp. Dreadful tempests sometimes happen through the winter, which often unroof the huts of the natives, destroy their boats, and cover the shores with immense heaps of sea-weeds, shells and drift timber.

And leaving nothing to the imagination, he advised the traveller wanting a really memorable experience of the sublime to station himself on a Harris headland at the height of a winter gale:

> The blast howls among the grim and desolate rocks around him. Black clouds are seen advancing from the west in fearful masses, pouring forth torrents of rain and hail. A sudden flash illuminates the gloom, and is followed by the deafening roar of the thunder, which gradually becomes fainter until the roar of the waves upon the shore prevails over it. Meantime as far as the eye can reach, the ocean boils and heaves, presenting one wide-extended field of foam, the spray from the summits of the billows sweeping along its surface like drifted snow. No sign of life is to be seen, save when a gull, labouring hard to bear itself against the blast, hovers overhead, or shoots athwart the gloom like a meteor. Long ranges of giant waves rush in succession towards the shores. The thunder of the shock echoes among the crevices and caves, the spray mounts along the face of the cliffs to an astonishing height; the rocks shake to their summit, and the baffled wave rolls back to meet its advancing successor. In the meantime the natives are snugly seated around their blazing peat-fires, amusing themselves with the tales and songs of other years, and enjoying the domestic harmony which no people can enjoy with less interruption than the Hebridean Celts.

With weather like that it was not unnatural that those endowed with time and money journeyed south not north. Dr James Johnson, in the preface to his account of a Highland journey, admitted that he had directed his steps into unfashionable parts: 'More of our nobility and gentry have ascended the Simplon and St Bernard than Ben-Cruachan and Ben-Lawers. They have become more familiar with Como and Lugano than with Loch Tay and Loch Lomond.'

This he thought was a great pity because 'at a small expenditure of time and money, our own islands present to the contemplative traveller or tourist in search of health, pleasure or information a series of scene and circumstances not much inferior to those which are presented on a foreign soil.'

Of course these scenes not infrequently gave cause for alarm. In 1832, when Johnson ventured north to Oban, although the age of steam had arrived its workings were still often eccentric. Johnson embarked for Staffa on the eleven-year-old *Highlander*, an eighty-foot steamer which was also equipped with a specious set of emergency sails:

> While passing the rock on which Ardtornish Castle once stood, and which is now a low jutting point that would not, for a moment, arrest a mariner's attention, the little *Highlander* doffed its cap, and every part of its clanking machinery was silent as the grave. Old stocking, rope-yarns, cords, nails, and every species of *Matériel* which the steamer could produce, were put in requisition to make the engine play – but all in vain! As there was a gentle breeze from the east, the sails were loosened from the yards; half of them flowed in streamers on the winds, and the remainder were so *holy*, as not to offer even 'passive resistance' to the gentlest gale. It was very fortunate for us that a fair wind wafted us towards Tobermory; for the *Highlander* lay a helpless log on the water, without engine to propel, or sails to guide us through the darksome Sound of Mull.

For the unflappable Johnson even appalling weather in Tobermory had its compensations:

> The howling of the winds, the pelting of the rains, the peals of thunder, the flashes of lightning, the dashings of the waves, and the clattering of the windows, combined to tranquillize the mind, and lull the tired traveller to profound repose.

Johnson would have made a first-rate copywriter for the Isle of Mull Tourist Association. On his autumnal pilgrimage round

Staffa and Iona, hard by the ruins of Duffstaffnage, the party was overwhelmed by thunder, lightning and rain:

> We quickly took shelter in a wretched-looking hut, built of rude stones, and thatched with heather. We found the interior much more comfortable than we expected. A good peat fire was blazing on the hearth, over which was suspended a pot of broth; while around the chimney hung more than a dozen of well-smoked salmon and other fish. A female and six staring, rather than smiling, children made instant accommodations for the Sassenachs, including two ladies. Pewter and wooden plates were soon rattling on the clean deal table, and the ladle was baling out the broth in the twinkling of an eye for the drenched strangers. Delight was pictured in every countenance of the Highland group, as well as of the guests; and never did I spend so happy a half hour beneath the sculptured domes of the great, as under the hospitable roof of this Highland hut! The poor family could not speak a word of English, nor we of Erse, to manifest the pleasure of the hostess and the gratitude of her guests – yet every thing went on in harmony and good nature!

Johnson pressed half a crown in the good wife's hand and she was all for getting down a salmon and boiling it for them on the spot. He used the story to illustrate the pleasures of travelling without the customary letters of introduction to the 'better classes':

> He who wishes to see as much as possible in the shortest space of time will not intrude on the domestic circle, or take up his abode for a week or two with each of his friends. Pennant, Macculloch, and fifty other Scottish tourists would have given us better delineations of man and the earth which he inhabits, had they worked harder and eaten less. Had they paid for everything they put into their mouths, the public would have had better and cheaper articles coming out of that reservoir.

It was advice followed by a Gloucestershire man, the Rev. Charles Lesingham Smith, Fellow of Christ's College, Cambridge, and the first of a long line of Oxbridge men who found their way with stout boots to Skye. Smith, who had the distinction of making in 1835 the first-ever scramble in the Cuillins, arrived by boat from Arisaig having walked the twelve miles from Kinloch Ailort. The charge for the ferry was a bottle of whisky – liquid currency was still preferred to money in those parts where stores were non-existent.

Two days later he managed to arrange for a boat to take him to Spar Cave and Loch Coruisk, but the rowers were beaten back by the wind. Thwarted, but by no means defeated, Smith set off in a hired cart for Sligachan Inn, which his guidebook described as uncomfortable:

> But to me it is a perfect palace, when contrasted with the cart in which I have been soaked and shaken. In fact it is a recent building, infinitely superior to the old one. Its situation is the dreariest spot that could have been selected for the abode of man: it stands at the base of the mountains, just in front of a torrent which, for a hundred yards on each side of its channel, has strewn the ground with fragments of rock, hurried down from the crags. Such is the view from my bed-room, which serves me for parlour also. The interior however is more cheerful, and I am enjoying extremely the humble luxury of a peat fire, while the clean napkin on the table and the fine coloured tea-things, invite me to a sober meal.

And that is the first account of what was to become the most famous climbing inn in Scotland; all the early Cuillin conquerors based themselves at Sligachan, following in the footsteps of Smith, who made his ascent almost by accident.

The following morning, 5 September, the sun was shining although the air had the keenness of winter. Outside the inn he fell into conversation with Lord Macdonald's forester, Duncan Macintyre, who told him it would take five hours to

walk to Loch Coruisk. Smith decided to think about it over
breakfast. Having despatched several mutton chops and eggs he
and Macintyre set off on their walk: the forester armed with a
telescope and a stout staff, Smith carrying his umbrella. On the
way Macintyre showed him Harta Corrie, 'a glen that some of
the gentlemen, who come to shoot, think finer than Coruisk'.

They reached Coruisk in two hours and a half. So impressed
was Macintyre by Smith's energy and agility that he suggested
they should return by a short cut over the Cuillins. 'This,' said
Smith, 'is a very weighty proposition, for to scale these rocks is
no trifle; so if you please, we'll sit down by this brook, and
take our dinner first, and then hold a council of war.'

They attacked their mutton, ham and biscuits, made what
Smith described as 'a considerable vacuum' in the whisky flask,
and set off. After a walk they came to a much steeper ascent
where they were obliged to crawl on their hands and knees:

> I here found my umbrella a sad nuisance; but the forester's
> two dogs were much worse, for they were constantly in
> my way. Sometimes we climbed up a cleft in the bare
> rock, just like a chimney; and sometimes the one was
> obliged to push the other up; and he in return, pulled up
> the first. A single false step would have hurled us to
> destruction and there was moreover very great danger that
> the first man would loosen some stone that might sweep
> down the hindmost. I once pushed down a tremendous
> rock, the percussion of which against the crag below, set
> up a strong smell of sulphur.

At length they stepped upon the topmost crag:

> And what a scene of unparalleled sublimity and grandeur
> was spread around us! On our right was the infernal chasm
> from which we had just emerged, paved by the waters of
> Coruishk; on the left we looked into Harticory, Lote-
> cory which is a continuation of it and Glen Sligachan,
> from which these two diverge. Immediately below us lay

the bays of Camasunary and Scavaig, the open sea and the isles of Eig and Rum with others of the Hebrides.

Duncan Macintyre was delighted with their achievement: 'You are the first gentleman,' he told Smith, 'that ever made this pass; nothing but a shepherd or a red deer has ever been here before us, take my word for that.'

And after a pause he added philosophically: 'I often think in my own mind that it is very strange you noblemen should come to see these wild hills of ours, and our noblemen should go to London to ruin themselves; but you've the best of it, Sir, for you gain health and strength, and our lords lose both that and fortune too.'

A year later Professor David James Forbes, making his first visit to Skye, was assured by Duncan Macintyre that Sgurr nan Gillean was still unconquered. On 7 July Forbes and Macintyre succeeded in gaining the top. 'Indeed,' said Forbes, an Alpine enthusiast, 'I have never seen a rock so adapted for clambering. At that time I erected a cairn and temporary flag, which stood, I was informed, a whole year.' When Smith and Forbes did those first two Cuillin climbs the only map of the hills was the one drawn by Arrowsmith in 1807 – Loch Coruisk was omitted altogether and the peaks were sketched in haphazardly. It fell to Forbes to compile the first accurate map of the most famous hills in Britain – a map for climbers drawn by a climber. A nineteenth-century *wunderkind*, Forbes achieved an international reputation for his work on glaciers and the polarization of heat and light. The youngest son of Sir William Forbes of Pitsligo, his mother had been the first love of Sir Walter Scott. At the remarkable age of nineteen he was elected to the Royal Society of Edinburgh and he became Professor of Natural History at the university there when he was only twenty-four.

Although Forbes had found Sgurr nan Gillean a far from difficult climb, his description of the Cuillins must have daunted many a mountaineer:

Their distance from countries usually visited is the least obstacle to their examination; their tops penetrating an almost ever stormy atmosphere, their bases bathed by a wild ever-chafing ocean, and their sides and peaks presenting more appearance of inaccessibility than perhaps any other mountains in Britain.

That inaccessibility and remoteness was to turn the Cuillins in the next few decades into a range as exciting for the climber as any in Europe. Skye indeed came to be preferred to Switzerland by many climbers who knew both well. A. P. Abraham, who scaled every peak between 1895 and 1907, numbered himself among them:

My memories of the Coolin are more pleasurable and lasting than those of the Alps. The happiness they have brought me has been greater; and in this I am not alone. Many there are who would rather forego for ever Switzerland than Skye; few there be who have once been there but have returned again in spite of the journey!

Forbes returned to Skye in 1845 to scramble up Bruach na Frithe and thereafter the peaks and pinnacles fell thick and fast: Blaven in 1857, Sgurr na Stri in 1859, Sgurr a' Ghreadaidh in 1870.

Between 1873 and 1874 Alexander Nicholson, a native of Husabost in Skye, despatched Sgurr na Banachdich, the eponymous Sgurr Alasdair and Sgurr Dubh Mor, feats which gave him so much pleasure that it's small wonder he wrote that famous quatrain:

> Jerusalem, Athens and Rome,
> I would see them before I die,
> But I'd rather not see any one of the three
> Than be exiled for ever from Skye!

The Cuillins wrung verse from many a hardened climber. The Pilkington brothers, Lawrence and Charles, who was later President of the Alpine Club, conquered Sgurr Mhic Coinnich,

Sgurr Thearlaich, Sgurr na h-Uamha and Clach Glas in 1887.
'Steep rocky hills are these,' wrote Lawrence Pilkington,

> Cliffs frowning on the seas
> With crest of indigo
> That mock the tides below –
> Dark clouds and sudden showers
> Breaking on wind-swept towers;
> Mist charged with rainbow light,
> Flung wide from height to height.

Some climbed from Sligachan Inn, some from Glen Brittle
House: medical students, surgeons, lawyers, and university pro-
fessors, like the celebrated Norman Collie who chose to be
buried in his beloved Skye alongside the most famous of Cuillin
guides, John Mackenzie of Sconser.

But there was one man, a frequent visitor to the Hebrides, who regarded mountains not, as Dr Johnson had done,
as protuberances, but as obstacles and obstructions. Joseph
Mitchell's career began in the days of sail and packhorse and
ended in the railway age. Born in 1803, he spent a large part of
his life travelling and building roads, bridges and railways all
over the Highlands. He visited Skye for the first time in 1816
and in 1883 he published at his own expense a memoir which
ran to just under a quarter of a million words: reminiscences of
lairds and landowners, of canal building, railway mania and
arduous journeys. In mid-September 1837 he was in Skye and
slept the first night in the inn at Broadford:

> It rained all night, and as we wound our way next morning
> along the Sound of Scalpa to Sconcer Inn, fifteen miles
> from Broadford, the sun rose and the sky brightened up to
> a clear azure blue, with here and there patches of cloud
> resting on the mountain tops.
>   The road ascends and descends, and is in many places a
> good deal elevated above the sea. Every new winding gives
> you a fresh grouping of headland, isle, and sea; and as it

was the herring season, the vessels and boats gave the scene life and animation.

There was a revenue cutter lying in the Scalpa Sound which we looked down upon. She fired a gun. There was a bustle on the deck, her sails were set, and she moved gracefully towards the Sound of Skye. The captain's son, we learned, had been appointed minister to a parish on the east of the island, and she was conveying some of the neighbouring clergy who had assisted at his ordination.

As there was a cattle-market being held at Sligachan, Mitchell found the inn at Sconser full of hungry farmers and cattle dealers:

The breakfast table of the inn groaned with viands – salmon, cod, mackerel, fowls, beef, and potatoes etc. At respectful intervals sundry stoups of whisky bitters (Skye being celebrated for its bitters, held an infallible antidote against the damp climate) with half-filled glasses standing beside them.

A good many market people were in the room. 'Now, Greshornish,' says a broad south-country voice, 'I'll gie ye £3 10s. for thae stots.'

'No, no,' said a stout, powerful man, dressed in rough shepherd's plaid, with a deep guttural voice, 'I must have the £3 15s.; what is the use of your higgling? I know you are for the seventy cows, so come to the point at once.'

'Oh, ye're a hard man, Greshornish, I canna think o' geeing you ony such price, it winna afeurd it. God bless you, mon, ye hae no notion hoo prices are doon i' the south. Just tak the money offered, and let's mak a bargain at yeance.'

'No, confound you, Macfarlane, you are offering for the stots, when I know you are for the cows also, so you better say £3 15s. for the whole over head.'

Such was the substance of a long conversation overheard while at breakfast, and which ended apparently in nothing, for they drove off together in the same gig for the market stanse at Sligachan.

These markets are of much importance in Skye. They are held at Portree, Sligachan, and Broadford at stated periods. The south country drovers attend and purchase from the breeders and farmers. The large farmer here generally disposes of his stock, the cottar his cow and stirk, and two or three sheep. The debts that are contracted at other periods of the year are here generally discharged, and there is thus a most heterogeneous collection of people – tacksmen, farmers, drovers, cottars, factors, shopkeepers, innkeepers, many women, and gillies great and small. There are, besides, the extensive droves of cattle and sheep, that are driven to these places to be sold and sent forward to the south.

At Sligachan the road was lined with tents. It was about eleven o'clock of the second day, and the tent-keepers were engaged in cooking broth, mutton, and potatoes for the country people inside, with the only drink, mountain dew. The tents, if they could be called such, were temporary, formed of blankets, and were miserable. The whole aspect of the place – a bare and barren mountain-side – was wild and savage. It had been raining all night, and as most of the people had been either up drinking or sleeping on the bare ground during the night, they had a dirty and dishevelled appearance. The gentlemen had a blowsy unshaven aspect, the horses were ungroomed and there being no stables, little gillies with kilts, bare heads, and bare legs were mounted, and with much glee were riding backwards and forwards along the road.

The cattle and sheep extending over an immense space were standing quietly looking at each other, while the gillies, their drovers, were leaning on their sticks or lying on the damp ground, their faithful collies at their feet, panting for employment. Such was the fair at Sligachan, which I viewed with no very favourable impression of the civilization of the people.

By this time, although sails still outnumbered funnels, steamboats were exciting little or no interest – they had become an accepted part of the seascape. The journey from Glasgow to Skye, which had taken ten days or more under sail, was now four times as fast. But although steamers were plying round the islands none had yet ventured as far as St Kilda. So when on 25 July 1838 the *Vulcan* left the Clyde on an excursion for St Kilda with thirty-four passengers she was making history. On board was author Lachlan Maclean, who left an account of the journey. On their way they called in at Lochmaddy where they found a group of emigrants waiting to sail on the brig *Corsair*. Maclean tried to persuade one of the two clergy-men on board to row across with him to the emigrant ship:

> Dr Macleod said his feelings could not stand it; and indeed it was a heart-rending scene. If he *had* gone, it would have marred his pleasure for the future part of the voyage, as indeed it did in part in my own case. Their berths seemed uncomfortable and ill aired – their tale of woe was harrow-ing to the feelings, and then the idea, notwithstanding of *their* golden dreams, the idea of so many fine fellows and fine women being decoyed to Cape Breton – the very St Kilda of America! At parting they gave us three cheers and a shower of blessings.

The main purpose of the voyage to St Kilda was spiritual. Dr Macleod had come to preach to the islanders, catechize them, and conduct a communion. On board as they steamed into Village Bay were two bedsteads for every house paying rent, one each for the poor widows and sundry chairs, stools, dressers, glass windows and pieces of Delftware. The manse and church had been built some eight years earlier, the work of the Rev. Neil Mackenzie who in 1829 had become the first resident minister on Hirta for over a hundred years.

When the gunner of the aptly named *Vulcan* fired a cannon and the band on board struck up the villagers ran for their lives to the manse to tell the minister that a boat on fire had entered the bay. It was the beginning of a memorable two days for St Kilda, one to be talked about for years to come. Maclean, a Gaelic speaker, was very conscious of the privations of the community. At the time of his visit eight out of ten babies died of tetanus within twelve days of birth. So insulated from the outside world was the minister (he had only received one newspaper in the previous three years) that he was still offering up prayers for William IV, dead for over a year. 'The writer took it upon him to advise Mr M'Kenzie to change the form from "our Majesty the King" or "Queen" to our *Sovereign* making no distinction as to *gender*.' He needn't have bothered: Victoria outlived the lot of them.

And then it was back from the strange world of the islanders to civilization. On 30 July Maclean was asking:

> Is this a dream or a reality? Have I been in St Kilda this *morning* and am I now at 11 o'clock at night in Oban, and reading the *Glasgow Herald of this morning's date*? It is a reality, for I see all my fellow-passengers around me except Dr Macleod whom we landed about three hours ago with sky-rockets and roar of cannon at *Fionnary*.

And there was the reality of the farewell *Deoch-an-doruis* at the Caledonia Hotel:

> Here while the Vulcan was taking in coal, we had three bottles of whisky made into toddy, one tumbler to each, for which we were charged six shillings a bottle, which is at the rate of thirty-six shillings a gallon, for what, making allowance for a pound of sugar and two pence worth of peat, never cost more than nine shillings. This is a profit with a vengeance. This is the third time I have been in this house, leaving it resolving and re-resolving. Our own excellent and attentive steward Mr Rose would have given us as good on board for something more than half.

And then, with an eye on the possibility of being at the Caledonia's mercy at some time in the future, Maclean diplomatically added: 'A pedestrian tourist, however, may be very glad to find an inn so respectable and commodious in the Highlands.'

The summers of 1835 and 1836 were particularly wet and stormy; the poor quality and quantity of the corn and potato harvest, coupled with a failure in the fisheries, was such that an appeal was launched at first in Scotland and subsequently throughout Britain to save the west coast from a fate approaching famine. The sum of £50,000 was subscribed and disaster averted. Allan Fullarton and Charles R. Baird, both members of the Statistical Society of Glasgow, were responsible for administering the fund and during the course of their work they came in possession of a mass of information which they laid before the public in 1838.

They gave a vivid description of the discomfort in which the people lived:

> The hut frequently, or rather generally, consists of a butt and a ben – one end is occupied by the family and the other by the little cow, if they have one, and the pig – the whole inhabitants entering by one door. The fire, which is composed of peat or turf, is in the centre of the floor and the smoke escapes by an aperture in the roof – very frequently formed by an old cask or barrel – and by the door and window, which last is seldom glazed, but is shut with straw or heather or wooden folding shutters. The roof is thatched and very warm – the floor is simply the soil, sometimes mixed with ashes and the walls, from their being in many instances formed of triturated or rounded stones and sometimes of turf, are very permeable and consequently admit a great quantity of air and moisture. There can be no question that such a residence enhanced in all its wretchedness by the vicinity of the family dung-hill and midden-dub has much in it of a tendency to degrade and brutalise the inhabitants.

The authors, both Protestants, singled out Barra for particular criticism. It was at the time up for sale. Its proprietor,

Colonel MacNeil, had established a large chemical manufactory to provide some form of employment when the kelp industry came to an end, but his speculation failed and the situation of the islanders was desperate:

> But, fearful as are the physical circumstances of the people, their intellectual condition is yet more deplorable. The savage-like ignorance in which they are suffered to live and die, will not be credited by persons at a distance. It looks like a tale invented for the purpose of exciting wonder and distress, in the minds of those who have enjoyed the blessings of mental cultivation, to state that, of the 2,200 inhabitants of one of the British Islands, only 200 are reported as being able to read, and that, although there is a parish clergyman, as well as a Catholic priest, resident in Barra, there is no effective school in that Island or its dependencies. Yet such is the fact. A fact disgraceful to the age in which we live, and peculiarly so to those who, although connected with the Islands, and themselves possessed of the blessings of education, have allowed, and are allowing, so many of their fellow-creatures to pass, from the cradle to the grave, in a state of ignorance as profound as that which characterises the New Zealander.*
>
> We trust that the time is not far distant when a brighter day will dawn upon this far distant Island of the sea and the inhabitants of Barra shall, in respect to education, be placed on a footing with the most highly-favoured of their neighbours.

The poverty which Fullarton and Baird found in the Hebrides was certainly aggravated by poor harvests but it stemmed in great part from the decline in the demand for kelp. Scott remarked upon the great prosperity that the burning of seaweed to produce kelp had brought to the Laird of Staffa; he was no exception. So lucrative was the trade that some farms paid their

---

* The authors were referring to the aboriginal Maoris not the European colonists.

rent solely from the sale of kelp; in 1818, 6,000 tons were produced in the Hebrides and every ton represented the ashes of 24 tons of seaweed.

The American War of Independence and the Napoleonic Wars pushed the price of kelp up to £22 a ton. But the Battle of Waterloo signalled the end of the kelp boom. Barilla could once again be imported from Europe, a much cheaper raw material to make soda, soap and glass from than the Hebridean kelp. The development of a cheap method of producing soda from salt and the discovery of vast deposits of sulphate of potash in Germany forced the price of kelp down even lower, to £2 a ton.

Lord Melbourne appointed a Select Committee to enquire into the problems created by the failure of the kelp industry and it emerged that the crofters who collected and burned the seaweed were frequently not paid in cash – they would be provided with meal and other articles of food and any credit left over would go to pay off their arrears in rent. Wages, when wages were paid, ranged from 1*s* to 1*s* 6*d* a day.

Giving evidence, Alexander Macdonald, a former kelp agent, told the committee that in the years 1808–10 he had given Lord Macdonald £14,000 a year as his share of the profits. 'I find', he said, 'that during the ten years down to the repeal of the kelp duty I paid the different proprietors within a trifle of £240,000.'

There were no overheads, no need to pay the natives more than the minimum, and the truck system ensured that almost all the profits went into the pockets of the proprietors.

A grim picture of the distress that ensued when kelp could no longer be sold has been left by Catherine Sinclair, who was not only a prolific author of such improving works as *The March of Intellect and Modern Society* but was one of the first woman writers* ever to visit the Hebrides. Like many of the

---

* She had been preceded by a Mrs Murray, whose *A Companion and Useful Guide to the Beauties of Scotland and the Hebrides* was published in 1810.

leisured classes, she was a constant traveller and wrote guides both to Wales and the Shetlands. But she is probably best remembered for her *Scotland and the Scotch*, an account of a journey made to the west in the late 1830s.

Like others before her, she was sensible that her steps were leading her into neglected parts:

> While the press abounds with interesting pages describing the present state of the Pawnees, Zoolus, Red Indians, Thugs, London pickpockets, New Zealanders and other barbarians, hardly one stray journal has ventured forth, these many years, respecting the almost unknown tribes of Caledonia.

She recognized that there were no cathedrals, opera houses or works of art in the Highlands and that the weather was not of the best, but as compensation there were 'old traditions, second sight, bagpipes, witchcraft, clans, tartan, whisky, heather, muir-fowl, red-deer and Jacobites'.

A relative of the Macdonalds of Sleat, she was luckier than most travellers. Hospitality at Armadale Castle was succeeded by a night with the Mackinnons of Coirechatachan, where she met a venerable old lady who remembered the visit of Boswell and Johnson. Then there was a pleasant sojourn with the Mackinnons of Strath. There was still no public transport in the Hebrides, and none of the inns had horses or carriages: 'travellers in Skye move about like the Ayrshire beggars who are laid helplessly down at a door, till, having been received and refreshed, they can be passed on to the nearest house beyond.' She continued:

> Nothing can be more depressing than to witness the ruinous effects produced in Skye by the disuse of kelp. Every change in our manufactures throws some people of course out of employment, and here, thousands who could once earn a competence, are now deprived of their only resource, while many whom we saw, having already exhausted all their provisions, were wandering along the

shore, picking up shell-fish as their sole means of existence. To the no small credit of those poor destitute people, not a sheep is ever stolen, nor an article of any kind missing, though two families, who were starving of cold and hunger, next door to each other, were reduced to live in one apartment, and to use the furniture of the rest for fuel.

Troops of men were flocking along the highway with a bag of meal, literally a single 'feed of oats,' slung over their shoulders, going to 'the Continent,' as they call Scotland, in search of work. Not one of these wanderers begged, and we were told, that the first account which generally reached home of their having got employment, is transmitted in company with a boll of meal, for the use of friends and parents left behind. One might have feared, that every warm and generous feeling of the heart would be chilled and frozen into selfishness by the intense suffering we witnessed, but it is far otherwise, and the magnanimous self-denial of Highlanders for the sake of their relations, is a beautiful trait of national character . . .

In every family here there are sons, brothers, or cousins, hurrying to Australia in search of the golden fleece. That country is the great lumber-room now for stowing away supernumerary people, and I was much interested, before we left the manse of Strath, to be present at the marriage of a young couple who intended making a wedding jaunt to the Antipodes. Mr Mackinnon, with his usual kindness, invited the whole friends and attendants into a parlour, where, for the first time, I heard the ceremony in Gaelic. It must have been, to judge from the agitation of all present, deeply impressive; and in less than ten minutes, the pretty interesting bride was metamorphosed from a Highland housemaid into an Australian shepherdess. Her friends were all dressed in the tartans of their various clans, looking most respectable, and evidently much awed by the compliment of being admitted into the manse, treading on the carpet as if it had been red-hot, and occupying the very smallest possible corner of their chairs. After a final benediction had been pronounced, the 'best man' poured out a glass of whisky, which we were expected to taste, wishing the bride happiness and prosperity in the far distant land where she was going in search of both.

At the time when Catherine Sinclair made her journey it would have been unthinkable for a lady of quality to have stayed in an inn, even had one presented itself. They were still few and far between and notorious for their bedbugs and fleas. Manses were often the only houses other than those of the gentry where a traveller could find reasonable accommodation. Their hospitality was almost limitless and in the summer a succession of guests would fill the bedrooms.

A fine description of such a manse has been left by Sir Archibald Geikie, who was born in Edinburgh in 1835 and at the age of twenty joined the Geological Survey. His studies took him on frequent expeditions to the Hebrides, where the minister was often the only member of the community with the advantages of a university education. For those who could neither read nor write such a person assumed great importance. The minister possessed not only a glebe but usually a farm as well – he was knowledgeable about agriculture and cattle breeding and combined the role of laird, clergyman and universal host. Such a man was John Mackinnon, who became minister of the parish of Strath in Skye in 1825:

He succeeded to the parish after his father, who had been its minister for fifty-two years, and he was followed in turn by his eldest son, the late Dr Donald, so that for three generations, or more than a hundred years, the care of the parish remained in the same family. Tall, erect, and wiry, he might have been taken for a retired military man. A gentleman by birth and breeding, he mingled on easy terms with the best society in the island, while at the same time his active discharge of his ministerial duties brought him into familiar relations with the parishioners all over the district. So entirely had he gained their respect and affections that, when the great Disruption of 1843 rent the Establishment over so much of the Highlands, he kept his flock in the old Church. He used to boast that Strath was thus the Sebastopol of that Church in Skye.

The old manse at Kilchrist, having become ruinous, was abandoned; and, as none was built to replace it, Mr Mackinnon rented the farm and house of Kilbride. There had once been a chapel there, dedicated to St Bridget, and her name still clings to the spot. Behind rises the group of the Red Hills; further over, the black serrated crests of Blaven, the most striking of all the Skye mountains, tower up into the north-western sky, while to the south the eye looks away down the inlet of Loch Slapin to the open sea, out of which rise the ridges of Rum and the Scuir of Eigg. The farm lay around the house and stretched into the low uplands on the southern side of the valley . . .

In the wide Highland parishes, where roads are few and communications must largely be kept up on foot, the minister's wife is sometimes hardly less important a personage than her husband, and it is to her that the social wants of the people are generally made known. Mrs Mackinnon belonged to another family of the same clan as the minister, and was in every way worthy of him. Tall and massive in build, with strength of character traced on every feature of her face, and a dignity of manner like that of a Highland chieftainess, she was born to rule in any sphere to which she might be called. Her habitual look was perhaps somewhat stern, with a touch of sadness, as if she had deeply realised the trials and transitoriness of life, and had braced herself to do her duty through it all to the end. But no Highland heart beat more warmly than hers. She was the mother of the whole parish, and seemed to have her eye on every cottage and cabin throughout its wide extent. To her every poor crofter looked for sympathy and help, and never looked in vain. Her clear blue eyes would at one moment fill with tears over the recital of some tale of suffering in the district, at another they would sparkle with glee as she listened to some of the droll narratives of her family or her visitors. She belonged to the family of Coirechatachan, and among her prized relics was the coverlet under which Samuel Johnson slept when he stayed in her grandfather's house . . .

The younger generation at Kilbride consisted of a large family of stalwart sons and daughters, whose careers have furnished a good illustration of the way in which the children of the manses of Scotland have succeeded in the world. The eldest son followed his father as minister of Strath; another became proprietor of the 'Melbourne Argus'; a third joined the army, served in the Crimea, and in the later years of his life was widely known and respected as Sir William Mackinnon, Director-General of the Army Medical Department, who left his fortune to the Royal Society for the furtherance of scientific research. Most of the family now lie with their parents under the green turf of the old burial-ground of Kilchrist.

FIVE: 1840–1850

ALTHOUGH QUEEN VICTORIA and Prince Albert did not make their first visit to Balmoral until 1848, as significant a year for royal patronage in the Highlands as it was for revolution in Europe, by the beginning of the 1840s Scotland had established itself as a fashionable place to be seen. 'The number of foreign, but chiefly English travellers,' Lord Cockburn observed in the autumn of 1840, 'is extraordinary. They fill every conveyance and every inn, attracted by scenery, curiosity, superfluous time and wealth, and the fascination of Scott, while attracted by grouse, the mansion-houses of half of our poor devils of Highland lairds are occupied by rich and titled Southrons.'

But the 1840s was still a pioneering period in the far Hebrides even though an increasing number of solitary tourists were setting off from Edinburgh and Glasgow bound not for the Swiss valleys or Tuscany but the mountainous regions to the north and west of Fort William. Among them was the Rev. Thomas Grierson, Minister of Kirkbean, his scanty wardrobe in a fishing basket, his favourite terrier frequently at his heels.

His regimen was spartan:

I would recommend early rising, and always turning over a good stage before breakfast. This I never failed to do when a young man, and even now I like walking before breakfast best when on a journey. Fifteen or twenty miles before nine o'clock was my ordinary arrangement.

His accounts of pedestrian tours in the Highlands and Islands were first published in the *Dumfries and Galloway Herald*. It was his custom to take a three-week break in the autumn: holidays which began in 1811 and continued to the 1850s when he was no longer able to 'pad the hoof' so vigorously.

Regular steamship sailings had made inter-island travel easier but, as was to be the pattern for many decades, the accommodation was always inadequate. In the summer it was often impossible to get a bed in Oban or Tobermory or Portree, and if you weren't first off the steamer you might find yourself sleeping on a sofa. Grierson recounts the story of the boat arriving at Oban crammed with passengers:

> one of them particularly intent on comfort sprung actively ashore and calling out 'Hurra! for the first bed' ran in the direction of a strong gas-light which he had ascertained was in front of the Caledonia Hotel. He succeeded in getting the *first bed* but it was just across the pier in ten or twelve feet of water from which he was not without difficulty extricated by some herring fishers who happened to be still astir.

Having found a bed in an inn, organizing a meal was often difficult. In Broadford the Rev. Grierson ordered breakfast but nothing happened for ages:

> After much delay and visiting the scene of action, the kitchen, I found that absolutely nothing was done! On expressing disappointment the reply was 'Oh! are ye in a hurry? we didna ken.'
> 'Can we have herrings and eggs?'
> 'You can get plenty o' eggs, but we hae nae herrings.'
> 'Indeed! the boat which set us ashore was so full of them that we could scarcely find room for our feet.'
> 'Weel, then, we'll see what can be done.'
> Not withstanding our utmost efforts, much time was lost before we could manage our point; and had we not lent a hand ourselves, it seemed questionable whether breakfast would ever have made its appearance. The people, generally speaking, in this island have no idea of the value of time. Many of them, unfortunately, having little

to do themselves, conceive all others similarly circum-
stanced, and their great object seems to be to spin out
every little job that occurs.

Even when there *was* food you weren't always sure of
getting a share of it. In 1840 Grierson had spent three days
rambling in Arran and found at Loch Ranza a comfortable little
inn:

> Upon entering I was glad to see a roast of mutton at the
> fire, but to my mortification was informed that it was
> preparing for two gentlemen who had ordered it some days
> before. Trusting to some favourable arrangement, I loitered
> about the shore for an hour or so, till the expected arrival
> when I was politely invited by the gentlemen to partake.
> Our dinner consisted also of excellent fresh haddock; so
> that we had no reason to complain of bad cheer. My
> companions were very genteel, agreeable young men –
> one had been ten years in India; and the other, the son of
> a gentleman connected with the island, had just returned
> from prosecuting his studies in England. We spent a very
> happy evening together, over some excellent whisky-toddy
> and tea which the Eastern soldier had been so provident
> as to send along with their luggage, not trusting to the
> resources of this sequestered spot for that delicate com-
> modity.

The prescribed tourist route round Skye in the 1840s was
limited to four main objects of curiosity: the Storr, the Quiraing, Spar Cave and Loch Coruisk. The terrain between these
attractions was usually dismissed as uninteresting and always at
the forefront of the traveller's mind was where he was going to
rest; as Grierson recalled of the season of 1849:

> On the night of the 4th September, the scramble for beds
> in Portree was almost unprecedented. Having secured ours
> however, before leaving it the previous day, we were
> not incommoded. Late in the evening, a coach-and-four
> arrived full of ladies, but how or where they were lodged

we could not conjecture, as every corner was occupied long before their arrival; very probably they were indebted for night-quarters to the vehicle in which they had travelled. This I know, that some half-dozen gentlemen were glad to wrap themselves up in their cloaks and plaids, and squat for the night on the floor of the sitting-room; there being no alternative, they wisely submitted with a good grace.

Much the easiest way to reach a place like Portree was by boat from Glasgow. Before the railways forged north to Strome Ferry and Mallaig, travelling overland was slow and costly. Henry Thomas Cockburn knew all about it: in 1834, at the age of fifty-five, he was promoted to the bench as one of the Lords of the Court of Sessions. From then until his death on the South Circuit in his seventy-fifth year he travelled thousands of wearisome miles round his native Scotland. He records that on one occasion in 1845 it took him six hours to cover eighteen miles. Between Fasnacloich and Oban there were the two ferries of Shean and Connel to cross. At Connel the boat, though bespoke, was on the wrong side:

And then the pulling and lifting the poor carriage, by Celtic arms alone, unaided by any machinery, the scolding and directing – all in Gaelic – and no man master! The expeditious passage of a Highland ferry would be a much greater miracle than the passage of the Red Sea.

By then Oban had become the steamship crossroads of the west. 'Each landing', Cockburn observed, 'creates a flutter which disturbs its solitude. It seems fuller of strangers than natives.' Some of the visitors were from abroad but the majority came from England. Cockburn had been prompted by the ambition to visit Iona and at six o'clock on a September morning in 1840 he and his family embarked on the steamer *Brenda*:

I saw little after the tenth or twelfth mile till I reached Iona, for my very unmaritime stomach was rebellious, and for about four hours I lay abusing my folly, and vowing that this should be my last voyage. In this state I was landed on that island, but my infirmity instantly ceased, and, getting into water like glass, it never came over me again during the day.

The ruins greatly surpassed my expectation. I thought that all I was to see was the mere stools of buildings, whereas I found as many legible old inscriptions, carved tombstones, and standing walls, as in most very ancient, fallen edifices. Being walked round by the Captain, and only an hour allowed, and a whole cargo of travellers to be satiated, it was not a visit that could do more than leave a general idea of the appearance of the place, and enable one to know hereafter what people are speaking about when they speak of Iona. Were it not absurd, after all that has been said and written, it would be irresistible for any one of ordinary sense or feeling to indulge in the visions which this remote and deserted little island is so well fitted to inspire.

But Cockburn was disgusted by the state of the ruins:

What a disgrace to their owners! who I understand are the Argyles. All the waters of Loch Fyne will not cleanse them from the shame of these neglected solemn ruins. They are the most interesting relics in the British Empire, and might, by mere attention, and with very little expenditure, have been protected for centuries; the flat, carved tombstones might have had their venerable letters saved from being worn out by regardless feet; and the grass might have been kept as smooth and pure as the turf at any of the Oxford colleges; but no foul beast ever trod a pearl in the dirt so unconsciously as these titled men have, for many ages, but particularly during the last hundred years, deliberately allowed fragments, that have been the wonder of thinking men, to be reduced to a worse condition than most pig-

styes. If proprietors who behave so had all the apology of
bankruptcy, this might be a consolation, for a well-disposed
mind could not fail to consider this as God's punishment
for their crime. But every one of them wastes yearly, on
contemptible importance, what would be quite sufficient
to transmit these sacred gifts of a former age to succeeding
ones, and in such a condition that they might be admired,
as they descend, without having the veneration they inspire
marred by unnecessary disgust. Even *the* Argyle is diminished in my sight.

And then on to Staffa, which Cockburn was in two minds
about. A friend of his who had been to see it described it as
'contemptible' but Cockburn was vastly impressed by the cave:

No thunder is more awful than the roar of the wave as it
breaks along the sides, and on the inner end of the cavern.
And then there is nothing human about it. It is all pure
nature. Not a single ass has even painted his name upon it.
The solitude and storminess of its position greatly enhance
its interest.

On the whole, I have rarely been more gratified than
by at last beholding these two sights, one the wonder of
nature, the other of man. I had been anxious to see them
almost all my life, and the recollection will now be more
exciting than the fancy of them was.

The rest of the sail was delightful. We moved over a
sea nearly of glass, past places, but particularly past islands
and points, and things called castles, the names of which
were familiar, and where the mere surprise of seeing what
one had so often heard of was a pleasure. In their present
state there is very little beauty in any one place along
that coast, and not a single old building of any architec-
tural interest. The great want is of wood, even of larch,
which however, for scenery, is rarely wood. Nor is it true
that wood would not grow on these tempest-beaten and
foam-dashed spots. A thousand small and exposed, but still
oak-clad islands, and promontories, and bays and knolls, and

ravines, but especially islands which are most in the way of the spray and the wind, attest that, even though not planted in great masses, the whole of the Hebrides might be adorned and warmed by trees. It is sheep and poverty, not the ocean or the storm, that keep them hard and uniform. What an Archipelago it would be had it only due summer!

A year later Cockburn is in Skye, 'as proud', he recorded in his diary on 3 September 1841, 'as Columbus when he landed in America.' Again there is one of nature's great geological feats to admire, the Cuillin hills and Loch Coruisk made famous by Macculloch and Scott. Cockburn, as he put it, was 'palpitating with anxiety' in case the object of his pilgrimage should prove to be an anticlimax:

I was foolish enough, considering what I knew, to feel a moment's disappointment at the smallness of the cupful of water. But it was only for a moment. And then I stood entranced by the scene before me. Subsequent examination and reflection were necessary for the details, but its general character was understood and felt at once.

The sunless darkness of the water, the precipitousness of the two sides and of the upper end, the hardness of their material, consisting almost entirely of large plates of smooth rock, from which all turf, if there ever was any, has been torn by the torrents; the dark pinnacles, the silence, deepened rather than diminished by the sound of a solitary stream, – above all, the solitude, – inspired a feeling of awe rather than of solemnity. No mind can resist this impression. Every prospect and every object is excluded, except what are held within that short and narrow valley; and within that there is nothing except the little loch, towered over by the high and grisly forms of these storm-defying and man-despising mountains.

Each of the hills seems to consist of one stone. They are not rocky mountains, but mountainous rocks. Hence the sharpness into which they have been cut, and hence the large plates, or rather fields, of smooth stone which the two sides exhibit. I need scarcely say that there is no path, no grazing, no human symptom. When it rains the sides must stream with water. But the surfaces are so steep that it soon runs off, and when I was there, there was not a rill either to be heard or seen; except one, which ran down an open grassy slope on the east side of the lake towards the lower end. The hills enclosing the upper end may, on being examined, be found to be not at all semicircular, or to have any approach to that form, but as seen either from the sea or Coruisk, they seemed to be curved inwards, and part of the seclusion of the place appeared to be owing to their doing so.

Cockburn spent an hour admiring the 'stern sterility' and then returned to the rowing boat for the journey back to the head of Loch Slapin where they had embarked.

As our bark receded from the shore, the Cuillins stood out again, and the increased brilliancy of the sun cast a thousand lights over Scavaig, and over all its associated islands, and promontories, and bays. The eastern side of everything was dark, while the opposite sides shone more intensely in front of the evening sun. One horn of the curved Cuillins, though quite clear, seemed almost black, while the opposite horn was blazing. The dark side of Rum was towards me, but its outlines, like all the other shaded summits, were made distinct by the glow behind them. And as far as the eye could reach, bright spots, especially light-touched rocks, attracted it; and almost the whole line of wall by which the eastern shores of everything but Scavaig were barriered, was gleaming in the distance. It was a glorious scene.

I should feel it as a sort of sacrilege to prefer, or even to compare anything to the Firth of Clyde. But one great difference between the sources of its beauty and that of Scavaig was forcibly impressed upon me. How much does Clyde owe to human association, to culture, to seats, to villages, to towns, to vessels! The peculiarity of the interest in Scavaig arose from the total absence of all human interference. The scene would have been the same had man not existed.

It is about this time that we begin to detect the faintly querulous note of those who are happy to share their impressions of distant places in print but not necessarily cheek by unwashed jowl with the masses. In Iona by the 1840s one not only had to contend with the jostling of fellow tourists but the avaricious inhabitants. Robert Carruthers, the editor of the *Inverness Courier*, visited Iona the year after Cockburn but in flat calm summer seas:

> The steam-boat had left Oban crowded with tourists – some from America, two Germans and a whole legion of 'the Sassenach.' The quiet beauty of the scene subdued the whole into silence – even the Americans who had *bored* us about their magnificent rivers, and steam-boats sailing twenty-five miles an hour. The sea was literally like a sheet of molten gold or silver. Not a breath agitated its surface as we surveyed it from beneath a temporary awning thrown up on the quarter-deck. The only live objects that caught the eye were an occasional wild fowl or porpoise.

Carruthers was overcome with the magical associations of the island; but not for long:

> As our vessel drew up to the usual landing-place, every cottage sent forth its inmates, young and old, and the beach was lined with spectators. The children came forward and stood on the crags and stones at the shore holding out collections of the small green and white pebbles and shells which abound in the island and vociferating 'twopence,' 'threepence,' 'fourpence' or 'sixpence' according to the amount of rarity of the store offered for sale.

There was then brisk altercation between two of the islanders, both claiming to be the official guide; one a ragged ancient, the other the local schoolmaster:

It was obvious that the schoolmaster was the real Simon Pure and that his rival was an idle, talkative old fellow who envied the dominie his glory and his gains. The party went on towards the religious buildings but the guides kept up a constant war of words, the pretender being, of course, the most noisy and most confident. The people crowded forward to settle the disputes of the guides, as to the history of the respective objects, all talking in Gaelic, while the passengers broke out into fits of laughter and the ragged children thrust in their hands and shells for money. The whole scene was so much at variance with the objects around and the feelings they are calculated to excite that we were glad to steal away from the rout and take a solitary perambulation among the mouldering tombs and churches.

No man was enabled to take more private and enviable perambulations of the Hebrides than Sir Thomas Dick Lauder of Fountainhall who, as Secretary to the Board of Fisheries, was commanded at public expense and in considerable comfort to investigate the natural history of the herring, the migratory fish on which much of the economy of the islands depended.

Lord Cockburn was one man who envied Sir Thomas his annual eight weeks' summer voyage deeply. He had been invited for a short cruise himself and noted the splendour of the hundred-ton cutter and its crew of twenty-three, commanded by a naval lieutenant. Cockburn wrote waspishly:

The voyages cost him nothing, or very little; they are dignified by a sort of pretence of public business; and their pleasures are not entirely maritime, for wherever a friend lives within reach of the coast, the herring secretary has only to anchor, to land and to reach him. Then the gratification of taking friends, including his daughter and other ladies on board and giving them trips and of wearing a blue jacket and trousers and letting the moustaches sprout; what can be more delightful to a sketching and geological man, whose digestion and slumber and reading, Neptune with his worst lurches cannot disturb.

On one of these summer cruises Sir Thomas took with him his 'sincere and faithful friend' James Wilson, and their circumnavigation from the Clyde round the north of Scotland and back to Leith lasted just over three months. Imagine a functionary of the Ministry of Agriculture, Fisheries and Food taking twelve weeks off to tour the North Sea fishing grounds today – more likely a quick reconnaissance in an RAF Nimrod, brief talks with union leaders and a dash back to the filing cabinets in Whitehall.

A 90,000-word chronicle of the expedition was written by Wilson and published in two volumes illustrated by steel etchings based on Sir Thomas's sketches of the passing scenery. What Daniell accomplished in aquatints, Wilson did in words. 'We had', he wrote, 'occasion to visit many localities not within the range of the ordinary tourist, as well as to explore those numerous isles and picturesque inlets for which our western shores especially are so remarkable.'

They visited Colonsay and dined off mutton 'kept to a minute, roasted to a turn', winding up the evening in gallant style with a Highland fling. Captain M'Neill of Colonsay pressed them to stay the night in his comfortable mansion, but the party were determined to return to the cutter in readiness for an early morning departure for Oronsay. Hebridean weather was no more predictable then than it is today; the night was filthy:

> We heard the rattling of the blast without as it rushed from tree to chimney, to show its impartial character, or howled past doors and windows, like a hungry wolf seeking what it might devour. We concluded with a small deoch-an-doruis from an ancient quaich, and bidding farewell to our hospitable friends, we buckled on our pea-jackets, drew our south-westers over our brows, tried to look grim and bold, and then sallied forth. The road by this time had been converted in many places to something like a muddy river. Our own clay assuredly was moist enough before we

got on board, but it is a sustaining thought to know that one is serving their Queen and country, and we ourself never cared much for rainwater at any time; so after looking a little at the cabin fire (which was bright and beautiful) and also at a red herring and a glass of ale, merely to encourage commerce, we retired to our respective places of repose.

From Oronsay they sailed to Tiree, Staffa, Iona and Mull and thence to the Small Isles. On Eigg they were shown the cave in which the entire population were smoked to death by a party of vengeful Macleods on a day trip from nearby Skye. Two hundred and fifty years later the grisly evidence was still lying around:

The bones of the victims lay scattered about the floor in various places, a considerable number at the far narrow end, to which it may be supposed the wretched creatures had retreated when the horrid choking smoke began to roll its fatal wreaths upon them. A good many lie also near the entrance, being the skeletons of those who had clung to the hope of fresh air or freedom or mercy from without. In the intermediate spaces they are few in number and apart, as if certain individuals from the huddled masses at either end had tried by a last desperate effort to change their respective positions when too late, and life had failed after a few faltering footsteps.

We found the scalp of a little child at the back of a large stone, and between the stone and the cavern side, close to its opening, as if it had been making a vain attempt to creep outward from the smoke, in ignorance of the clearer though not less deadly breath of 'the lightning of fiery flame.' Most of the skulls were gone, and what struck us as curious, there were scarcely any teeth lying among the stones. These melancholy remains consist chiefly of the bones of legs and arms and a good supply of shoulder blades.

That they are a high-minded and romantic race these

islanders, and extremely tenacious of their ancestral glories, is evident from this, that during the potato harvest the pigs are put out of the way of doing mischief by being all cooped up in this same ancestral cave – and fine mumbling work they will make of it, while grumphing to each other – *de mortuis nil nisi bones.* Now as the people eat the pigs and the pigs the people's predecessors, it follows logically that the present natives are a race of cannibals of the very worst description.

Yet they seemed a pleasant, courteous, good-looking set of lads, such of them as we came in contact with, and one little fellow of about ten years of age, who followed us into the cave, was most assiduous in dragging out the hind-legs of an old lady from an obscure corner, into which she had probably retired to be out of the crowd during the night of the great fire. He told us that strange sights were sometimes dimly seen flitting about the mouth of the cavern during the darker hours, and that dreadful groans and shrieks, especially of women, were often heard. We were really glad to embark again on board the Cutter.

During their June and July jaunt in among the Western Isles they encountered atrocious weather as they tacked from Skye to the coastline of Wester Ross and out to the Long Island. When they reached Stornoway they were impressed by the mounds of salted cod, ling and saithe spread out on the beach for curing:

As we walked along the beach towards the stacks in question the air became sensibly odoriferous. We found them neatly built, the fish being carefully laid flat, layer above layer and each kind being made up in separate stacks each consisting of a couple of tons. Previous to curing they are bled, cut open, nicely cleansed and the back-bone for nearly two-thirds of its length from the head cut away. They are then immersed for a certain time in large pickling tubs and finally spread out to dry upon the stony beach which seemed excellently adapted to the purpose. The country people make a kind of coarse *finnans* of their fish by smoking them and filling the orbits of the eyes with salt, which descending down the spine forms a pervading and preserving brine. This practice originated formerly when salt was dear and is now continued by habit in preference to any other.

We passed a kraal of wretched looking huts, some of them so small and sad, so resembling decayed portions of mother earth upheaved by accident that we did not at first regard them as human dwellings, till we observed a single pane of glass in one sticking in the thatch. Some were attached together and thickly built up with sods in such a way as to look like natural green hummocks over the tops of which chance had thrown a scanty covering of dirty straw. The interiors were very miserable. Yet the people had a healthy aspect on the whole and seemed in no way deficient in muscular strength. Black eyes, dark hair and a somewhat swarthy complexion were more common than we expected in a country where the Scandinavian blood so long prevailed.

From Lewis they cruised back to Skye to continue their circumnavigation of the island. On sailing up Loch Follart, now known as Loch Dunvegan, they found the castle undergoing extensive renovations, the first since 1812. Norman, the twenty-second chief of the clan Macleod, had succeeded to the chiefship in 1835 and it was he who in a few years' time, with the failure of the potato crop of 1845, would be faced with ruin and forced to find a post as a civil servant in Whitehall. But in the summer of 1841 there was still plenty of money in the Macleod coffers:

The ancient castle of Dunvegan rose before us, close upon the northern shores of a small embayment of the sea. The weather moderating slightly in the forenoon we landed for the purpose of inspection, as well as to despatch our letters. Though the general pile is imposing from its size and situation, from its dark rocks below, almost surrounded by the wild ocean waters, and its massive square towers, in part thickly mantled by luxuriant ivy, yet is less picturesque than might be expected, chiefly we daresay from some of its more modern additions being built in an unaccommodating *house-like* form not amalgamating with the prevailing character of the scene. We also saw the whole concern, both in and out, to disadvantage, as a few weeks ago an immense range of buildings had been taken down, and there were at the moment about a score of south-country masons, (large athletic, fair-haired, fresh-complexioned men, at once distinguishable from the surrounding and more swarthy Celts) at work upon the premises. These were consequently bespattered with lime, the flooring of many rooms uplifted, and halls crowded and passages almost blocked up with various ranges of hewn stones and cut timber. The last Laird of Macleod lived long in London, and little attention had been paid to this ancient dwelling for a length of time either before or since his death; but his son, a young married man, is now effecting great improvements. We could scarcely judge of the character of the rooms, with their dusty furniture, broken plaster, rent pannelling, and all those other discomforts which precede the remodelling now in agitation. This Castle has evidently great capabilities, and a judicious combination of ancient baronial splendour, with the more luxurious and refined comforts of modern elegance, will render it a princely place: but the Secretary (whose fine taste and feeling on such points may well be relied on) seemed sorely distressed that a principal portion of the interior, containing a magnificent old hall 80 feet in length by 20, had been taken down.

It was all in great contrast to the destitution and distress which characterized the island at the time – a lot of which, Wilson suggested, the people had brought upon themselves. In addition to the decline in kelp manufacture and the diminished herring shoals, apathy lay like a malaise on the land:

Their indolence and inactivity, except by fits and starts, cannot be denied, and their dark, moist, dirty dwellings, with the unseemly byre as a hall of entrance, are surely their own free choice rather than nature's doom. It may be mentioned as a good example of the prejudice produced by long-formed habits, that for some years after the construction of roads in Skye, the common people refused to travel on them, alleging that the hard surface of stone and gravel wore their shoes, and bruised their feet, and so they long continued to follow the old uneven paths. The most distressful feature of the poverty of these people is its demoralising influence. The flocks of sheep farmers are yearly thinned by the reckless hand of want, goaded on by approaching famine, and uncontrolled by the now nearly dissevered chains of feudal affection.

Ironically, as the fisheries cutter weighed anchor, Dick Lauder and James Wilson were able to observe five or six boats from Banff making excellent catches of cod and ling. The fish was there but the men of Skye were lacking in boats.

Famine apart, the most far-reaching and radical event of the 1840s was the religious schism which came to be known as the Disruption. In the growing conflict between landowners and peasants the ministers of the Established Church had aligned themselves on the side of patronage. Spurred on by a new wave of earnestness, piety and evangelical revivalism, congregations began to question the right of landowners to foist ministers upon them, and particularly ministers who condoned the worst excesses of forcible eviction.

The Church had failed the people and in 1843, after congregations were denied the right to choose their own ministers, 474 members of the clergy seceded and formed the Free Church. Their people came out with them and while the old parish kirks stood empty the new congregations gathered in barns and in the open air to hold their services. Many proprietors refused them sites to build new churches and extraordinary alternatives were resorted to. The people of

Strontian, denied land to erect a church by Sir James Riddell, the owner of Ardnamurchan, raised £1,400 to build a floating church which was anchored offshore: 'it was found that for every hundred hearers, the vessel sank an inch in the water. Nothing therefore, could be easier than to keep the register. They could tell to an inch the popularity of every minister who came.'

A similar state of affairs in the Small Isles led the Free Church minister, Mr Swanson, to buy a small boat, the *Betsey*, which came to be known as the floating manse. He was persistently denied a site for a home by the owner of Eigg, Professor Macpherson of Aberdeen, a staunch upholder of the established Church. A vivid account of Swanson's travails has been left by Hugh Miller, himself an even more remarkable man.

Miller, born in 1802, was apprenticed to a stonemason, and acquiring more than the usual interest in the materials he was chiselling, moved on to become an eminent geologist, an author, and editor of the *Witness*, one of the few papers in Scotland to champion the cause of the Free Church. Invited by the Rev. Swanson to pursue his geological studies on board the thirty-foot *Betsey*, Miller joined his friend in Tobermory for a three-week cruise in June 1844. The cabin reflected the dual role of his host as minister and mariner:

A well-thumbed chart of the Western Islands lay across an equally well-thumbed volume of Henry's 'Commentary'; there was a Polyglot and a spy-glass in one corner, and a copy of Calvin's 'Institutes,' with the latest edition of 'The Coaster's Sailing Directions,' in another; while in an adjoining stateroom, nearly large enough to accommodate an arm-chair, if the chair could have but contrived to get into it, I caught a glimpse of my friend's printing-press and his case of types canopied overhead by the blue ensign of the vessel, bearing in stately six-inch letters on white bunting, the legend 'FREE CHURCH YACHT'.

From Tobermory they beat out into the Sound, rounded the headland of Ardnamurchan, passed Muck and anchored late at night some fifty yards from the shore of Eigg:

We were now at home, — the only home which the proprietor of the island permits to the islanders' minister; and, after getting warm and comfortable over the stove and a cup of tea, we did what all sensible men do in their own homes when the night wears late, — got into bed.

We had rich tea this morning. The minister was among his people; and our first evidence of the fact came in the agreeable form of three bottles of fine fresh cream from the shore. Then followed an ample baking of nice oaten cakes. The material out of which the cakes were manufactured had been sent from the minister's store aboard, — for oatmeal in Eigg is rather a scarce commodity in the middle of July; but they had borrowed a crispness and flavour from the island, that the meal, left to its own resources, could scarcely have communicated; and the golden-coloured cylinder of fresh butter which accompanied them was all the island's own. There was an ample supply of eggs too, as one not quite a conjuror might have expected from a country bearing such a name, — eggs with the milk in them; and, with cream, butter, oaten cakes, eggs, and tea, all of the best, and with sharp-set sea-air appetites to boot, we fared sumptuously. . . .

Among the various things brought aboard this morning, there was a pair of island shoes for the minister's cabin use, that struck my fancy not a little. They were all around of a deep madder-red colour, soles, welts, and uppers; and, though somewhat resembling in form the little yawl of the *Betsey*, were sewed not unskilfully with thongs; and their peculiar style of tie seemed of a kind suited to furnish with new idea a fashionable shoemaker of the metropolis. They were altogether the production of Eigg, from the skin out of which they had been cut, with the lime that had prepared it for the tan, and the root by which the tan had been furnished, down to the last on which they had been moulded, and the artizan that had cast them off, a pair of finished shoes. There are few trees, and, of course, no bark to spare, in the island; but the islanders find a substitute in the astringent lobiferous root of the Tormentilla erecta, which they dig out for the purpose among the heath, at no inconsiderable expense of time and trouble. I was informed by John Stewart, an adept in all the multifarious arts of the island, from the tanning of leather and the tilling of land, to the building of a house or the working of a ship, that the infusion of root had to be thrice changed for every skin, and that it took a man nearly a day to gather roots enough for a single infusion. I was further informed that it was not unusual for the owner of a skin to give it to some neighbour to tan, and that, the process finished, it was divided equally between them, the time and trouble bestowed on it by the one being deemed equivalent to the property held in it by the other. I wished to call a pair of these primitive-looking shoes my own, and no sooner was the wish expressed than straightway one islander furnished me with leather, and another set to work upon the shoes. When I came to speak of remuneration, however, the islanders shook their heads. 'No, no, not from the *Witness*: there are not many that take our part, and the *Witness* does.' I hold the shoes, therefore, as my first retainer, determined, on all occasions of just quarrel, to make common cause with the poor islanders.

Two years later the Hebrides, indeed the whole of the north-west, suffered the loss of the potato crop; the famine, mirrored in the west of Ireland, excited considerable attention both in Parliament and in the Press. Among those who investigated the extent of the distress was Robert Somers, whose *Tour of Inquiry* was published *seriatim* in the radical *North British Daily Mail*.

Somers, an implacable opponent of the non-improving landlord, ironically owed his swift passage to the west coast to one of the biggest landowners of all, Macleod of Macleod, who ran a handsome stage-coach three times a week from the Highland capital of Inverness to the gates of his castle at Dunvegan; this journey of 144½ miles was accomplished in little more than twenty hours.

Somers found Skye in a worse condition than any part of the mainland:

> Had war or pestilence swept over the island eight or ten years ago, cutting down all the strong and the able bodied, and leaving none but little boys and old women to do the labour of the field, Skye, in these circumstances, would have been much the same in its external appearance as under its present alleged redundancy of population. An immense proportion of the soil fit for tillage lies in all the rude waste of nature. Every object wears the desolate aspect of a place deserted by the hand of industry. Land unploughed and unenclosed; houses bare, dilapidated, and unapproached by roads or foot-paths; ditches chokefull of weeds and stagnant water; huge mosses and heathy uplands, relieved only by dreary tracts of withered and whitened pasture, from which the few remaining traces of former tillage are rapidly disappearing, only make the desolation more striking by calling up the remembrance of busier and happier times. Man, instead of conquering the difficulties of the soil, has here permitted the difficulties of the soil to conquer him. You look in vain for any signs of a firm, bold, masterly dominion of the soil. There is none of that Titan energy which drains swamps, levels heights, fills up hollows, grinds the very rocks, and stamps images of power, order, and beauty upon the face of Nature. The agriculture of Skye on the contrary is feeble as the feebleness of infancy – more indeed like the puny scratching of savages than the powerful agriculture of civilised life.

Simplistically perhaps, Somers put the blame entirely on the shoulders of the landlords. He found Macleod's ownership of the only shop on his estate attended with some of the evils of the truck system:

> Macleod is also a sheep-farmer, an innkeeper, a coach-proprietor, and a ship-owner; and by this multiplicity of engagements, he only fulfils what seems to be an essential condition of rank and importance in Skye. In every part of the island you find the most multifarious and incongruous professions conjoined in the same person. The sheep-graziers are also cloth-merchants, factors, meal-mongers, and inspectors of the poor; and the very ministers of the sanctuary are seen chaffering as store-farmers in the wool and the flesh markets. This system is injurious in every respect. It divides society into two extreme classes, one of which it exalts and the other it humiliates. In Skye the rich monopolise all profits and emoluments, while the reins of social oppression are tightened to the utmost stretch of endurance over the necks of the poor.

Somers attacked the clan chiefs for clinging on to the very power which had impressed young Stanhope forty years previously. Where Stanhope had seen romance and glamour in the deference paid to Lord Macdonald, Somers saw only corruption:

> Towards the close of the last century, the rise of rents and the profits of kelp brought the Highland chiefs within the reach of the same temptations to which the English and Lowland barons had yielded a century earlier. They introduced them into the splendid warehouses and saloons of London, filled with the richest handiwork and the rarest and costliest luxuries which the ingenuity of man could devise, or the unwearied energies of commerce could collect. There, too, were the English aristocracy, with their princely equipages, and their glittering wealth, to excite emulation and ruffle pride. The effect was the same as when a hawker of the backwoods spreads out his toys and trinkets and firewaters before a tribe of Indians. The vanity

of the Highland chiefs was intoxicated and the solid advantages which the new tide in their affairs had opened up to them were bartered for the merest baubles. There is a staircase-window in Lord Macdonald's mansion in Skye which is said to have cost £500.

The misery which Somers recorded was to explode later in the century in the Land League riots and the appointment of a Commission of Enquiry into the grievances of the people. But not yet; not for another forty years.

When two years later Queen Victoria and the Prince Consort made a cruise through western waters they were carefully insulated from any scenes that might distress them. The small squadron attending on the Royal Yacht *Victoria and Albert* included the *Black Eagle, Garland, Undine, Fairy* and *Scourge*. With her the Queen had her two eldest children, the Duke and Duchess of Norfolk, her Secretary of State Lord Grey and assorted courtiers.

They left Osborne pier in the Isle of Wight on 11 Aug 1847 and rounded the Mull of Kintyre seven days later. It was, the Queen recorded, a calm and pleasant evening: 'We dined and went on deck; and the blaze of the numerous bonfires – the half moon, the stars, and the extreme stillness of the night – had a charming effect.'

On the following day, a Thursday, they left Crinan at nine in the morning and began to thread their way through the islands:

We passed first up the Sound of Jura, where numbers of people met us in small boats, decorated with little flags; then up the Pass of Kerrera to Oban, one of the finest spots we have seen, with the ruins of the old Castle of Dunolly and a range of high mountains in the distance. We then came into the Sound of Mull by Tobermory, a small place prettily situated, and from thence the view continued beautiful. At one o'clock we were in sight of the Isles of Rum, Eigg and Muck (rather large islands, which Lord

Salisbury bought a few years ago). Next we passed the long, flat, curious islands of Coll and Tiree. The inhabitants of these islands have, unhappily, been terrible sufferers during the last winter from famine.

At three in the afternoon the Royal Yacht anchored close to Staffa and the Queen and her party entered the barge and were rowed towards the cave:

It looked almost awful as we entered and the barge heaved up and down on the swell of the sea. The rocks under water were all colours – pink, blue, and green – which had a most beautiful and varied effect. It was the first time the British standard with a Queen of Great Britain, and her husband and children, had ever entered Fingal's Cave and the men gave three cheers, which sounded very impressive there.

Like most people who led comfortable lives, Victoria remained strangely unmoved by the wretchedness and misery that she could, had she desired, have observed in the Hebrides. Where Somers had found islands full of people in the last stages of famine and destitution, she found islands 'full of poetry and romance, traditions and historical associations'.

The Queen closed her eyes to things which would not amuse her. She was not amused by political agitators like Somers and her advisers took pains to protect her from any unpleasantness. She sketched the picturesque not the poor and remained unimpressed by facts or events that she could not fit into her domestic view of life. Even Albert's enthusiasm couldn't tempt her to land on Iona, that most holy and historic island; she was quite content to stay on deck and execute an indifferent sketch. 'I must,' she confided to her journal, 'see it some other time.'

But there was not to be another time. She never ventured into Hebridean waters again and when the hour came for the crofters to rise she had no sympathy for them at all.

SIX: 1850–1870

IN THE MID-NINETEENTH CENTURY there were an extraordinarily large number of physically active men who had
absolutely nothing to do. In London they could be seen
embalmed in the windows of West End clubs reading the
papers, their lips sometimes moving silently; when in the
country they were usually engaged in exterminating wildlife.
One such man of leisure was a Wiltshire parson, the Rev.
George Hely Hutchinson, who concealed his identity under
the pen-name of 'Sixty One'. One morning in June 1850 he
was staying at Borthwick Brae with two friends when Snowie's
list of shootings arrived in the post. Among the advertisements was one for some shooting in Lewis and Harris. 'The
space seemed large, the rents small. Accordingly, instanter the
phaeton was ordered to the door; to the nearest station we
drove and were in Edinburgh in time to find our gentleman at
Home.'

As a result of the meeting Hutchinson and his two sporting
chums leased 130,000 acres. For three years they slaughtered
whatever moved within a fifteen-mile radius of Aline and then
Hutchinson moved to Soval Lodge, nine miles from Stornoway, and until 1869 flushed its 75,000 acres – stags, grouse,
sea trout, salmon, geese and woodcocks were pursued with
schoolboy zeal.

He found the natives most helpful: 'The Highlander is a
gentleman at heart, and never forgets his respect for you, so
long as you respect yourself.' When it was time for him to
leave the keepers and stalkers and gillies wrung his hand in
gratitude: 'there was truth in that grasp – nay, even in the tear
that stood in the eye of some, and certainly in my own.'

It was a hectic and tireless two decades; birds plummeted from the sky, fish were whisked from the water, deer buckled to the ground as Hutchinson let fly in all directions. Not even the whales were safe:

We were all sitting together one of those fine days when there is nothing to be done but admire the prospect – if the midges will let you – with just mist enough on the hills to prevent stalking, no breeze for fishing, and grouse too small to shoot, when our notice was attracted by several boats appearing at the mouth of Loch Seaforth. Out went the prospects, and McAulay was summoned; after a long look through his glass, he remarked, shutting it up, with emphasis, and with that look of pleasure and determination which gleams in his eye when he sees a good royal: – 'It's just the whales.' An electric shock seemed to pass through the whole party, and in less than no time every craft in the establishment was manned, and everybody seized every conceivable weapon of offence, and hurried into the boats. The whale boat, our own particular conveyance across Loch Seaforth, was manned by the best crew, under the special guidance of McAulay, who hoisted his flag on board of it, and then took command of the whole squadron, to watch the movements. The whales had been descried off West Tarbert Loch, in Harris, when all the inhabitants got into their boats, and, following them, 'put them,' as it is termed, 'into Loch Seaforth.' . . . Having thus induced them to enter such a loch, you follow them up in the same manner, slowly and distantly, cautiously outflanking, but never pressing or disturbing them. Thus, as it were, left to themselves, they gradually advance up the loch, following their leader; and, if the tide and shoal and all be propitious, he will of his own accord take the shoal water, even sometimes beach himself on the sandy spit, when the whole band will follow him like a flock of sheep, and strand themselves. . . .

Now, Loch Seaforth is admirably adapted for a whale-hunt. The loch runs up from the Minch straight to Seaforth Island, about six or seven miles, pretty well iron-bound on both sides. At Seaforth Island, which is nearly opposite Aline, the loch turns almost at right angles, and runs by Aribhruich, where are some sharp rapids, up to Skipnaclet, its head. Here, or on the shoals above – the Aribhruich Narrows, as they are called – is the best place for stranding the bottle-noses. . . .

The whales passed round the island without hesitation, and pursued their way upwards, our boats following slowly. There was little delay or stoppage till we came to the Narrows. There the whales paused, and did not much seem to relish the idea of putting their noses to the steam. We, of course, rested on our oars, awaiting their determination, and there we waited all night.

Towards dawn, as it was low water then, and it was quite clear that the whales were waiting for water, or something before proceeding higher – once past the Narrows, they were ours – and that could not come for some time, we, who had started shortly after our breakfasts without any luncheon, were getting hungry; so we rowed back to Aline to soothe our very clamorous stomachs, and, that done, returned without delay.

During our absence a reinforcement had joined our fleet, and a curious, and, as it turned out, a most unfortunate one it was. It was in the shape of one of the dirtiest, crankiest tubs of a boat, with the roundness, not the steadiness, of what was called at Westminster, in my day, 'a punch-bowl,' and as little hold in the water as a skiff. How it got round from Tarbert-in-Harris, whence it was said to come, I cannot imagine. The crew consisted of three of the ugliest, noisiest, most ill-conditioned-looking viragoes of women I ever looked upon. No one knew, or, if they did know, would own them. There they were, perched up in their boat, like so many witches, barring their broomsticks . . . The tide was now making fast. The rocks over which the rapids had been foaming were disappearing. We could see the leaders of the band of the bottle-noses moving about, and gradually feeling their way as to taking the Narrows. Half-an-hour's patience now, and our troubles would be repaid, and this band, like the last that had visited Loch Seaforth a few years before, would be ours; when, just at this critical moment, this triumvirate of demons, deaf to all entreaties, to offers of bribes innumerable, to threats (for it was proposed to fire across their bows to bring them to) – these demons, with an indescribable yell, broke loose, and being on the outside, but nearest, flank to the whales, rushed their boat at the Narrows with the incoming tide. Deep were our imprecations, for in a second the whales turned, and the game was up. . . .

There was nothing to be done now but to join in the chase. We could not succeed in turning or making any hand of the band, and they made good their retreat to sea again. A good many shots were fired, and apparently a good many whales received rifle-bullets, which drew blood; but they sank, and I do not think that eventually more than three or four carcasses were recovered.

There were many more in the Hebrides like Hutchinson, happy to potter and pop off at anything that moved from a stag to a snipe. Armed with the deadly and beautiful toys hand-made by Purdey, Lancaster, Westley Richards and Boss they went out with their gillies and keepers looking as much for quantity as quality. John Colquhoun came to Skye with his horse and dog-cart looking, above all, for the white-tailed sea eagle which was, as he put it, 'a deficit in my collection'. The sea eagle, thanks to the vigilance of shepherds and the rapacity of Victorian Colquhouns, is now a national deficit; it became extinct in the islands at the turn of the century. But in the early 1860s their eyries could still be found all over Skye and there was a price of 10s on their head, since it was popularly believed that they regarded new-born lambs as a delicacy. The keeper at Glenbrittle admitted to a reporter from the *Glasgow Evening*

News in 1865 that he had killed upwards of sixty eagles in the previous few years.

On reaching Staffin Colquhoun contacted a keeper who told him that there were three breeding pairs around but that their eyries were not yet discovered.

> These sea-eagles are neither so rare nor so savage as the golden, but, although more vulture-like in their spirits and tastes, are still destructive and ferocious birds. Their liking for fish and water-fowl makes them choose a range in the neighbourhood of the sea or of a fresh-water loch. They will not scruple to attack a full-grown goose, although I have never been able to prove their power to lift one. The time for the sea-eagle's fishing is when the warm weather brings its prey to the surface. I have known a shepherd lad secure a good breakfast every day while the eaglets were rearing, simply by watching the feeding hour and robbing the eyrie.

Colquhoun himself was robbed of any opportunity to bag a sea eagle in Skye, but he made up for it amply on 11 May 1879 when he shot one of the only pair nesting near Cape Wrath. The other bird was seen to frequent the old site for a year or two afterwards, but then it, too, disappeared. Perhaps had Colquhoun operated from the sea and not the cliffs he would have been able to wreak even more destruction – having a boat meant you could double your sporting opportunities. Sir Randal Roberts was a frequent writer in the *Field* who bagged anything that came within bullet range, edible or otherwise. When the birds migrated he could always fall back on the seals. One autumn, aboard the *Sprite*, a sixty-foot yawl, Sir Randal and his cronies set off from their base in Mull for the seal islands in Loch Sunart:

> Having come to anchor, had our dinner and made every-thing snug, we began to think what we should do for the rest of the afternoon. I proposed taking the gig and pulling up the loch to see what seals there were. Accordingly,

leaving all on board, I took Angus with me and pulled up the loch in search of sport. Cautiously we advanced, Angus taking a couple of sculls, whilst I sat in the bows with my glass in hand, and swept the loch and shores as we advanced. A low sound from Angus and the stopping of the oars made me turn round when I saw two seals right in our wake, about 100 yards' distance, looking at us with their large thoughtful eyes. Bidding Angus crouch down, I stealthily took up my rifle, whistling a few sharp notes. The smallest seal immediately advanced some few yards towards the boat, when I pulled the trigger and fired, the bullet sped true, and the splash and commotion told me that I had hit him. When we arrived at the place the blood and oil on the water showed plainly that I had hit my mark; but although the water was clear, and scarcely three fathoms in depth, we could see no signs of the seal. This is the usual disappointment the seal-shooter encounters, unless he is so fortunate as to shoot one either on a rock whilst he lies basking, or in shallow water, and he kills him dead.

Sir Randal did not reveal to his readers what you actually do with a seal when you have killed it. They would make very mournful, indeed reproachful trophies for the gunroom or library, and the west coast seals wouldn't even have interested Lady Roberts: 'the skin being of too coarse a texture to admit of its being used for ladies' cloaks, muff, or tippets.'

The following day the *Sprite* anchored off Canna and the sportsmen managed to creep up silently to an island where a dozen seals lay, 'some asleep, others stretched lazily on the rocks'. Resting his polygroove twelve-bore Rigby muzzle-loader on a rock, Sir Randal put up the 100 yards sight and drew bead:

I touched the trigger, the bullet sped true and with a thud entered the seal's body. It rolled into the water, dyeing the surface with blood and oil and lashing about in a furious manner; but his struggles were soon over and I saw his carcass lying inanimate, half-submerged.

It was a bull seal, five feet five inches in length. And then it was back to the shooting lodge on Mull and the pleasures of the table:

Dinner was always an institution at Glenmahra, with its fore and after accompaniments. Somehow or another, you always turned into the dining-room before going into the drawing-room and there, curious enough, you always found Mr Jones with his back to the fire and a couple of bottles on each side of the fender, at a respectful distance from too much heat. There too, on the sideboard was a certain bottle with a quill through the cork and a great deal of 'writing about it,' as Angus said, yclept Angostura Bitters, flanked by a bottle of sherry and some wine-glasses, standing invitingly on the sideboard. It is astonishing what the force of habit will do; for not withstanding Highland appetites, you never can withstand sherry and bitters.

'So you've had a pleasant trip?' said Mrs Jones as she helped the soup.

'We've had the jolliest in the world,' answered Johnson; 'and I shan't easily forget the *Sprite*, the rocky shores of the Western Isles and the pleasant events of the last few days.'

It was quite possible to have a really jolly time in the Hebrides if you kept your eyes firmly closed to everything other than the sights of your rifle. Unless you looked for wretchedness you didn't necessarily need to see it and if you didn't see it then it didn't exist. However, some there were who came to find misery and there were others who had it thrust upon them.

Among the first was Lady Macaskill, a noted philanthropist, who found so much penury and hunger that her strongly worded report induced the usually imperturbable Queen Victoria to send her £100 towards relieving conditions in the islands.

In Portree in 1851 Lady Macaskill watched the poor women of the village knitting in Hogg's Woollen Manufactory. The mill, still in use as a showroom selling tweeds and woollen goods to tourists, had been built with the remains of a fund collected for the destitute Highlanders and its main function was to benefit and employ the destitute poor of Skye.

'Now then,' wrote Lady Macaskill in her business-like way, 'the poor knitters are paid thus:- Two pence halfpenny for each pair of stockings, full men's size; gloves and comforters and waistcoats and all other things in the same proportion. Thus a good knitter may earn with diligence and industry something less than a penny a day! Ample remuneration! – great profits – but in what quarter? Into whose pockets does the money flow?'

Part of the answer was explained a few years later to a group of undergraduates from Oxford, the guests of Thomas Brassey Jr whose father had made a prodigious fortune building railways all over the world. He lavished money on his son and bought him a fifty-six-ton yacht, the *Cymba*. It was, wrote Thomas with youthful pride, 'of most elegant form and marvellous speed. She is so swift that for many summers yachting writers in the columns of the "Life" have been pleased to confer upon her the epithets "peerless" and "unmatched".'

Even at that age Thomas Brassey settled only for the best. In twenty years' time he was to build the famous *Sunbeam,*[*] a sail and steam schooner ten times bigger than *Cymba*, and embark on an eleven-month voyage round the world with his wife and family. Brassey received an earldom, became a civil lord of the Admiralty and a Governor of Victoria. But picture him on Sunday 13 July 1856, just turned twenty, anchored off Canna, about to have a few simple truths thrust upon him:

> After a late breakfast, we had the awning put up on deck
> and luxuriated beneath its shade, reading and thinking and

* See page 195.

doing nothing. Our pilot who had conducted us from Tobermory was very loquacious and prattled away, at first to our great annoyance, though the remarkable nature of his information concerning the social state of the great lairds of the Western Isles soon made him more interesting. Almost every great proprietor whom he mentioned, and they were many and rich, was born, was living, or had died under mysterious circumstances. Land or island owners, glorying in their £60,000 per annum, hardly wrung from a poverty-stricken tenantry, so far from endeavouring to improve the condition of their tenants, are wont to expend their whole substance in the gaieties of the London season; while the entire care of the property appears to be entrusted to a set of factors who, to the sole advantage of their privy purse, habitually exact double rental. No means of redress exists for the unhappy tenants, whose complaints, addressed to the proprietor are, by him, of course, referred to the astute and pitiless factor. Such were the wailings of the pilot. The uncouth and wretched appearance of such of the inhabitants as we encountered amply fortified his statement.

Another early intimation that amid the beauty of the islands there existed the very depths of poverty was imparted to young Osgood Hanbury Mackenzie in June 1853. He and his uncle, Dr John Mackenzie of Inverewe, had been on an expedition to St Kilda. Although he was only eleven years old at the time, one particular impression remained engraved on his mind. It was a Saturday when, on their return from Hirta, they made a landfall at Obbe on the west coast of Harris. They had no milk on board for their Sunday porridge so young Osgood was sent ashore with Simon Hector the butler to try and obtain some. They chose a thatched house and entering by a door near one end made their way through dung and straw past the eight or ten cows to where a fire was burning against the gable and where there was what appeared to be a bed:

We were most politely and hospitably welcomed. The good wife, like all the Harris people, had most charming manners, but she was busy preparing the family breakfast, and bade us sit down on little low stools at the fire and wait till she could milk the cows for us.

Then occurred a curious scene, such as one could hardly have witnessed elsewhere than in a Kaffir kraal or an Eskimo tent or Red Indian tepee. There was a big pot hanging by a chain over the peat fire, and a creel heaped up with short heather, which the women tear up by the root on the hillsides and with which they bed the cows. The wife took an armful of this heather and deposited it at the feet of the nearest cow, which was tied up within two or three yards of the fire, to form a drainer. Then lifting the pot off the fire, she emptied it on to the heather; the hot water disappeared and ran away among the cow's legs, but the contents of the pot consisting of potatoes and fish boiled together, remained on the top of the heather. Then from a very black-looking bed three stark naked boys arose one by one, aged, I should say, from six to ten years, and made for the fish and potatoes, each youngster carrying off as much as both his hands could contain. Back they went to their bed, and started devouring their breakfast with apparently great appetites under the blankets! No wonder the bed did not look tempting! We got our milk in course of time, but I do not think it was altogether relished after the scene we had witnessed, which impressed me so much that I have never forgotten it!

At this time in the century the two most daunting aspects of travel in the Highlands and Islands were the wretchedness of the accommodation and the elastic timetables of the shipping companies. Take poor Charles Bond, Secretary of the Royal Patriotic and Industrial Society, who embarked on the *Duntroon Castle* on Christmas Day 1851 bound for the islands to investigate means of ameliorating the almost universal destitution.

Dense fogs delayed the departure of the vessel from Greenock until lunchtime on Boxing Day. Then at six o'clock in the evening when they were three miles to the east of Sanda there was an ominous crack — the main shaft of the engine had fractured and the steamer became disabled. A sail was spread and the ship slowly made its way to a safe anchorage in Campbeltown Loch. As there was no other steamer to Skye until the following week, Bond returned to Glasgow where in self-defence he took to his bed with a violent cold. On the first of January he set off again, this time to *sail* from Oban to Skye, deciding no doubt that the uncertainty of the wind was preferable to the wonders of steam.

Perhaps even more uncertain was the prospect of trying to find a bed when you eventually did arrive. When Charles Richard Weld, writer of guidebooks and Alpine climber, visited the north in the summer of 1859 he found Sutherland particularly bereft of accommodation. The Duke, he was told, was resolved to build no more inns: 'probably from a desire to keep his vast county in a state of primitive wildness, deer being more considered than men.' Worse even than Sutherland were the inns on Skye. 'It is tantalising', wrote Weld, 'to be always near the sea and have fish very seldom. When you ask for fish the answer generally is that the sea is too rough to enable the boats to go out — a statement that you cannot conscientiously contradict. Mutton, mutton, mutton — on this the traveller must feed, happy if he can get a potato with his meat.'

The nadir of his journey was reached in the inn at Sligachan where he was the only guest for four days, two of which were so stormy that he was unable to venture forth. The inn is still there, centrally heated now and ultra-comfortable, but in 1859 —

> Sligachan inn at no period of the year can be a lively abode, but when the clouds, surcharged with vapours from the Atlantic, pour their contents on the Cuchullins, the steep sides of which are ribbed by innumerable water-falls, you may suppose that its few eligibilities are very much at a discount.

It was not rain that fell, but periodical water-spouts that

swept from the hill-tops down the glen with such force and fury that you would have believed you were in the zone of typhoons. A water-course through the glen, which, during fair weather, is a mere brook, was swollen to the dimensions of a mighty river, which rushed down, roaring, to the head of the bay. Add to these disagreements that the inn is situated in the midst of barren moorland, treeless, and with nothing to break the sterile prospect but a bridge backed by Bein Glamaig, which, during the greater part of the time that I was at Sligachan, was shrouded in mist, and that the house itself was extremely uncomfortable, and you will see that it requires considerable philosophy to support the ennui of a four days' residence at Sligachan.

How soon you can detect the influence of a clever and clean hostess, and that of the reverse. It was very easy to see that the domesticities of Sligachan were out of joint, for the landlady neglected her duty, and the landlord went about the house with a heavy heart. And no wonder, for when you hear that his wife was not allowed access to the liquor closet, you will understand that she was not fit for the office of landlady.

The day after my arrival was Sunday, and although the weather was as bad as can be conceived, I contrived, in the spirit of hoping and enduring all things, to get through the day. Twice, availing myself of the retreat of the storm blasts in the gorges of the hills, I went out, but had scarcely walked a hundred yards from the house when the enemy was down upon me with a fury that sent me reeling back to the inn. Some hours were spent in ingenious devices to make the peat smoke ascend the chimney, and occasionally I found occupation in re-lighting the fire, which had been suddenly extinguished by a waterfall down the chimney.

But still, as you may suppose, the time hung heavy; for although in a snug cosy inn you may be able to realise what Washington Irving calls a feeling of territorial consequence when taking your ease before the fire, I am quite sure, if you see Skye through such a medium of mist and gloom as I did, you will have no desire to be the possessor of an acre of land in it. Of course I held long parleys with the landlord; but he being a Ross-shire man, and a recent dweller in Skye, knew but little folk or local lore, and indeed he had no inclination to talk of anything but his own sorrows.

Weld, sometime Secretary of the Royal Society and member of the Alpine Club, was one of the pioneer Cuillin climbers; making the first recorded ascent of Sgurr na Stri in 1859. But there were others who came to Skye armed not with ropes but easels. Among the earliest was the painter known as Turner of Oxford. I have a watercolour of the Cuillins which he executed in 1824; nothing is missing that the southerner would expect in a Highland scene – Harta Corrie is wreathed in mist, an eagle hovers in the air, a stag and a hind stand poised for flight; in the foreground purple heather and on the jagged peaks ominous racing clouds. It is like the Cuillins but it is not the Cuillins, if you take my meaning. Turner's namesake, J. M. W., produced an even more impressionist painting of Loch Coruisk when he came to Skye. It was as if the wild smoky peaks of the Cuillins were too much for the palette of Academicians used to softer and more cultivated landscapes.

In the 1850s Walter Cooper Dendy made a striking series of illustrations to accompany his guidebook *The Wild Hebrides*. He was not only a President of the Medical Society of London but a practising and very practical doctor. 'Bannocks and whisky essential for the pedestrian', is one of his more notable pieces of therapeutic advice for those on walking tours. His verbal flights are as eccentric as the strokes of his brush:

> Early morning, and Armidale smiles in the sun. The architecture is in poor style, but it boasts a large staircase window with a painting of the mighty Somerled. Its umbrageous woods are hanging on the mountain side and shelving down to the beach are dipping over grey rocks

into the pure green water that is rolling over the stones. The black-cock is springing from the heather, and the heavens are intensely blue. . . . Skye is deemed a land of deluge, but in truth it is no more so than that of Clyde, or even the English Lake District and North Devon.

Then for sport this land of Skye is of the richest variety: there are Lord Macdonald's deer forests, full of stags and hinds and harts; and heathery moors where the caolacs or grouse, dhu or rheadh, are roused at every step, and yonder under those purple peaks, lie the lochs of Coruisk and Na Creach, and there are the black lakes under Ben a Charn Mhor, by Broadford and four tarns in Scalpa teeming with mountain trout, and in the sea lochs especially, under the torrents in Loch Scavig, salmon and grilse so game and eager for the fly, that we may load a creel in an hour.

One isn't quite sure with Dendy's book which came first – the pictures or the prose; both are romantically exaggerated. The stream from Loch Coruisk, in real life quite a modest affair, is pictured by Dendy as a rival to the celebrated Schaffhausen Falls with boulders tumbling to the sea like so many granite dragees: Loch Coruisk is girdled with peaks of Himalayan stature. The prose is on an even grander scale:

The deeper we penetrate into Scavig the more majestic are the buttresses which adorn it. It is a deep dark cove, studded with spectral blocks and pillars; and with the flickering of light and shadow as they play on one and another of these fairy blocks the changeful hues and shades constitute the scene one beautiful dioramic picture. And there are two burnies in the depth of the bay; the tiny Althaich on the left, and on the right the stream from Loch Coruisk, roll down in yon torrent of foam over the deep amber rocks like a shower of shivering pearls, as high as the mast of a tall bark, that may almost close on the cliff, so abrupt is its bold face, and so deep the pure green water at its very base; yet Scavig, shut in as it is by these giant rocks on the Atlantic, and by its breakwater, the bank of Soa, may be calm and glassy as a Cumbrian lake. . . .

We climb to a bold and horizontal crag, and the glorious scene bursts forth in all its perfection, the sable peaks of the Cuchullins peer up into the clouds, which are floating down low into the valley; there are dark umber corries and clefts, and silver ribbon streamlets. And there, in the depth of the ravine lies the dark mirror of Loch Coruisk, black as Acheron, running up two miles at the base of perpendicular precipices 600 feet in direct height. We are looking into, through it, in all its dark translucent beauty – no reflected ray to mar its mystery; there are millions of globules, but, as far as vision goes, they lie asleep amid the gloom of this gulf of desolation. There is, seemingly, no life, aquatic or aerial: an osprey or white eagle soars round it instinctively, or like the birds over the Dead Sea, it might drop into the dark water. And there is an elemental silence – the rushing streams are mute to us, so high and distant are we poised: yet it seemed we might have leaped from our ledge into the cauldron at a bound.

An author who was privy to more that went on in Skye than anyone else in the 1850s was Alexander Smith, who at the age of twenty-eight married a Skye girl, Flora Macdonald of Ord, a descendant of the celebrated Flora who had compromised herself politically with Bonnie Prince Charlie. Smith was a poet, and writer of dramas, essays and a book based on his annual visits to his wife's home called *A Summer in Skye*. Everything he wrote is now unread apart from this one book. It celebrates not the unacceptable face of lairdism that Lady Macaskill saw but the old values of paternalism. Smith's father-in-law was an ex-army officer who on retirement had taken a tack of land in Sleat in the south end of Skye. From Ord House, where he lived, he ruled his roost with the same kind of mild concern that characterized the squire in an English village:

When old men or children were sick, cordials and medicine were sent from the house; when an old man or child died, Mr M'Ian never failed to attend the funeral. He was a Justice of the Peace; and when disputes arise amongst his own cotters, or amongst the cotters of others, the contending parties were sure to come before my friend: and many a rude court of justice I have seen him hold at the door of his porch.

It was a comfortable status quo which of course men like M'Ian actively fostered. Although he gave his time and attention to his tenants they in turn were expected to look after him, often for no more than a kindly word in return:

The most active of the girls were maids of various degree in Mr M'Ian's house; the cleverest and strongest of the lads acted as shepherds. When required, Mr M'Ian demands the services of these people just as he would the services of his household servants, and they comply quite as readily. If the crows are to be kept out of the corn, or the cows out of the turnip-field, an urchin is remorselessly reft away from his games and companions. If a boat is out of repair, old Dugald is deputed to do the job, and when his task is completed, he is rewarded with ten minutes' chat and a glass of spirits up at the house. When fine weather comes, every man, woman and child is ordered to the hay-field, and Mr M'Ian potters amongst them the whole day, and takes care that no one shirks his duty. When the corn or barley is ripe the cotters cut it, and when the harvest operations are completed, he gives the entire cotter population a dance and harvest-home.

But, as Smith pointed out, his father-in-law didn't pay a penny for all this mandatory labour:

between Mr M'Ian and his cotters no money passes; by a tacit understanding he is to give them house, corn-ground, potato-ground, and they are to remunerate him with labour. Mr M'Ian, it will be seen, is a conservative, and hates change; and the social system by which he is surrounded wears an ancient and patriarchal aspect to a modern eye. It is a remnant of the system of clanship.

It was a remnant which was perpetuated in the 1850s and 1860s all through the Hebrides; a system which exploited the landless cotters in much the same way that the peasants in Tsarist Russia were exploited – dependent on the landowner, they could never do more than survive.

Smith was far too intelligent and sensitive a man not to perceive the corroding effects of this form of feudalism, but it was his wife's father who was keeping it alive, a man whose hospitality and friendship he had embraced. This is how he steered the difficult course between condemnation and approval:

> No doubt Mr M'Ian's system has grave defect: it perpetuates comparative wretchedness on the part of the cotters, it paralyses personal exertion, it begets an ignoble contentment: but on the other hand it sweetens sordid conditions, so far as they can be sweetened, by kindliness and good services. If Mr M'Ian's system is bad, he makes the best of it, and draws as much comfort and satisfaction out of it, both for himself and for others, as is perhaps possible.

Thus might a latter-day Smith defend apartheid or any social order founded on the principle of exploitation. I was not going to quote any further from Alexander Smith, whose classic *A Summer in Skye* can still, I'm glad to say, be found in any second-hand bookshop. (It was a work which ran into edition after edition and one which captured the spirit of Skye from the privileged point of view more precisely than any other book of its time.) However, I've found a piece that Smith wrote for the magazine *Temple Bar* three years before *A Summer in Skye* was published. He called it 'Rambling In the Hebrides', and as it has never been reprinted I give an extract:

The month of August is to the year what Sunday is to the week. During that month a section of the working world rests. Bradshaw is consulted, portmanteaus are packed, knapsacks are strapped on, steamboats and railway-carriages are crammed, and from Calais to Venice the tourist saunters and looks about him.

Early in the month in which English tourists descend on the Continent in a shower of gold, I was heaving in the *Clansman* steamer round the headland of Ardnamurchan, bound for the Hebrides. It was not my first visit to the islands, nor yet my second. And when, rolling round that iron coast, – on which the big Atlantic billow smites, then leaps up in a column of foam fifty feet high, – you catch the islands beyond, I think I never beheld a finer sight. Muck is in front, then Eigg, with its high towering rock, like a curling wave about to break, associated with one of the bloodiest stories of the old Highland time; then farther on Rum and Skye; and in the latter island, as the steamer advances, you may behold the clouds and the Cuchullins holding strange commerce together. I confess to a strong affection for those remote regions. Jaded and nervous with eleven months' labour or disappointment, there will you find the medicine of silence and repose. Pleasant, after poring over books, to watch the cormorant at early morning flying with outstretched neck over the sleek firth; pleasant, lying in some sunny hollow at noon, to hear the sheep bleating above; pleasant at evening to listen to wild stories of the isles, told by the peat-fires; and pleasantest of all, lying awake at midnight, to catch, muffled by the distance, the dull thunder of the Northern Sea, and to think of all the ears the sound has filled. The country is thinly peopled, and its solitude is felt as a burden. The scenery is wild; the sound of the vexed sea is ever in your ears; the wind is gusty on the moor, and ever and anon the craggy jags of the hills are obscured by swirls of fiercely-blown rain.

Of all the Islands, Skye is the most renowned for its

scenery, and certainly its aspect is remarkable and memorable enough. During the past summer the writer resided for four weeks in the Island, and had, during that period, only four days of partial rain – rain being incessant during the other twenty-seven. There was but little pleasure in consequence; and yet there were compensations. To that rainy weather I am indebted for the edification arising from an attentive perusal of Dr. Isaac Watts on the 'Human Mind' and travelling in steam-boats and mail-cars, I saw certain effects of wind and rain and gleams of light which, were I a painter and able to reproduce, would astonish the critics of the next Royal Society's Exhibition. People standing before my streaming canvas would put up their umbrellas. How I would dazzle their eyes with my wet cliff smitten by a passing sunlight! How I would bring my rainbow out of the gloom, the burning angel of the shower!

SEVEN: 1870–1880

AFTER ALEXANDER SMITH the most celebrated poet of the age in Scotland was Robert Buchanan. Half Scots, a quarter Welsh and a quarter English, Buchanan was born in 1841, the son of a Glasgow journalist. He published his first volume of verse in 1864 and from then until his death in 1901 produced a series of poems, plays and novels.

To our taste his writing may be prolix, and when he came to write about Scotland and in particular the Western Isles he felt it necessary to rise continuously to the occasion: 'any description of landscape that is not poetical must, for artistic reasons, be worthless and untrue.' *The Hebrid Isles*, published in 1872, was an account of his voyages in a seven-ton yacht, the *Tern*, through waters still largely unvisited. As Buchanan reminded his readers:

> the typical tourist seldom quits the inner chain of mainland lakes, save perhaps when a solitary 'Saturday Reviewer' oozes dull and bored out of the mist at Broadford or Portree, takes a rapid glare at the chilly Cuchullins and shivering with enthusiasm hurries back to the South. The heights of Rum, the kelp-caverns of Islay, the fantastic cliffs of Eig, scarcely ever draw the sightseer; Canna lies unvisited in the solitary sea; and as for the Outer Hebrides – from Stornoway to Barra Head – they dwell ever lonely in a mist, warning off all fair-weather wanderers. A little, a very little has been said about these Isles; but to all ordinary people they are less familiar than Cairo, and farther off than Calcutta.

Buchanan set out deliberately to steer away from the beaten track of steamers like the *Clydesdale* and the *Clansman* which left Glasgow twice a week, for the island run to Oban, Tobermory, Portree and Stornoway. He was able to drop anchor in private places like Rum which the tourist could never reach:

Our slumbers are sweet though short, and ere long we are up on deck, looking around on Loch Scresort. Viewed in the soft sparkling light of a windless summer morning, it is as sweet a little nook as ever Ulysses mooned away a day in, during his memorable voyage homeward. Though merely a small bay, about a mile in breadth, and curving inland for a mile and a half, it is quite sheltered from all winds save the east, being flanked to the south and west by Haskeval and Hondeval, and guarded on the northern side by a low range of heathery slopes. In this sunny time the sheep are bleating from the shores, the yacht lies double, yacht and shadow, and the still bay is painted richly with the clear reflection of the mountains:

> Not a feature of the hills
> Is in the mirror slighted.

On the northern point of the loch, where the old red sandstone is piled in torn fantastic heaps high over the sea, gulls innumerable sit and bask. 'Croak! croak!' cries the monstrous hooded crow at their backs, perched like an evil spirit on the very head of the cliffs and squinting fiercely at the far-off sheep. A bee drones drowsily past the yacht, completing the sense of stillness and pastoral life.

Scattered along the southern side of the bay are a few poor cottages, rudely built of stone and roofed with peat turfs, and at the head of the loch is a comfortable whitewashed house, the abode of Captain Macleod of Dunvegan, the tenant of the island. There is, moreover, a rude stone pier, where a small vessel might lie secure in any weather, and off which a battered old brigantine is even now unloading oatmeal and flour. Casting loose the punt, we row over to the vessel, and begin a chat with the shrewd-looking ancient skipper, who is superintending the passage of the sacks into a skiff alongside. In that extraordinary dialect called Gaelic-English, which may be described as a wild mingling of Gaelic, bad Irish, and Lowland Scotch, he gives us to understand that he is at once the owner and master of his craft, and that he cruises from island to island during the summer, bartering his cargo of food for whatever marketable commodities the poor folk of the place may have prepared. His great trade is with the fishers, who pay him in dried fish, chiefly ling and cod; but all is fish that comes to his net, and can be anyhow cashed in the South. Doubtless, the odds of the bargains are quite on his side. In answer to our queries as to the general condition of the islanders, he shakes his grey head dismally, and gives us to understand that but for him, and for such as he, many a poor household would perish of starvation.

Starvation, however, does not seem the order of the day in Loch Scresort. On landing, and making for the first hut at hand, we find the cow, with her calf by her side, tethered a few yards from the dwelling, two pigs wallowing in the peat-mire close by, and at least a dozen cocks, hens, and chickens, running to and fro across the threshold, where a fresh, well-fed matron, with a smile for the stranger, salutes us in the Gaelic speech. With that fine old grace of hospitality which has fled for ever from busier scenes, she leads us into her cottage – a 'but' and a 'ben', The apartment into which we are shown, despite the damp earthen floor and mildewy walls, is quite a palace for the Highlands; for it has a wooden press bed, wooden chairs and table, and a rude cupboard, shapen like a wardrobe; and the walls are adorned, moreover, by a penny almanac and a picture cut out of the *Illustrated London News*. Drink fit for the gods is speedily handed round, in the shape of foaming bowls of new milk fresh from the udder – a cup of welcome invariably offered to the traveller in any Highland dwelling that can afford it. A few friendly words warm up the good woman's heart, and she begins to prattle and to question. She is a childless widow, and her 'man' was drowned. She dwells here all alone; for all her relatives have emigrated to Canada, where she hopes some day to join them. On hearing that we have passed through Glasgow, she asks eagerly if we know a woman called Maggie, who sells eggs; the woman's surname she does not remember, but we must have noticed her, as she is splay-footed and has red hair. She has never been farther south than Eig, and hence her notion of big cities. She longs very much to see Tobermory and its great shops – also to look up a distant kinsman, who has flourished there in trade. She tells us much of the laird and his family – the 'folk in the big house'; they are decent, pious people, and kind to the poor. Will she sell us some eggs? Well, she has not heard the price of eggs this season, but will let us have some at fivepence a dozen. She loads the pilot with a basketful of monsters, and we go on our way rejoicing.

And rejoice he did in the physical beauty of the world about him as the *Tern* sped through the waves from Rum to nearby Canna,

now dipping with a stealthy motion into the green hollow of the waves, then rising, shivering on their crest, and glancing this way and that like a startled bird; drifting sidelong for a moment as if wounded and faint, with the tip of her white wing trailing in the water, and again, at the wind's whistle, springing up and onward, and tilting the foam from her breast in showers of silver spray.

And on Canna Buchanan found a fair-minded precursor of the present owner, John Lorne Campbell. A hundred years ago Canna, 'fat and fertile, full of excellent sheep-pastures and patches of fine arable ground', had an equally sympathetic landlord:

The Laird of Canna might fitly be styled its King; for over that lonely domain he exercises quite regal authority, and he is luckier in one respect than most monarchs – he keeps all the cash. His subjects number four score – men, women, and children. Some till his land, some herd his sheep. For him the long-line fishers row along the stormy coasts of Rum; for him the wild boors batter out the brains of seals on the neighbouring rocks of Haskeir; the flocks on the crags are his, and the two smacks in the bay; every roof and tenement for man or beast pays him rent of some sort. The solid modern building, surrounded by the civilized brick wall, is his palace – a recent erection, strangely out of keeping with the rude cabins and heather houses in the vicinity. Yet the Laird of Canna is not proud. He toiled hard with his hands long before the stroke of good fortune which made him the heritor of the isle, and even now he communes freely with the lowliest subject, and is not above boarding the trading-vessel in the bay in his shirt-sleeves. A shrewd, active, broad-shouldered man is the Laird, still young, and as active as a goat. Though he sits late at night among his books he is up with the greyest dawn to look after his fields. You meet him everywhere over the island, mounted royally on his sturdy little sheltie, and gazing around him with a face which says plainly –

> I am monarch of all I survey;
> My right there is none to dispute.

But at times he sails far away southward in his own boats, speculating with the shrewdest, and surely keeping his own. In the midst of his happy sway he has a fine smile and a kindly heart for the stranger, as we can testify. The great can afford to be generous, though, of course, if greatness were to be measured by mere amount of income, the Laird, though a 'warm' man, would have to be ranked among the lowly. He has in abundance what all the Stuarts tried in vain to feel – the perfect sense of solitary sway.

Buchanan was as poetically enthusiastic about the islands as W. Anderson Smith was down to earth. A Corresponding

Member of the Natural History and Geological societies of Glasgow he won prizes for his essays on such subjects as 'Pisciculture as a Source of National Wealth' and 'Oyster Culture in Scotland'. When he went to the Isle of Lewis in 1870 he would more than likely have been one of the first to travel on the new Dingwall & Skye Railway.

Until 19 August 1870 the quickest and most comfortable way to travel to the isles of Skye and Lewis was by swift steamer from the Clyde. But on that day the fifty-three miles of line connecting Dingwall with Strome Ferry on the shores of Loch Carron was opened to passengers. On Saturday 20 August advertisements in all the Scottish newspapers heralded this remarkable advance in travel.

For the first time the west coast had been linked to the east – you could leave Inverness at ten in the morning and be at Strome by lunchtime. From there the steamship *Oscar* would convey passengers every day of the week except Sunday to Portree and the *Jura* made three sailings a week to Stornoway. Portree was now only fifteen hours' travelling time from Edinburgh, and Stornoway could be reached within twenty-four hours.

Anderson Smith described how the highest-paid workers in the islands were the herring girls from Essex and Newcastle who worked on the quays at Stornoway, earning sixteen shillings a week for gutting fish. Riches indeed at a time when a labourer in Lewis would be paid between 7s 6d and 9s a week and a girl in service could expect to receive no more than £3 a year and her keep. At home she would certainly work longer and harder than any man:

As soon as the family is astir in the morning, the grown-up girl, or whoever is entrusted with the duty, prepares to go to the stack of peats on the moor for a supply of fuel. Before setting out with her creel, she partakes of the roasted potatoes which it is the common custom of the country people to place in the ashes of the day's fire before turning in for the night. On her return the fire is made up and cooking commences, which consists in boiling a huge pot of potatoes to be eaten with butter or milk by the family; or perhaps a piece of fish, fresh or salted, should the men be fishermen; or a few herring, brought over last season from Wick or Fraserburgh. If the potatoes are finished, as they will be in spring, porridge takes their place, this breakfast being eaten about ten or eleven in winter. These dishes form the principal part of their diet, to which may be added, when the family is well off, eggs from their poultry, together with the universal, wholesome, and palatable barley bread, and of late years an occasional cup of tea. A repetition of this meal again about six in the evening may be said to constitute the customary diet.

Like the day, the year had an ordained and largely unvarying pattern. During the winter after a stormy night the women would go down to the shore and bring back creels of seawrack to make a compost, along with fish offal, for the spring sowing of the barley. When the good weather came the whole family took part in turning over their small patches of land ready for sowing. The winter's accumulation of manure was removed from inside the black houses and taken out to the fields. Then the roof of barley roots and straw, impregnated with peat soot and half rotted by the winter rains, was taken off and carried out in creels and spread on the potato patches.

When the seed was in, the sheep and cattle were driven to the shielings where the girls of each family spent up to two months of the year.

The men take every opportunity to go courting them, as their sweethearts on those occasions always deluge them with the richest of milk and sweetest of butter. It is almost impossible to get girls to go to service at this time, seeing it is looked forward to as *par excellence* the courting time. No inducement will entice them to forego this long period of free picnicing amid the heather.

It was at this time of the year that the men packed their canvas bags and took the steamer for the Caithness fisheries, at ports like Wick and Fraserburgh. If the fishing was good they returned in September with £20 to £30 –

> a very large sum for a Lewis man and sufficient to support his family in comfort for the remainder of the year. Although they are always back in time for the harvest it is the women who do most of the work, as indeed they do at seed-time. The potatoes are dug up and creeled home to be pitted near the houses; the oats are cut down with the sickle and the barley drawn up by the roots.

And then the winter, a stimulating time especially for the young and lusty – bundling was still a universal practice in Lewis, both from choice and necessity.

> Most of the unmarried young men pass the winter nights with their sweethearts. The want of light in most dwellings, the numbers of dark corners even in daylight, and the general habit among the people of throwing themselves down on the straw, simply divested of their outer garment, gives every facility for courtship in the Hebridean fashion. As the girls are, at the same time, 'very kind,' courting assiduously, and are possessed of far greater energy than the men, they acquire a great hold on their affections and seriously influence those youths who might otherwise have enterprise enough to emigrate to the colonies and attempt to better their condition.

Anderson Smith convinced himself that Lewis was a kind of wild Arcadia, a landscape of harmony and happiness:

> Rarely does one hear of unfaithful wife or cruel husband: nay, we verily believe that a happier class of people, a people thinking less of to-morrow and enjoying themselves more to-day does not exist. Illegitimacy in the country is so rare as to be merely nominal, while most married couples are eminently fruitful: the children are fat, intelligent and

frolicsome; the men stout, hearty, keen-witted; their active good dames crowning a social edifice of health, peace, and contentment, though it be of the humblest. We thank Providence that women may be fond and men affectionate to an extent of mutual confidence long expelled from the more civilised regions of the earth.

As we have seen, the first steamboats began operating among the islands in 1820, but it was not until the late 1860s that iron and steam eclipsed wood and canvas. Even in 1870, 30 per cent of British-registered ships were still under sail, a method of navigation which left you frequently powerless in the face of strong winds, and often immobile and at the mercy of currents and tide when the wind failed to blow at all. As some indication of the ubiquity of sailing brigs and barques right up to the turn of the century, it is worth noting that between 1870 and 1900 all the fourteen large vessels which foundered on Fair Isle (a rocky hazard lying in the main shipping lane between the Baltic ports and North America) were under sail.

So when R. Angus Smith set out from Durris House in Aberdeen to visit St Kilda in 1873 it was on board a sailing yacht, the *Nyanza*, a quiet but nevertheless still unpredictable way to travel. They tacked through the Pentland Firth, rounded Cape Wrath and the Butt of Lewis, and ran down the east coast of Harris:

> The breeze grew stronger and we moved more rapidly; the sun still shone over a sky unclouded, except in the distance before us where we saw a mass of bright woolly clouds heaped up on one spot, and gradually sinking down on one side where they continued far over on the ocean as in a thin line: St Kilda below the clouds. We moved nearer and saw land growing as it were beneath the accumulation and gradually lifting the cloud higher above it. The heap was remarkable; it seemed as if the cold island had first made a cloud and then the cold cloud had condensed

more, and so on until the thickness had accumulated to a depth of many hundred feet, so far as we could judge; and what is still more curious, rising like a cone in the centre, somewhat imitating the shape of the island.

Smith's description of the approach to St Kilda is one of the most powerful I have read:

The dusky precipices jutting out on every side from the mist were lost in the dense clouds above and seemed like pillars holding some awful roof, threatening to fall down on our heads, the pillars themselves shedding equal awe. A wild opening appeared between St Kilda and Borrera which gradually became less gloomy and showed us two long lines of cloud stretching like a mighty entrance to halls that would fit beings who could lift up mountains. And so we wandered round the dark columns that seemed to be supporting the gloomy roof. Had it been a land of demons it could not have appeared more dreadful and had we not heard of it before we should have said that, if inhabited, it must be by monsters.

All night they sailed backwards and forwards along the West Bay waiting for a wind which would allow a landing in the East Bay. On the following day the cloud had gone and the natives were all astir. They always hoped that when a large yacht appeared it would contain persons of influence who would wave a wand to dispel their chronic deprivation. As soon as the initial greetings had been disposed of the visitors were more than likely to be exposed to a long shopping list of articles in short supply:

As we stood before his house, a crowd of inhabitants were round their teacher, dictating requests to us which he put into English. First, 'It is hoped that you may be able, when you return, to do something for the poor people of this island.' We were rather in difficulties as to meeting the requirements or giving a suitable answer; it was a new sensation, as if on a small scale a nation demanded help.

Sweetmeats, tea, sugar and tobacco, were distributed much as coloured beads might have been offered to blackamoors on some remote tropical isle: 'Acting on information obtained in Stornoway, we had brought a little thread, with a few needles, pins, and thimbles; and finding that they were really appreciated were only sorry that we had not brought more.'

The minister, the Reverend John Mackay who had been on the island for seven years and who had turned the St Kildan Sabbath into a marathon of mournful gloom, told them the men would like fishing lines. They had already petitioned for a nine-ton boat but without any success. As a result of Smith's visit a five-ton vessel was sent to St Kilda but that was not considered adequate. Smith was a great believer in the virtues of peat-agriculture in the north and on his return to the mainland tried to use his influence to have the St Kildans instructed in the cutting of peat. Six years later he recorded laconically: 'The very latest news from St Kilda is that they want 36 tons of coals, and they expect this to be sent to them. They have not taken the lesson – they have not cut the peat.'

★

I've never yet opened a book of yachting memoirs without great expectations; seldom closed one without disappointment. When all the episodes of dragged anchors, splintered booms and storm-tossed nights are eliminated there's not much left.

Victorian yachtsmen were a hungry lot, and a lot of their time was taken up with the minutiae of trying to get something to eat. Here's John Inglis, who wrote under the pen-name 'The Governor' and cruised in western waters in the 1870s. In Tobermory he and his companions searched in vain for a butcher's shop and were about to return on board,

> when we were accosted by an old aborigine with 'Thus wass a fine day' – we assenting most cordially he ventured to guess 'you will be from the yatt,' to which impreach-ment we owned. His motive for opening communications

then appeared from his concluding that we were in want of what he called 'some good mittens', and we thereupon recognised in him the local butcher, and proceeded with him to his establishment, where heads and joints of sheep reposed in strange juxtaposition with boots and bibles, hardware and hosiery, tapes, threads, treacle, testaments and such incongruous necessaries.

If it be true that the nearer the bone the sweeter the meat, no mutton could have been sweeter than that of Tobermory.

Our opinion of the resources of the place was altogether more extended after this episode and Andy proposed we should ferret out a confectioner who would achieve for us a *chef d'oeuvre* of his art to grace our dinner-table. After a long search a man of dough was found who declared himself competent to execute any order of the kind having served his apprenticeship in Glasgow; but as the requisite materials were not obtainable in the island our negotiations suddenly collapsed.

There is an amused condescension in these yachtsmen's diaries which mirrored the natural superiority of the educated classes when confronted with feckless natives who spoke English with difficulty and made unintentionally comic remarks.

They wrote of their adventures much as an explorer might when sailing down the Gold Coast. Substitute *kraal* for *crofthouse* and this might be an excerpt from Stanley's *In Darkest Africa*. It was Isle Ornsay, Skye:

Stooping under the lowly lintel we entered, and after our eyes had become accustomed to the dim light, we began to make out the details of the menage. On a seat made of the root of a larch tree sat a very old woman, leisurely washing from her feet the incrustations of the past few weeks in an iron pot which on other occasions most probably cooked the family porridge. On a rough bench sat an older man in an attitude suggestive of the cobbler, his actual vocation as it proved. In a corner was some coarse sacking stuffed with filthy straw – the nuptial couch of the ancient couple. In and out there pattered some draggled hens, while three or four ducks with their flat feet mixed the accidental impurities with the damp mud of the floor into a charming compost. The scanty peat fire smouldered in the middle of the apartment, the pungent reek finding its way out by the numerous apertures in the roof, through which not a little rain entered. A young calf had strayed in for shelter and met us in the doorway as it made its exit. There was no pig to be seen, although the hovel was everything a pig could desire.

Crossing from Stornoway to Ullapool the other day on Cal-Mac's *Suilven*, a glorified container ship designed to carry vehicles, I happened to have for light reading a book published to celebrate a 'pleasant cruise on board the *Elena* in the autumn of 1876'. I fetched myself a plastic cup of tea from the help-yourself cafeteria and lamented the absence of the good homely food and drink that was such an admirable part of west coast steamers even in my youth. I compared my spartan crossing of the Minch with the author's description of his short trip on the *Iona*, 'a fine saloon steamer, which waits for the train at Greenock, and thence careers along the Western Coast, leaving her passengers at various ports.' J. Ewing Ritchie, author of *The Cruise of the* Elena, was on the way to join his host, a wealthy Glasgow businessman and philanthropist, at Kirn:

> To breakfast on board the *Iona* is one of the first duties of man, and one of the noblest of woman's rights. Oh, that breakfast! To do it justice requires an abler pen than mine. Never did I part with a florin – the sum charged for breakfast – with greater pleasure. We all know breakfasts are one of those things they manage well in Scotland, and the breakfast on board the *Iona* is the latest and most triumphant vindication of the fact. Cutlets of salmon fresh from the water, sausages of a tenderness and delicacy of which the benighted cockney who fills his paunch with

the flabby and plethoric article sold under that title by the provision dealer can have no idea; coffee hot and aromatic, and suggestive of Araby the blest; marmalades of all kinds, with bread-and-butter and toast all equally good, and served up by the cleanest and most civil of stewards.

On the *Elena* itself the food without doubt would have been even better. The yacht was one of the most magnificent that ever sailed down the Clyde:

It is rarely one sees a yacht more tastefully fitted-up, and we have a ladies' drawing-room on board not unworthy of Belgravia itself. She is slightly rakish in build, but not disagreeably so. Her tonnage is 200 tons, and her crew consist, including the stoker and steward, of some eight clever-looking, sailor-like men.

The *Elena* cruised from Oban to Tobermory and from there to Portree and on to Stornoway. It was, according to Ritchie, a move in the right direction:

As a town, Stornoway is an immense improvement on Portree. It rejoices in churches, and the shops are numerous, and abound with all sorts of useful articles. The chief streets are paved. It has here and there a gas lamp, and the proprietor of the chief hotel boasted to me that so excellent were his culinary arrangements, that actually the ladies from the yachts come and dine there. On Saturday night the shops swarmed with customers, chiefly peasant women – who put their boots on when they came into town, and who took them off again and walked barefoot as soon as they had left the town behind – and ancient mariners with a very fish-like smell.

John T. Reid, author, artist and self-confessed 'graduate in Dame Nature's schools', spent several months in Skye in the 1870s but he didn't travel in such style as Mr Ewing Ritchie. At that period most of the shipping in the Hebrides was in the hands of David Hutchenson & Co., the partners of which were David and Alexander Hutchenson and David Macbrayne.

There were smaller enterprises like the Western Isles Steam Packet Company, which had begun trading in 1873 with a paddle steamer called *St Clair of the Isles*. There is a belief in the Hebrides that these sturdy little inter-island boats sailed in all weathers and seldom came to grief, but a month after entering service with the company *St Clair of the Isles* struck a rock in Loch Sunart and was badly holed. Two years later she was auctioned and her place taken by a screw steamer launched in April 1876 also called *St Clair*.

The following year the new *St Clair* went aground in Loch Bracadale in Skye. In September 1878 she was stranded again, this time at Salen in Loch Sunart when she heeled over, and filled with water. Her final disaster was not far off – in October 1880, after only four years' service, she struck a submerged rock at Coll and sank. An unlucky ship with an unlucky master.

The *St Clair* carried cattle and general cargo and Reid joined her at Oban from whence they proceeded in a leisurely way to Tobermory, Salen, Croag in Mull and on to Coll:

> We got an accession to our passengers there, and this rendered our company as much as our cabin could accommodate with seat-room at meal-hours. We had a bachelor party on board, who were out for a little merrymaking: an island marriage ball had wooed them from the desk of the counting-house, and having had a taste of the free air of these parts, and being good fellows well met, a few more days of healthful roving gave a gleeful appendix to the gaieties of the wedding. There was, as a matter of course, a clever punster and an old joker, and no end of reminiscences with a strong spicing of the comic element in them. The steward was not left to mourn that his bottles found no custom: there was treating and return treating, and one humble Highlander who could sing Gaelic songs was made the sink into which was poured the spirits bought

by sundry odd pence; and, to the satisfaction of those who deem it a noble accomplishment the filling a man drunk, this Celt was brought into that pitiable condition, and manifested the power of the spirits over his brain in rather a curious way, – he was for kissing all round.

We had in addition to this party, – a doctor coming to visit his mother, who lived in Coll; a young Englishman with a fishing-rod, who had left a medical practice for a few days to whip the burns of Coll and breathe the fine air; a minister's wife; a retired minister and his wife, both in delicate health; the Fiscal of Tobermory, who had a farm in Tiree; the Chief Constable and Sheriff Clerk from Mull, who came to investigate a case of suspected cattle poisoning; and a young Glasgow teacher, who came to be the guest of the Fiscal aforementioned.

It was Saturday evening as we neared the low-lying reaches of sandy shore and the outlying rocks of Tiree, and the sun was setting peacefully as our steamer came along-side the stone pier at Scaranish Harbour, and we saw a sand-environed bay with some veteran sloops fixed in the sand – no more to mount o'er the waves of ocean, and spread ample sails to the breeze of heaven – left there, I am told, because it would not be deemed lucky to break them up. A flag-staff was fixed on a sand-hill; some of the homes were within the circuit of the bay; a store-house was near the pier, and a large bare-looking stone building, with slated roof and large windows, at the other side, was pointed out as the Temperance Hotel – the only hotel in the island, and but seldom patronized; so those who want spirits find in the steamboat a house 'licensed to retail spirits, porter, and all' and drouthy customers have thus a special interest in the steamboat sailings. I got a room in the inn, and despite the windiness of the house and the army of earwigs that peopled it, I was very snug; a friend who has been there in winter gives amusing particulars regarding the draughts that are vocal as well as felt in this palace of the winds; he found it necessary to nail up his

bed-room windows with many piles of blanket, and thus
to allow day and night to glide un-noted past, for all was
dark – yet were not the breathings of the winds hushed!

As you can see, Reid was an exponent of the inverted verb
and he also suffered from varicose verbiage. 'I saw the sunset',
he could write with scarce a blush, 'in glowing red behind the
range of mountain-peaks ere they were crowned with misty
wreathes.' His *Art Rambles* was intended to be of an improving
nature and Reid spent much of his time in Skye, when he
wasn't being eaten by midges, noting examples of Christian
eccentricity.

Then as now sectarian differences added a dash of religious
spice to the monotonous daily round. Where you worshipped
was more important than whom you worshipped and there
was a pecking order of piety of consuming importance to the
professionally devout. 'I am told', Reid recorded, 'there are
two sisters who dwell under one roof' – on Stormy Hill in
Portree – 'who cannot speak to one another, for the one is a
Free Churcher and the other is a Baptist; and that one gave to
the other cause of great offence, having put cream in the tea of
the other when such kind office was not desired. I mention the
case of the Free Church and the Baptist adherent because,
although it is a very extreme case, it unfolds to us what exists
to a large extent in the Highlands of Scotland – a strong
sectarian rivalry.'

It is of course a story which unfolds to the agnostic yet one
more reason for reserving his judgment. Indeed many of Reid's
tales of piety were concerned with those of patently enfeebled
wits who came to no good end through drinking too deeply of
the Christian spirit:

There used to be a young man with a weak mind, who
lived in one of the humble cottages that skirted the inner
portion of Portree Bay: he was known as John the Preacher
and was remarkable for the sunny joyfulness of expression
that lit up his sparkling small dark eyes. He often got a

barrel out of one of the shops, and taking his stand at a corner of the street, spoke long though not very connectedly, yet his words were full of Scripture truth. . . . Some were fond of teasing him and tried to make him lose his temper; but that proved fruitless labour. Sometimes he took preaching tours, and for this purpose he visited the mainland. I am told his body was found by the roadside in a snow storm while he was on one of these tours.

Reid spent several weeks in Staffin staying at Stenscholl Inn and climbing up as often as he could to paint the Needle Rock. He was frequently deterred by boisterous weather and on one of the days it was too wet and windy to climb the Quiraing he visited a Gaelic school in the neighbourhood:

On pacing the mile of cart-road between the inn and this school, some of the native cottages are seen, and I often saw a lunatic – a man of middle height, about thirty years of age, with bare head and bosom and bare legs, a garb of claret-coloured homespun tweed of indescribable cut. This day he seemed to vie with the ducks in the enjoyment of the drenching rain. Drooket Skye wives and maidens I met going to and coming from the mill with the last of the corn or barley from the stack. . . .

The streamlets from Cuiraing were full and foaming; the burn by the Gaelic school-house had overflowed its banks, and inside the building we saw one of the quaintest gatherings of kilted lads and sweet wee Skye girls, not over-warmly clad, some of the more delicate shivering with cold; and one or two, for lack of other, with clothes greatly bigger than themselves. In a circle they gathered round the fire. It is not one of the most pleasing occupations listening to a Gaelic lesson, though in this case the master's mouth was itself a study as he threw out the sounds for the little ones to imitate. In honour of a stranger visiting the school he bade them cheer and clap their hands. They were good at that. Not so at the after exercise, viz, a singing lesson. The master had neither a musical ear nor

a musical voice, and he made sad, sad work of 'There is a
happy land far, far away.' The schoolhouse singing would
not awake the most joyful anticipations of the bliss promised in the line, 'There we shall sweetly sing.' I am told he
is a good Gaelic teacher and he was a good man, whose
character was everywhere esteemed but underpaid. These
schools are fast disappearing and giving place to better. The
labourer is worthy of his hire; and those who devote their
lives to this most arduous work have need to be maintained
comfortably.

A better artist, and, for that matter, a better writer was
Sidney Cooper, a Victorian painter who specialized in sheep
and cows (*In the Meadows at Noon, The Fleecy Charge, Cooing the
Hoof*) and who became a great favourite from 1833 onwards at
the annual Royal Academy exhibitions. My aunt, who owned
one of his watercolours, claimed that his only failing was that
he was no good at animals' feet. This may be scurrilous libel
but it is strange that a large number of his four-footed subjects
are discovered either standing in conveniently long grass or up
to their fetlocks in water. In 1890 Cooper published a two-
volume autobiography in which he described his visit to Skye
in what he says was the summer of 1882. But this was his only
visit and it must have taken place earlier than he recollects
because in the Academy of 1877 he exhibited *A Sketch in Skye*
and in the following year among seven of his works accepted
was *Up on the Cuchullin Hills*. The artist travelled by rail to
Strome Ferry with his son and here they embarked on the
steamer for Skye:

> It was a most beautiful afternoon, with a bright sun shining,
> and our route lay by the narrow channel of Loch Carron,
> through the western portion of Ross-shire. In the course
> of half an hour we reached the open water, when the most
> wonderful and enchanting view burst upon us.
>   In the distance, over the calm water appeared a mass of
> mountains against a light, warm sky, they being of the pale

grey colour – so faint in tone as to look like the ghosts of mountains. I have never witnessed such a lovely scene before, either in nature or in the illustrations of any books of travel that I have come across. As we neared Skye, boats came out to row us to the shore at Broadford, the water being too shallow for the steamer to approach the land, at which place we found a small but comfortable hotel, which we reached in time for dinner, and there we put up for the night.

The next day we began to look about us, and soon found plenty for the palette and for drawing. About four miles from Broadford we entered a glen, through which a stream flowed, with rough broken rocks on either side. There were patches of cultivation here and there, but the mountains seen beyond, or rather over, these rocks were bare of herbage from bottom to top, and were of wonderful form and colour. Of this view I made a careful study in oils.

The following day we proceeded to the next village – Sligachan – and truly the road thither was full of wonders. The scenery was grand and sublime. The whole way to Sligachan was wonderfully beautiful; the glens through which we passed one after the other were all of the grand type, and I saw no scenery in Switzerland so suited for pictures as this part of Great Britain. The beautiful and grand scenery of the Isle of Skye is often talked of yet but few have visited it for the purpose of sketching, and I cannot do better than advise landscape painters to make themselves acquainted with this spot, which I consider unparalleled for the study of their branch of art.

My son and I procured a pony each, and, with a guide, we ascended the Cuchullin Hills, which was the most uneasy bit of travelling I ever experienced. Sometimes, as we went up a steep part of the ascent, the heads of the ponies would touch us; at others we had to take great care to prevent ourselves slipping over their heads. The whole country was broken up into enormous pieces of rock in a most wonderful manner. It seemed extraordinary how they got there. The view as we got higher and higher was grand and beautiful – quite beyond my power to describe. When at an altitude of about 1200 feet, I made a sketch of a passage in the rocks, from which I have often desired to paint a picture, but as yet time and opportunity to do so have failed me.

It was easy to see why Skye was such a magnet for painters in Victorian times. It had all the romantic associations of the lost Jacobite cause, it had the grandest scenery in the Hebrides, and it had a rail link which meant you could travel comfortably by train from London almost to the shores of the island. Oban was not to be joined by rail to Glasgow until 1880, so Skye was a much easier option than Mull or any of the Outer Hebrides.

From Mull to Skye in those days was a very simple sea trip; today using public transport it wouldn't take you much longer but it would take you twice as far and involve two car ferries and a long drive on mainland roads. Two steamers sailed to Skye from Mull every week, the *Clansman* and *Clydesdale*. So when Tina Brooke and Bell Munro, cousins who were spending part of the summer of 1872 in Mull with friends, decided to visit Skye they telegraphed for ponies to be awaiting them at Sligachan and booked their rooms at the inn.

The trip got off to a bad start: the *Clydesdale* was five hours late arriving at Craignure to pick them up and although the sea was flat the steamer never really seemed to get any speed up. In those days there were as many ports of call as wayside halts on a rural railway line: 'At one wild-looking place,' the cousins recorded, 'Arisaig, in particular the steamer waited a very long time and Tina was much astonished to notice the great boxes of soap that were here landed, and more especially as there only appeared to be one human habitation within sight, and that a small inn.'

Next a diversion was made up Loch Nevis to land passengers destined for the shooting lodge: 'It was quite a little variety to watch the party going on shore which they did in little boats, rowed by such smart-looking sailors belonging to Mr Baird's fine yacht, which lay close at hand.'

The cabin they had ordered failed to materialize and they descended to the saloon where they tried, amidst the whisky-toddy drinking, the laughter and conversation, to sleep. By midnight the heat became so stifling that the cousins sat up and ordered the steward to fetch some sherry and lemonade.

About three o'clock in the morning they reached Portree, and finding both hotels full, they settled for a couple of sofas. In the morning when they rose the dining-room was full as well. Their visit to Loch Coruisk ('A most remarkable little inland lake ... the pervading tint all round being a sort of dreary-looking brown') was also far from solitary.

They had been deposited in Skye in the small hours of the morning and when they came to leave Broadford, two days later, once again they were expected to be ready when most people were still abed. At 5 a.m. they made their way to the pier but the steamer didn't appear round the eastern side of Scalpay until seven: 'then it became evident that the passengers were to row out to her, though how they were to get down into the small boat awaiting them seemed a difficult question to solve, for, the tide being low, the pier was at least six feet above the water!'

The transfer was somehow accomplished and the two young ladies found themselves back on board the *Clydesdale* 'among a motley crew of other tourists, Cockney and un-Cockney. As there was a general air of discomfort pervading everywhere, and the decks were still in a very moist state from their recent scrubbing, Tina suggested retiring at once to the deck-cabin, which they had previously secured.'

Once more there were stops, this time to load wool at Inverie in Loch Nevis, a job that took a full two hours. But their unhurried progress had advantages not found aboard the car ferries of today: 'just ere leaving the captain called out something in Gaelic to the men in one of the boats and instantly a large net was lowered and a great draught of fine fresh herrings put on board. They appeared on the table for evening tea.'

A young lady of about the same age as Tina and Bell came to Skye a few years later. Her name was Alice Liddell and as a nubile nymphet she had inspired Charles Lutwidge Dodgson to write the most famous children's book ever published. *Alice in Wonderland* lives on but it wasn't until a few years ago that a diary turned up among some family papers in Gloucestershire in which Alice, then twenty-six, recorded her adventures while staying as a guest in Dunvegan Castle in Skye.

They travelled from London in style. 'Had dinner', she wrote, 'at King's Cross Hotel and started in a saloon kindly ordered for us by Lord Colville at 8.30 by the Scotch Express for Inverness.' The family took two maids with them as befitted their situation; Alice's father was Dean of Christ Church, nephew of Lord Ravensworth and a former chaplain to Prince Albert.

Unfortunately they arrived in Portree on the day of the annual Skye Games, an event attended by large crowds and moderate intemperance. Alice noted:

We had been warned by Macleod of these games, but had understood we were safe till after the 4th inst. Still hoping in the efficacy of our letter ordering rooms, Mama and Alice scrambled off the steamer, up a precipitous path, off to the Portree Hotel, leaving Papa, Rhoda & the two maids to struggle with the luggage, to bring up which there appeared neither porters, carts, nor any other means of transport and the reason became quickly apparent on reaching the 'main street' of this populous and important town, as all the inhabitants seemed turned out to see the judging & awarding of the prizes, an important ceremony without doubt, but creating a somewhat alarming crowd & a still more alarming ring round the front door of the Hotel as Mama & Alice bowed their way in search of some place of abode.

Dunvegan Castle proved to be a more sheltered retreat. The evenings were passed with selections from Gilbert and Sullivan accompanied on the smoking-room piano, billiards, whist and Dumb Crambo. One of the highlights of their Skye holiday was a visit to the Quiraing. Already, and this was exactly a hundred years ago, the 'honeypots' of Hebridean tourism were defining themselves – the Quiraing, and Loch Coruisk in Skye, and the isles of Staffa and Iona off Mull. Embarking for a day trip at Oban in August was as much of a jostle as taking a cross-Channel ferry at Dover in high summer today. The steamer for Staffa and Iona left at seven thirty every morning:

> The hundred tourists look as if they had all risen too early, and were trying to appear wide awake by unwinking eyelids. People who could not make up their minds in time, or who were lazy, come running breathlessly as the last bell rings a resolute departure; and I am afraid that we who have been exemplary in earliness find a grim satisfaction in contemplating their hurry and confusion. One lady has forgotten a provision basket and lingers at the gangway, undecided whether to sacrifice her sandwiches or take her chance of being left behind; till the steamer brings the matter to issue by casting off cable.

Thus an article in the *Leisure Hour* of the period, though the trip certainly wasn't leisurely:

> the loud snort of escaping steam and the sailors let down the boats. Now the majority of our over hundred tourists are seized with a panic apprehension that there will not be opportunity for all to land, and that a crowding and crushing forward will vastly facilitate matters. The minority who lean contentedly on the taffrail, waiting for their turn quietly and improving their leisure by securing a memory of Iona as a lifelong picture, get ashore on the rude wharf

with less éclat to be sure but with considerable more comfort.

There was no doubt left in the reader's mind that the author was numbered among those leaning in a superior fashion on the taffrail! Once ashore the shoving and pushing grows worse:

Like a swarm of bees about their queen, the mass of our tourists crowd after a guide, and listen to the venerable history of Iona discoursed in the tones of an auctioneer. A few odd people, like the writer, prefer rambling at will among the ruins for the allotted hour, with a guide-book as silent and reliable companion.

To escape from the summer crowds it was necessary to go to the comparative seclusion of the Outer Isles. As a writer expressed it in *St Paul's Magazine* in 1872, to get away from it all you must:

look westward far out into the seas where, like a monstrous serpent crawling northward and dimly distinguishable in the weltering waste of water the Hebrides stretch in utter loneliness, visited by no passing ship and holding scarce any communication with the world of man.

If you did find your way to the Outer Isles at the time of the herring harvest, and you were used only to the sedate interiors of Temperance hotels in Oban, you might have been slightly shaken. For fear no doubt of being thrown in the sea if he returned, one author preferred to remain anonymous and even invented a mythical location for his fishing port. 'Storport' was probably Lochmaddy. Wherever it was, the fair held every Spring would have been worthy of a Hebridean Hogarth:

The broken-down-looking inn of Storport, a one storey edifice without 'sign' of any sort, stands at the head of a large pier or wharf, and for nine months out of ten stares with two glazed and fishy-looking eyes at the cheerless waters, broken with damp green islands, projecting reefs and floating weed. The landlord wanders away wherever business or pleasure leads him, and a dirty servant roams to and fro through rooms innocent of the taste of whiskey or the smell of smoke. But suddenly, in the spring of the year, the fishy eyes of the inn begin to sparkle and to blaze late on into the evening with a red and festive glare. The herring-fishers, like a swarm of locusts, have descended upon Loch Storport and the whole district is alive with the signs of life. The air is full of the smell of fish, the bones of boiled fish are scattered everywhere on the ground, fish are drying on the beach and on the stones above the village, the boats at the quay are full of fish newly caught – fish everywhere, and the smell of fish; tempted by which, a crowd of gulls, hundreds upon hundreds, are hovering and darting above Storport with discordant screams.

Everywhere close to the water's edge and in the water, fish, fishermen, fishing-boats, wild women, nets, ropes, and oars: a confused moving patchwork which fatigues the eye and bewilders the brain.

Through the crowd which besieges the quay walks Father Macdonald, the priest of Uribol, his white head towering over all, and his face looking at once grave, benignant, and kind. Mingled up with the crowds of strange fishermen and fisherwomen are drovers and their dogs, mendicants, shepherds out for a holiday, farm servants in gaudy finery, cattle-dealers with their pockets stuffed full of one-pound notes, and ragged cotters of the isles. Hand after hand is thrust out to grasp that of the priest; greeting after greeting is showered upon him; and many a kind word and respectful salutation is thrown after him.

Along the winding country road, as far as eye can see, the people are coming in a thin stream; troops of cattle driven by shouting dogs, and ever breaking from the track; poor women leading their solitary cows to the market by straw-ropes; ... tacksmen mounted on their sturdy ponies, and crofters toiling barefoot; groups of men, women, and children, gaily dressed, jolting in rude springless carts behind old horses that creep along at the pace of snails.

On the knolls above the quay, where the cattle are legion, groups of cattle-dealers and farmers are now wrangling together and bargaining at the height of their voices. The dirty inn is already crowded with drinkers, and the excitement is beginning.

Sellers and buyers have done their business, and all have now abandoned themselves to merriment – that is to say, to furious drinking. The lowing of the cattle, the crying and singing of the men, the shrill voices of the women, make day hideous. On a smooth bit of green above the inn a ragged bagpiper and a blind fiddler are playing different tunes, and shepherds, herd-girls, farmwomen, and drovers are dancing like mad people, with the usual shrieks that accompany the Highland reel. Here a couple of men are fighting, not in the knock-down English fashion but rearing, screaming, and clinging to each other's throats like wild cats. The dirty inn is crammed, and the sound of roaring and singing comes from the rickety door. Half-naked Highlandmen in kilts are rushing about everywhere with bottles of whiskey in their hands, beseeching their friends to drink.

If any curious observer or midnight dreamer should be wandering to-night among the hills and knolls surrounding Storport, he will be startled every now and then by stumbling over a corpse-like recumbent figure, which will either grunt out a sleepy disapproval, or, springing to its feet, spar tipsily at the disturber of its slumber. Most of these figures will be armed with black bottles of whiskey. The highway, too, will be sprinkled with drowsy bacchanalians. More than one well-to-do farmer is already lying tranquilly asleep on the road, still gripping the bridle of the horse from which he has gently rolled, while the quiet beast, used to its master's eccentricity, is patiently nibbling the scanty herbage on the side of the road; and a little way off, his head shepherd perhaps, quite as respectable-looking and quite as respectably clothed as his master, is sleeping too, with his tired dog curled up close to his head. With very few exceptions, there are no female night-birds of the tipsy kind, though out on the lonely hillside more than one girl is lying coiled up in her lover's plaid, far too sick and weary to take the dark road home.

Before daybreak, however, all the thirsty plants are cooled by a drenching shower, and when the sun rises, or rather when he looks out of the clouds with a ghastly countenance, just like one who has been keeping it up overnight and is suffering for it in the morning – when light comes, and the herring-boats are again at anchor, and the pier and the shores are glittering with fresh fish, almost all the bacchanalians have disappeared from the hills and knolls, and the inn has subsided into its chronic state of dirt, darkness, languor and general misery.

EIGHT: 1880–1890

THE EXTRAORDINARY LUST for property which marked the arriviste in Victorian times provides a theme for a great deal that was written about the Highlands in the period of Britain's industrial ascendancy. Anxiety to gain land, fear of losing it, a desire to enjoy it as conspicuously as possible, are obsessions which recur again and again.

It was an age when the Forsyte with foresight could convert the profits from factory, brewery and mill into something both substantial and romantic. A Highland estate with an imposing baronial shooting lodge and limitless acres on which to stalk, shoot, and fish was considered as essential a piece of scaffolding for the social climber as a steam yacht and a town house in Belgravia.

Owning an island was, of course, the ultimate luxury. A picnic for your guests could be turned advantageously into a circumnavigation of the property; the glittering yacht could be admired, the investment enviably displayed. Whole regions of the Highlands and Islands were locked up for private use and understandably the people living there (over and above convenient hands needed as domestic servants, gillies, stalkers and boatmen) were regarded as a most frightful nuisance.

An additional nuisance came from tourists, who began to appear in increasing numbers as cheap excursions flourished. Particularly resented by owners of Scottish estates was the Access to Mountains (Scotland) Bill of 1884 promoted by James Bryce, later to become British Ambassador in Washington. Bryce failed to obtain public right of access to the wildernesses despite a clause (aimed at placating owners plagued by poachers) restricting access to the hours of daylight.

The hysteria which greeted Bryce's Bill has never really subsided. To this day, so entrenched is the landowning lobby that Scotland remains the only part of Britain without any national parks. But ninety years ago fury at this newest intrusion on the traditional freedom of the Highland laird was unbridled. That great swashbuckling sportsman W. Bromley-Davenport raised a quill trembling with anger:

> It was simply an open and undisguised attempt to injure Highland proprietors, and so reduce the value of their estates as to make them almost worthless. For who would hire a deer forest or a grouse moor if he were liable at any time, at the conclusion of a long stalk perhaps, to see the hideous apparition of 'Arry in appalling checks on the sky-line in full view of the deer? Or on a windy day with the grouse rather wild, to see the same estimable being, with more or less kindred spirits, whooping and holloaing across the sheltered flat on to which the luckless sportsman had driven the bulk of his birds, expecting there to 'make up his bag' in the afternoon, and where now he sees them wheeling off in affrighted packs from the unaccustomed sights and discordant sounds?
>
> Says the Bill: 'in case of any action of interdict, etc., etc., founded on alleged trespass it shall be a sufficient defence that the lands referred to were uncultivated mountain or moor lands, and that the respondent entered thereon only for the purposes or recreation or of scientific or artistic study.' So 'Arry, when challenged as to his business on the sky-line of the deer forest, has only to pull out an old betting-book, which for the nonce he turns into a sketch-book, and proudly proclaim himself to be a 'Hartis' and when questioned on his proceedings on the grouse moor, he replies that he's 'a recreating of himself'. True he is not allowed to carry a gun, and a 'blooming shame' that is, but he'll take care that no one else shall do so to any effect.

Bromley-Davenport prophesied the economic collapse of the countryside if the Bill became law:

The wretched proprietor or lessee will have to give up, the one his profit, the other his pleasure, at the bidding of the senseless sentimentality of fanatical socialists, and at the sacrifice of hundreds of honest thousands of pounds sterling which Scotland now annually receives from English sporting enterprise.

But despite the agitation of land reformers and the activities of politicians like James Bryce, the attractions of buying land remained undiminished. In 1883 a series of articles in *The Times* drew attention to the very real opportunities still open to the man with ready cash in his hand. But the author, Alexander Shand, warned potential speculators what sort of difficulties they might run into if they bought in the Hebrides:

The question of the irrepressible crofter is a more serious element; nor is it possible to avoid glancing at it in passing. Broadly-speaking there is a fairly well-defined line dividing these properties into two distinct categories. There are most of the properties in the Western Isles and perhaps on a few of the sea lochs on the mainland which may be said to be more or less swamped in squatters. These properties must necessarily hang on the market. The poor-rates at the best of times are out of all proportion to those in the mainland parishes; while in the worse seasons the purchasers will have the privilege of accumulating hopeless arrears of rent and feeding a population of starving paupers, who may abuse him for a tyrant when the pressure has gone by. A case in point is that of the late Sir James Matheson who probably expended for the benefit of Lewis nearly as much as the original purchase-money, and whose heirs, in return for his generous sowing, have been reaping a rich harvest of ingratitude.

And the writer saw little advantage in trying to invest in islands like Skye:

Even were it offered for sale, except for the savage stern grandeur of the scenery in certain districts, it can scarcely be called attractive. The grouse-shooting is generally poor, though in some places it is very good; and although Lord Macdonald has devoted large ranges of his country to deer, they do not take kindly to the soil or climate. The heads are by no means fine and the harts are far from heavy.

But there were exceptions, like the neighbouring island of Raasay, twenty miles long, three in breadth, 'a sporting Hebridean paradise':

Steaming along its shores, one is struck by the richness of the heather, which covers, with scarcely a break, the long low line of the western slopes, and its chief value must come from the sporting rental; although for many years, near the mansion, it has been beautified by the proprietors. In a recent season, 1250 brace of grouse had been killed – an extraordinary bag for a Hebridean shooting; as for woodcock, it is, perhaps, the best ground in Scotland, since they come thither in great flights when the weather is unusually severe on the mainland. Seven hundred have been shot in a single year, five hundred is by no means an unusual number. And the black game have been at least as abundant as they used to be when Boswell walked over the island with old Mr Malcolm Macleod; although, as black game are seldom constant to their haunts, I believe that of late years they have been rather less numerous. As for the proprietor's residence, it seems the most attractive in all these Western Isles, Lord Macdonald's more imposing castle at Armadale not excepted. It is such a handsome modern building as you might expect to see surrounded by the timber of an English deer-park. It faces the sunny quarter of the west; it is surrounded by ornamental plantations and highly respectable trees; while smooth-mown lawns of the richest green run down between the gardens to the shingly beach. The place has been embellished by successive capitalists since the last of the Macleods left his ancestral seat. Between forty and fifty years ago Macleod sold it to Mr Rainy for £12,000. Mr Rainy held it for about twenty-five years; his son who succeeded him died within the year, and then the island was bought by Mr Mackay, the Inverness engineer, who speculated largely in Highland land. The purchase-money at that time was £55,000. Mr Mackay sold it to Mr Armistead, who disposed of it very shortly afterwards to Mr Wood, the present owner, at a very large advance.

Edward Herbert Wood, a Warwickshire landowner, took possession of Raasay in 1876. The family had made their fortune at Burslem in the Potteries where Enoch Wood had been a friend and contemporary of the great Josiah Wedgwood. The private sporting estate in the Hebrides was the final and logical step for a country gentleman like Wood, but he soon found that although emigration in earlier days had been brisk, like many another island paradise Raasay was plagued by far too many unwanted tenants.

The last Chief of the Macleods of Raasay had, through penury, been forced to sell the island in 1843 for 35,000 guineas. When the potato crop failed in the Hungry Forties the new owner, George Rainy, decided to convert as much arable land as he could to more profitable sheep runs. An autocratic proprietor, he practised a simple but effective form of population control – he forbade young people to marry. If they wished to breed they must leave. By 1852 two boatloads of emigrants had been sent to America and twelve townships had been cleared. In 1865 another 125 Raasay men and women took a last trip down the Sound to Glasgow where they boarded an emigrant ship bound for Australia.

The Highland Emigration Society, supported by landowners anxious to improve the market value of their properties, encouraged even more islanders to seek a new life overseas. Raasay passed through a succession of hands until Edward Wood appeared and his reign marked the beginning of the end for Raasay as an agricultural community. The land which had been cleared by Rainy for sheep was now to be used almost exclusively for private sport. Pheasants were reared for the guns of the family and visiting guests, deer were encouraged, and the rabbit population allowed to multiply. The islanders were forbidden to shoot either vermin or game.

The conflict between the 'natives' and the proprietor of an estate was almost insoluble. He wanted his land for sporting purposes; the crofters and cottars wanted to grow food and graze their cattle and sheep. The Irish Land League formed by Michael Davitt and his militant friends in 1879 was certainly instrumental in rousing the people of the Hebrides to take more direct action to secure some kind of agrarian reform, and in the early 1880s many people cancelled their summer holidays in the Hebrides, fearing that they might become involved in violence.

The Gaelic-speaking author Malcolm Ferguson, who visited Skye in the summer of 1882, was firmly on the side of the landlords and he described how some of the Glendale crofters had taken forcible possession of a farm in order to extend their grazings:

> The Glendale shootings, which are reported to be very good, and used to be regularly rented, are unlet this season, incurring a considerable loss to the proprietor. I believe that owing to the crofters' ill-advised squabbles with their land-lords, parties in the south did not care to venture amongst them; and I have been repeatedly informed by hotel-keepers that the crofters' doings have been the direct cause of preventing many tourists visiting Skye this year – probably the dullest season experienced for years by hotel-keepers. I know from personal knowledge that not a few parties in London and the south had written to friends asking them if they thought it would be safe to visit Skye this summer.

Like many Lowland Scots, Ferguson was inclined to believe that the people of the islands, if only they bestirred themselves, could better their lot overnight without any recourse to land-raiding:

As a rule, they appear to be fairly well fed and clad, and I fancy that their greatest drawback and discomfort is the wretchedly miserable hovels of houses they live in, which, however with a small amount of labour and taste, could be greatly improved and made more comfortable. I have been in several of their houses, where I saw aged people tortured with rheumatism, sitting amidst thick volumes of blinding peat reek, the only window in the apartment being an open aperture in the wall without any glass, the wind blowing in and whirling the reek hither and thither, and out at the door.

Being a good-hearted man, Ferguson spoke to several crofters and explained to them how with a little thought they could make their cottages much more tidy and comfortable. They told him that as none of them had a holding on their house for longer than a year any improvements would in the end be only to the landlord's benefit. Even well-to-do small farmers who had built themselves slated houses had no guarantee of possession beyond a year.

Glendale itself was an isolated community. Few of the people Ferguson spoke to had any English and in the ten townships that made up the district of Glendale only the two schoolmasters and the miller were franchised.

There are no 'upper ten' nor middle-class people, neither clergyman, doctor, nor big shopkeeper in all the Glen. While wending our way towards the miller's house, after spending most of the day visiting various parts of the district, we observed our coachman standing on the top of a knowe on the look-out for us. He waved and made signs to us to come down to the miller's house and on entering we at once saw that the kindly-hearted and hospitable miller had prepared a sumptuous dinner for us. Mountains of mealy tatties laughing in their jackets and fresh-boiled salmon, sufficient to satisfy the inner-man's cravings of at least half-a-dozen hungry mortals of ordinary capacity, lots of nice sappy barley bannocks, and thick, crispy oatmeal cakes, jugfuls of thick sweet milk or rather cream, from the miller's Highland cows that daily browse among the bonnie, blooming Highland heather. After partaking of an excellent dinner we had a long crack with our kind host who told us that the last time he was beyond the boundaries of his native Glen was on the occasion of the last Parliamentary election when he got a 'hurl' in a carriage and pair to Portree, where he was entertained for a couple of nights and driven home again.

Ferguson was told that it was common talk all over Glendale that when the men returned from the herring fishing they would retake possession of the farm in dispute which had been handed back to the landlord by law officials during their absence at sea. The rising tide of public indignation against the use and abuse of land in the Highlands eventually overflowed into Westminster. In March 1883 when three crofters from Skye, dubbed the Glendale Martyrs by the radical Press, were sentenced to two months' imprisonment in Edinburgh for what many people saw as a courageous and completely justified stand against the tyranny of a proprietor, there was overwhelming pressure for some kind of government action.

Gladstone set up a Commission of Inquiry headed by Baron Napier and Ettrick to investigate the condition of the people. Lord Napier, a landowner himself, was assisted in his task by two other landed gentlemen, Sir Kenneth Mackenzie and Donald Cameron of Lochiel. The Commission was completed by the radical MP Charles Fraser-Macintosh, Donald Mackinnon, Professor of Celtic in Edinburgh, and the popular Sheriff Alexander Nicolson of Skye.

The six men and their entourage travelled through the Hebrides that summer taking and accepting evidence. It was only the second visit ever made to the Hebrides by a Parliamentary Commission. In April 1851 Sir John M'Neill had toured the islands in HMS *Comet* seeking the causes of destitution. As his interviews were almost entirely with proprietors and factors it was not unexpected that his recommendations were in favour of emigration to the colonies for the surplus population; a verdict which would have been applauded by his father, the Laird of Colonsay, if not by the islanders.

But now the conspiracy of silence about the real state of affairs in the Hebrides was to be broken. The islanders' inability to express their grievances fluently in English, the language of parliamentary democracy, had all too frequently kept their voice unheard. 'It has been said', wrote Hugh Miller, 'that the Gaelic language removed a district more effectually from the influence of English opinion than an ocean of three thousand miles and that the British public know better what is doing in New York than what is doing in Lewis or Skye.' When the Commission began to receive evidence it was remarkably conflicting. The crofters and those who espoused their cause spoke of evictions, unrealistic rents, harassment, exploitation and intolerable hardships. Establishment opinion was convinced that the crofters were being misled by political activists. As Macleod of Macleod put it in his evidence to the Commission: 'For some considerable time there have been agitators in every corner of the island, circulating the most communist doctrines, and endeavouring to set tenants against their landlords.'

Such sentiments would have been vigorously applauded by a remarkable man who was, like many visitors to the Hebrides, passionately addicted to the pursuit of field sports. Captain J. T. Newall was a hyperactive paraplegic who, unable to afford the expensive moors of Perthshire and the well-stocked Highland deer forests, had settled for a relatively cheap shoot in Lewis. A riding accident in India had left him unable to walk or even stand, but paralysed as he was, he refused to admit defeat. He had constructed for himself an iron framework chair which could be lifted on poles:

With one man in the shafts, in front, and one similarly placed behind, with two, one on each side, to assist the latter, he having the principal weight, I can manage to ascend high hills, and get carried to places and over ground which would have been quite inaccessible to a pony. In fine, I shoot over dogs, and even stalk deer with success, though of course it is shooting under difficulties.

In 1880 he and his eldest brother, General Newall, rented the shooting of Scaliscro, on the eastern shore of Little Loch Roag in Lewis, and for four happy years he spent his summers there:

> The most northern island of the outer Hebrides may appear a somewhat distant *locale* to select by a man in my position; but one has to go far afield now-a-days, unless endowed with such means as render expense no object. Moreover, I had shot in Lewis, where the birds lie close throughout the season, a great object to one situated as I am; I love a wild country also. Above all, on the Scaliscro ground, I knew that there was every chance of getting deer without having to pay forest prices.

In case you imagine that Captain Newall was totally impoverished, you must remember that when a man described himself as being of limited means he didn't mean *that* limited. There was always enough money to travel in style:

> I found that by taking a deck-cabin on the *Claymore*, or one of Mr Macbrayne's other steamers from Glasgow, I got to Stornoway with far less change and worry than if travelling the same distance by land. With our own servants on board, we were able to get our meals brought to our airy cabin. There existed, therefore, no necessity to descend into the hot, whisky and food-stricken atmosphere of the regions below. The beauty too of the scenery as the steamer threads its way among the various islands, repays one for many inconveniences; for some of the finest scenery in Scotland exists among those fjords with which the wild west coast and its islands are so frequently and deeply indented.

Newall's book *Scottish Moors and Indian Jungles* records the deaths and escapes of stags, salmon, woodcock and snipe in the Lews and bigger game (bears, panthers and tigers) in what the author calls 'the spiced Indian air'. At Scaliscro the shikaris and beaters were replaced by stout gillies every bit as deft as Indian bearers.

'My team soon had me out of the cart and strapped and buckled all right on to the carrying apparatus.' It took four men to manoeuvre the Captain into position for a shot: 'They were all good and kindly fellows, and we learned to regard them with a genuine and most friendly interest, which I think was reciprocated.' Donald was a fine, good-looking fellow who 'lifted his cap when courtesy so required, with all the grace of the old régime, as contradistinguished to the quick jerk and sweep which is the custom now-a-days in more fashionable circles'.

Like most visiting sportsmen, the Captain did not feel it was part of his duty to become involved in local politics. But even he could not ignore the gunboat that had to be sent to Loch Roag at the time of the Land League disturbances. He revealed that he had 'a great feeling of interest in, and sympathy for, this simple, brave, and struggling people'. And he felt it worth placing on record, in case any of his readers might have formed a contrary impression, that 'human beings, and especially human beings of such a type as these Hebridean men, are of more consideration than grouse and deer, or even sheep'.

The Captain was pained to see the poor people being led astray by fanatical zealots 'ever keen to rouse clashing interests, or stir up ill feeling between class and class'. As a military man he realized the importance of the islands but if emigration was the answer so be it:

From an Imperial point of view, any unnecessary expatriation of the islanders would be, as it has been, a national loss. These islands, Skye especially, once formed a depôt from which was drawn some of the finest fighting material in the British Army. At present, in the Lews, there is a considerable number of Navy Reserve men. But, however desirable it may be to retain such valuable material for the use of the public services, the land cannot support it. Even were landlords willing to surrender their rights at the dictation of those who have no sort of sympathy with them, the congestion must be relieved ere long, and the difficulty to be faced only postponed.

Captain Newall and others like him, who saw the Hebrides as a cheap source of sporting pleasure and a reservoir of manpower for the army and navy, must have been dismayed by the Napier Commission's report, which was ready within a year of their initial appointment. It spoke officially, for the first time, of 'a state of misery, of wrong-doing, and of patient long-suffering, without parallel in the history of our country'.

The Commission's recommendations led to legislation which gave even the poorest crofter fixity of tenure and seemed at the time to herald a new era for the crofting counties. Indeed the Crofters Holdings Act of 1886 has been, erroneously to my mind, described as a Magna Carta of the Hebrides. But was it?

By perpetuating small and uneconomic holdings crofting was gradually turned into a way of life insulated from the mainstream of agriculture. The sacred plot of family ground handed down by legal right from father to son has assumed an importance more emotional than economic. From a farming point of view crofting land is both unproductive and unprofitable – only seven per cent of it is cultivated today and emigration has not been arrested. Far too many crofters are old-age pensioners whose children and grandchildren live in high-rise flats in the Lowlands.

What the islands needed desperately in the 1880s was development; what they were offered was assisted stagnation. Outwardly little changed; there was still a great deal of poverty and more or less unlimited opportunities for those armed with rod and gun. A constant visitor to the Western Isles at this time was Charles Peel, not only a Fellow of the Zoological Society and the Royal Geographical Society but the very model of an English sporting gent. The Outer Hebrides was, he thought, a paradise for the study of animals and birds but one where much of the pleasure of killing the wildlife was still spoilt by the natives:

> It is not conducive to sport [he complained] to be followed by a gang of men and ordered out of the country, nor is it pleasant to be cursed in Gaelic by a crowd of irate old women, even if you do not understand every word they say. They accused us of shooting their horses and sheep, filled in the pits which we dug in the sandhills for geese, shouted to put up geese when we were stalking, cut up the canvas and broke the seats of our folding-boat, and tried in every possible way to spoil our sport. They were especially insolent and troublesome in Benbecula and Barra. Taking them as a whole, the crofters are an ignorant lot of creatures and the less said about them the better.

Mr Peel wrote widely for such journals as *Rod and Gun*, *Land and Water* and the *Field* and was that common mixture of Victorian naturalist, both collector and predator. In the same sentence he will describe with admiration the flight of the curlew and then add, 'I very soon bagged a couple'. He admired rabbits too ('in a short day we once bagged 105 bunnies with the aid of only a couple of ferrets') and Bewick's swans ('I shot a fine specimen in Benbecula') and the great northern diver ('I raced up and down that pool for over three-quarters of an hour, when I at length got him with a shot through the neck').

One feels it would have given him great satisfaction to wing a few of what he usually referred to, remembering perhaps his safaris in Africa, as 'the natives'. He recalled, for instance, the flotsam washed up one year on the west coast of North Uist:

> several 60 lb cheeses, tins of vaseline, cases of champagne, beans from the West Indies, a turtle from the sub-tropical

seas, and an incandescent lamp quite uninjured! The vaseline was much appreciated by the natives who spread it in thick layers on their bread, and ate it with great relish.

Mr Peel approached all creatures great and small with relish, none more so than the grey seal (*Halichoerus grypus*):

When basking in the sun on the rocks grey seals are very difficult to stalk, and must be shot dead, or they invariably slide off the rock into the sea and escape. When in the water they are very inquisitive, following a boat for a great distance. If the water is not too deep you may try a shot, but when struck in the head they immediately sink. A hook at the end of an oar or pole will fetch them up easily from the bottom. Seal oil is much prized by the natives of the Outer Hebrides, and is considered superior to cod-liver oil.

The common seal (*Phoca vitulina*) is a much smaller animal than the grey seal, its average length from tip of nose to end of tail being 4½ feet. Two specimens shot by me measured 4 feet 4¼ inches and 4 feet respectively. The adult animal is of a silvery or yellow-grey, with black spots, the spots being smaller than those on the grey seal. The belly is yellowish-white. The young also are of a pale yellow colour. These animals are also of a very inquisitive nature. One which was struck on the head with an oar behaved in a most extraordinary manner, turning over and over in the water, and rolling like a porpoise. It eventually recovered, and went away as if nothing had happened.

Seals afford very good sport, for they are as difficult to stalk as red deer. I was once landed out of a boat upon a small island which was literally covered with them. By dint of much crawling on hands and knees on the hard rock (a very painful operation), and taking my boots off, I got an unexpectedly close shot. I was crawling for a lot of six, when, on creeping round a rock, I suddenly became aware of a large eye looking sideways at me at very close quarters. I was obliged to fire at him, although a small one, or he would have put the others away. He rolled over dead, and, on running up to the edge of the rock, I saw the others swimming about in the water, looking curiously at me. I fired my left-hand barrel at the nearest one, and he sank in about eight feet of water. Going back to the first, I measured the distance, and found it was ten feet from me when I fired at it.

It is very seldom an adult seal will allow you to approach to such close quarters, their sense of smell being very acute. I brought the boat round to the spot where the second one had sunk. The weed was so thick at the bottom that I did not like the idea of diving for it; but with the aid of a long pole, with three large sea-hooks attached, we dragged it up at the first attempt. Thus I bagged my 'right and left' at seals.

Another visitor who came on a more peaceable and silent mission also bagged a first and if 'Nauticus',* as he styled himself, doesn't merit a footnote in Hebridean history, he would certainly be worth a paragraph in the official records of British cycling. In the summer of 1880 he became the first man to pedal a tricycle through Skye, the climax of a 2,462-mile journey round Scotland on his Coventry-built Cheylesmore (as supplied to HRH the Prince of Wales).

During his tour he carried three shirts, one pair of trousers, one waistcoat, three pairs of socks, six handkerchiefs, collars, slippers, washing-gear, note and guidebooks and 'a muffler to put on when standing about.'

He encountered a fellow bicyclist in the Highlands but saw not one other tricycle. The only island he visited on his tour was Skye where his arrival created a minor sensation. He was ferried over from Glenelg to Kylerhea in exchange for a shilling and had great difficulty in ascending the precipitous road of

---

* It is possible that 'Nauticus' was Sir Owen Seaman (1861–1936), then an undergraduate at Cambridge and later editor of *Punch*.

Bealach Udal in the shadow of Beinn na Caillich. He calculated the angle as being about 70 degrees:

> Though I have since been told that this was impossible, the gradient was such as to make me fear that I should have to take my tricycle to pieces and carry it up bit by bit; notwithstanding I determined to have a good try first.

Putting his shoulder under the saddle he managed gradually to push the heavy machine to the summit. But there were fresh perils yet in store:

> Having mounted, I was just commencing to move, when a sudden squall burst upon me, and in a second I was being whirled along by a furious gust of wind. To my horror, I discovered that I was being carried at railway speed down a steep pitch, with only a low wall between me and a frightful precipice; moreover the road twisted in and out in a succession of sharp corners. It was an anxious moment! Had I lost my head for a second nothing could have saved me.

Staying the night at a cottage in Broadford, he pedalled the following day in ominous weather to Sligachan. Pouring rain, black storm-clouds and capricious winds made his climb over Druim nan Cleochd fraught with peril, and on arrival at Sligachan Inn he found his fellow guests had been stormbound for several days:

> In the smoking room, an Oxonian, travelling with his tutor, related their misfortunes. Three times had they started for Loch Coruisk, and on each occasion were driven back by the weather, and the Cuchullins, which they had specially wished to see, had not once been clear during their stay in Skye.

And then on to Portree and a change in the weather:

> As I came nearer, the appearance of Portree with the yachts lying in the harbour had a very pleasing effect and my

advent into the town was of a lively description. The
working population were basking in the sun after the toils
of the day; on sighting me a shout arose, a simultaneous
rush was made from all quarters in my direction and an
excited crowd escorted me to the door of the 'Royal'
hotel. When walking to the post-office afterwards I heard
several people discussing the latest arrival, and disputing as
to the number of wheels, etc.

'Nauticus' was more interested in covering ground than
observing it closely. He visited the Quiraing and Coruisk, but
it was the travelling rather than the arriving that preoccupied
him: 'I knew all the time that my left tyre was getting shaky,
and now on examination I found that it was once more loose
all round.'

Highlight of his visit to Skye was a race with a dog-cart:

'Ho, ho!' thought I, 'if you are not going faster than that,
and the road remains good, there is a chance of our seeing
the mountain together after all, my friends.' Suiting the
action to the thought, I put on a spurt, and gradually over-
hauled and passed them. This proceeding put the driver
on his mettle, for sounds of the whip met my ear, and on
coming to a stony bit, they shot ahead of me.

There were lots of stony bits in those days and it must have
come as no surprise to 'Nauticus' to find when he returned to
the mainland from Kyleakin that he had blazed a pioneering
trail: 'I crossed the ferry very well in the ordinary boat (1s.).
The man told me that he had once had two bicyclists on board,
who apparently are the only wheelmen who have ever visited
Skye.'

Even on a tricycle it was much easier for a male tourist to
make his way alone round the islands than a woman, but that
didn't deter a remarkable lady who came to sketch, to paint
and to write at about this time. Constance Gordon Cumming
was a compulsive traveller and when her Hebridean memoirs
were published in 1883 she had already written *At Home in Fiji*

and *A Lady's Cruise in a French Man-of-War,* after a wet but productive summer in the Western Isles she set off indefatigably for the Himalayas.

She had a sharp if romantic eye and her account of the cattle market at Lochmaddy is a more gentle antidote to the bacchanalian orgy described at the end of Chapter Seven. At that time the population of North Uist was four thousand and it seemed that almost all of them had come for this great annual gathering:

I doubt if any other spot could show so picturesque a cattle-fair. In the first place, all the cattle had to be brought from neighbouring isles to this common centre, and, as each boat arrived, with its rich brown sails and living cargo of wild rough Highland cattle of all possible colours, the unloading was summarily accomplished by just throwing them overboard and leaving them to swim ashore.

Besides the fishers' brown-sailed boats, several tiny white-winged yachts had brought customers to the market and added to the general stir – a stir which must have so amazed the lone sea-birds, which are wont to claim these waters as their own, for, as a general rule, a more utterly lonely spot than this dull flat shore could scarcely be found.

Now, however, an incredible number of islanders had assembled. It seemed a fair matter for wonder where they could all have come from, but a tidier, more respectable lot of people I have never seen. These people of North Uist – now, alas! like their neighbours, so sorely oppressed by downright want – generally rank among the most prosperous of the Outer Islesmen, their patient industry being proverbial.

Naturally, there was a liberal consumption of 'the barley bree' at the market, but, the consumers being all hardened vessels, no one appeared any the worse, nor even any the livelier – and liveliness is by no means a characteristic of these gentle quiet folk, most of whom seem to be naturally of a somewhat melancholy temperament. Men and women alike have a grave expression – not exactly careworn, for in truth they are generally ready to accept their hardships with amazing philosophy, but a far-away look, as those whose life-long teachers have been the winds and waves, – solemn spiritual influences which have sunk deep into their souls.

A whole-hearted son of the Isles has just told me that I have misinterpreted his countrymen, and that the gravity is a quality of modern growth, carefully fostered by 'Free Kirk' influences. He maintains that the true nature is that which only peeps out occasionally, when the barley-bree has shaken off the acquired gravity, and encouraged the singing of rollicking songs and dancing in the energetic fashion of olden days, compared with which our most inspiriting 'Reels of Tulloch' are tame indeed.

I am bound to believe these words of a true Gael, but I speak of the people as they seemed to me, and this great cattle-market afforded a very fair opportunity for judging.

Perhaps the truth lies somewhere in between the fictional fair of Storport and the rectitude of Constance Gordon Cumming's Lochmaddy. Had she lingered later than mid-afternoon she might have received some livelier impressions.

One woman who did have some lively adventures on her frequent journeys from her home in Cardross to the Hebrides was Mrs Frances Murray who, with her family, spent six summers in the big house on Oronsay, an idyllic retreat whose enjoyment was spiced with some long-drawn-out arrivals and departures. 'Many a time we have stayed up all night,' recalled Mrs Murray, 'on the *qui vivre* for the hoarse whistle which signalled the ferryman to hasten to get all aboard the boat.'

And the boat on which they relied was seldom on time:

There was always the risk of weather too rough for landing, and in the season of ferrying cattle the steamer was often late through calling at all sorts of odd places. Such a boat may advertise to leave at seven in the evening and yet keep you waiting till seven in the morning without any manner of apology. This was the more inconvenient in our case as not only had we six miles to drive, but we were also obliged to cross the strand when the tide suited which sometimes caused us to leave some hours before the time advertised for the steamer's arrival.

And then there were the all-too-frequent occasions 'when the steamer neglected to put out the meat, bread and groceries at Scallaoig and it was all taken north to Harris and only landed on the return trip.'

Such minor inconveniences paled before the shipwreck which Frances Murray experienced in September 1882. A woman of courage and backbone, she rose even above that. When the boat went aground off Islay everyone struggled ashore, tarpaulins were raised on oars to provide shelter from the wind and rain and the passengers crouched for twelve hours in their makeshift tent before they were rescued.

While the Napier Commission was considering the future of the crofters, Mrs Murray entertained the members of her local Church of Scotland Literary and Scientific Society with an account of her adventures in the Hebrides and in particular a yachting trip she had made that summer through the islands on board the forty-five-ton schooner *Aglaia*. There were no slides to show, but Mrs Murray (accompanied by her daughter at the piano) sang a few Jacobite songs with, according to the *Helensburgh and Gareloch Times*, 'alternate fire and pathos'.

She described some of the curious habits of the natives [*Laughter*], her own views on the present position of the Highlands [*Applause*] and delivered some verses on the pleasures of yachting:

> Farewell *Aglaia!* and your crew
> Fairest of schooners, fare you well!
> For we must haste away from you,
> Far from old ocean's changing blue,
> Far from the billows heaving swell.
> [*Loud Applause*]

Back in their comfortable homes that night, kept spotless perhaps by domestics from the islands, Mrs Murray's audience may well have, in their bedside prayers, thanked the Lord that He had given them warmth and comfort and not the kind of desolate dwelling that their lecturer had seen on Mingulay:

> An old woman at her time-blackened spinning-wheel sitting on a lump of the naked rock beside the peat-fire; a hen mother and some chickens foraging over the earth floor; a small pig scratching his apparently clean little back under the bench of driftwood supported by turf on which we were sitting. A little table but no dresser; one small chair, one three-legged pot and a kettle. This is about all.

But in spite of their lack of material possessions, Mrs Murray had found the crofters 'kind, gentle, courteous and very hospitable. It was indeed touching to receive out of their poverty, presents of milk, eggs and potatoes, though sometimes the milk or bottle of cream tasted so of peat that we could hardly make it palatable.'

Mrs Murray had left her audience on a note of hope. Perhaps, she told them, when the Napier Commission had finished its work there would be a large voluntary emigration which would relieve congestion in the islands:

> In the meantime, let what of the land can be given, be given to the crofters, and that not the worst but the best, putting townships before sheep farmers wherever this can be done. These are some of the means to win back to loyalty a strong generous and splendid race, which has filled our armies with recruits of the best kind and our families with valuable servants. [*Applause*]

A more politically motivated voyager round the Hebrides was Charles Fraser-Macintosh, who came to collect not impressions but votes. Known as 'The People's Candidate', he travelled round the islands in the thirty-seven-ton *Carlotta* accompanied by Hector Rose Mackenzie, son of Alexander Mackenzie, editor of the *Celtic Magazine*. Hector Rose wrote an account of their campaigning voyage and he describes how after embarking at Strome Ferry they sailed into Loch Duich. Here late on Sunday night Sir Thomas Brassey's yacht steamed majestically towards them and anchored. Brassey had owned many a yacht since his first voyage through Hebridean waters twenty-nine years earlier in the *Cymba* but in 1885 nothing more splendid than his *Sunbeam* sailed the pleasure lanes. Young Mackenzie was overwhelmed by the opulence which the multi-millionaire Brasseys had created for themselves:

> The *Sunbeam* is quite a floating palace fitted up in the most luxurious manner. Her many saloons and sleeping-cabins are marvels of elegance and comfort, while the taste of Lady Brassey is displayed in the numberless pictures and curios which adorn the walls and tables in the different apartments. On deck, as below, everything is the perfection of neatness and tidiness. The crew numbers twenty-seven and the yacht carries six boats.

The paradox of the *Sunbeam* in all its glittering ostentation sailing among islands where the population lay entrapped in the permanent miseries of penury escaped Hector Rose's pen. There were meetings all over the Outer Isles and at various places in Skye. Here Fraser-Macintosh met the celebrated Glendale Martyr, John Macpherson, who had led the crofters of the west coast of Skye in their battle for the right to be treated as human beings. As the *Carlotta* entered Loch Colbost they saw that the *Dunara Castle* had just arrived and was putting ashore a number of Glendale men who had been at the east coast fishing:

> Groups of women were hurrying down to the seashore, and as each man stepped from the boat, he was hugged and kissed by his wife, mother, or sweetheart, as the case might be, in the most affectionate manner, while a torrent of welcoming and endearing terms was poured forth with all

the fervour of which the Gaelic language alone is capable. Driving on, we met several more women on the road, coming to meet their friends. A young man who was trudging along in front of us with his heavy trunk upon his broad shoulders, seemed to be a particular favourite, and received a cordial greeting from everyone he met. At length we saw a good-looking young woman running towards him as fast as she could while at the same time the young man dropped his trunk and ran to meet her. A close embrace, a sounding kiss, and a few affectionate enquiries, and then the two, with entwined arms, returned to where the trunk had been so unceremoniously abandoned. The last I saw, as a turn of the road hid them from sight, was the two walking briskly along, carrying the trunk between them, and conversing with great animation. They were sweethearts, our driver informed us, waiting patiently until better days should enable them to marry.

The men of Glendale are, without doubt, the finest looking fellows I have come in contact with. The majority are tall and broad-shouldered. They are industrious, well-clothed and courteous to strangers. John Macpherson, the 'Glendale Martyr' and leader of the people, is a good type of the average Glendale-man. He is a broad-shouldered, hardy-looking Celt, with a bushy brown beard, just tinged with grey. His forehead betokens considerable brainpower, his eyes are brimful of intelligence and his hard-set chin and firm lips denote decision of character. But it is as a speaker that John Macpherson is seen at his best. When thundering forth his denunciations of the oppressor and the tyrant to an enthusiastic audience of his own countrymen, at one moment rousing them to the highest pitch with some faithfully drawn picture of the wrongs suffered by the people, at another causing roars of merriment by some apt simile or well-aimed hit – it is then that one can fully realise and appreciate the power which Macpherson possesses over the minds and feelings of his fellow-Highlanders.

In the early part of 1883, Macpherson was apprehended, with two other Glendale-men for breach of interdict, and sentenced, by Lord Shand, in the High Court of Justiciary, Edinburgh, to two months imprisonment. From this circumstance, he has ever since been known at home and abroad as the 'Glendale Martyr,' a name of which he is naturally proud.

It was a highly successful cruise and when the election results were declared on 5 December 1885 Fraser-Mackintosh topped the poll with twice as many votes as his two opponents, the Macleod of Macleod and Sir Kenneth Mackenzie.

None of the candidates of course had ventured as far as St Kilda, indeed it is doubtful if the islanders even had a vote to cast. For much of the year, in the period of the winter gales, the island was completely cut off from all communication with the rest of Britain. The only way to attract attention was to wait for a good wind from the west and cast a message on to the waters in the hope that it would be picked up on the Long Island or the west coast of Scotland.

The St Kilda mail-boats, as they were known, had been cast up as far away as Orkney and even Norway. They were simple but effective: a boat-shaped piece of driftwood in which was hollowed out a cavity big enough to take a small tin or bottle containing a letter. A wooden hatch was nailed over the tiny hold and the words 'Please Open' cut into the wood. A sheep's bladder filled with air served as both float and something to catch the eye and a coin or two was enclosed to pay the postal expenses of the finder.

On the last Thursday of September in 1885, one of these St Kilda mail-boats was washed ashore near Gallan Point in the Uig district of Lewis and the letter inside described the great damage which had been done to the crops on Hirta by an unprecedented storm. Shortly afterwards another mail-boat was retrieved on the mainland containing a letter from the minister which ran as follows:

I beg leave to intimate to you that I am directed by the people under my charge on this island to tell you that their corn, barley, and potatoes are destroyed by a great storm which passed over the island on Saturday and Sabbath last. You will be kind enough to apply to Government in order to send us a supply of corn seed, barley and potatoes. This year's crop is quite useless. They never before saw such a storm at this time of the year. They have lost one of their boats; but happily there was no loss of life.

The letter was addressed to the Rev. Dr Rainy of the Free Church and he and Sir William Collins of Glasgow decided to provide aid at once for the islanders. They chartered the *Hebridean* and sent a cargo to the value of £110 to the rescue. The only passenger on board was Robert Connell, a journalist employed by the *Glasgow Herald*.

They steamed into the bay of St Kilda at half-past four in the afternoon, on Sunday 18 October. The events that followed furnished Connell with a series of articles which were subsequently published in book form. He wrote about the islanders' sheep-plucking expeditions to Boreray, their methods of self-government, their massacre of sea birds, their desperate addiction to church-going and their susceptibility to alien germs:

> You are not long on St Kilda before you hear of the *cnatan na gall*. This is variously interpreted as the strangers' cough, the strangers' cold, the boat-cold, or the Harris cold. The very day our party arrived on the island one of the natives insinuated that we would no doubt have brought, among other good things, a dose of the *cnatan na gall*. This was said as a 'feeler' and the immediate excuse for its being said was that one of our number had been observed to sneeze. Happily the culprit understood thoroughly the idiosyncrasies of the islanders, and he was able to meet them on their own ground. He convinced them that if he really was suffering from the *cnatan na gall* he must have caught it since setting foot on the island that very morning. The

incident was not lost upon us. We were all careful afterwards never to sneeze in public.

Surprisingly, Connell could not understand that the St
Kildans were indeed being highly accurate in their diagnosis of
the boat-cold. It manifested itself in the form of stiffness in the
jaw muscles, a headache and a feeling of depression. The cough
which developed was occasionally a killer and very often the
entire island was laid low. Connell was told that if the infec-
tion was brought by a vessel from Glasgow or Liverpool the
'cold' was not so severe as if it came from Harris which had
the reputation of sending the worst type of virus. Virus was not
a word then in vogue and most visitors thought that the St
Kildans had invented their symptoms.

Connell quoted John Sands, who had visited St Kilda ten
years earlier and who had at first laughed at the concept of a
boat-cold:

> But yet, he adds 'after all there may be some truth in it'
> and he solemnly records the fact that on the arrival of the
> factor's smack in 1876 every one of the natives caught this
> peculiar cold, as they did again at the beginning of the
> following year, when a shipwrecked Austrian crew landed
> on the island.

But the 'boat-cold' was a mild affliction compared with
what was known on St Kilda as the 'eight-day sickness':

> Roughly speaking, one-half of the children born on the
> island came into the world only to die of this terrible
> scourge when they are a few days old. Medical men
> have been casting about for the cause of this frightful
> mortality, while pious men of a certain type have been
> peacefully folding their hands, endeavouring to console
> themselves with the fatalistic reflection, quite worthy of the
> unspeakable Turk, that after all it is the Almighty's business,
> not theirs.

Only a year or two ago, Miss Macleod, sister of the

proprietor, on one of her visits to the island, made a suggestion to the people that a properly qualified female nurse should be sent to them, but a certain old man, who shall here be nameless, met the proposal with the devout exclamation – 'If it's God's will that babies should die nothing you can do will save them!' Mr Sands bears testimony to the fact that he has 'heard more than one pious gentleman suggest that this distemper was probably a wise provision of Providence for preventing a redundant population on a rock where food was limited.'

I have heard the same idea expressed even more dogmatically. On my way home from St Kilda I had the pleasure of meeting a great gun of the Free Church – a gentleman who makes the Assembly Hall ring with his ponderous voice every year. Learning from a mutual friend that I had been to St Kilda, he had many questions to ask about the minister and the people. On the subject of this terrible lockjaw he became particularly loquacious. With a knowing air, and evidently wishing the company to understand that he was coaching me with my facts, he was not ashamed to say that this lockjaw was a wise device of the Almighty for keeping the population within the resources of the island. When I asked him how he could reconcile this theory with the two facts that not so very long ago the population was nearly three times as large as it is to-day, and that as a fishing station the island could easily maintain two or three thousand people he was dumb. His dispensation to speak of the ways of Providence evidently did not carry him so far as this.

At about this time an American couple, Joseph and Elizabeth Robins Pennell, were touring the Hebrides collecting material for a series of articles to be published in *Harper's Magazine*. The destitution of the inhabitants of St Kilda would have provided even more ammunition for them than the wretchedness and misery they found in other parts of the Hebrides. 'We were not blind to the beauty, the sternness, the wildness of the country,' they wrote in their preface to *Our Journey To The Hebrides*, 'but the sadness and sorrows of its people impressed us even more than the wonder and beauty of their land.'

Despite the fact that the *Scotsman* had for months been reporting the privations and grievances of the crofters, their reviewer dismissed the book as 'culpable misrepresentation' and 'amazing impertinence'. But what the Pennells recorded was not only pertinent but probably one of the most accurate and objective impressions of Hebridean life in the 1880s. From Tobermory, where the couple spent 'two interminable days', they boarded the *Dunara Castle* and sailed north to Tarbert in Harris:

> The principal building in the village was the large white manse, half hidden in trees. A parson's first care, even if he went to the Cannibal Islands, would be, I fancy, to make himself, or have made for him at somebody else's expense, a comfortable home. There were also on the outskirts of the village two or three new, well-built cottages for men in Lady Scott's, the landlord's, direct service, and a large, excellent hotel, the only place in Tarbert where spirits could be bought. The rich may have their vices, though the poor cannot. Beyond was misery. Wherever we went in the island we found a rocky wilderness, the mountains black as I have never seen them anywhere else, their tops so bare of even soil that in the sunlight they glistened as if ice-bound. Here and there, around the lochs and sloping with the lower rocky hills, were weed-choked patches of grain and huts wreathed in smoke, their backs turned hopelessly to the road. Near Tarbert there was one bur-rowed out like a rabbit-hole, its thatched roof set upon the grass and weeds of the hill-side. Just below, in the loch, Lady Scott's steam-yacht came and went. Beyond, her deer forest, a range of black mountains, stretched for miles. Within sight and low on the water were the thick woods, in the heart of which stands her shooting-lodge. The

contrast gave the last bitter touch to the condition of the people. They starve on tiny crofts, their only homes; their landlord holds broad acres as play-ground for a few short weeks.

The hovels were as cheerless within as without. I do not know why it is that one takes liberties with the poor which one would not dare take with the rich. It is no small evil of poverty that it is everybody's privilege to stare at it. The people of Harris are hospitable, and receive the stranger with courtesy, but you can see that they resent the intrusion. It is not, I fear, to our credit that curiosity got the better of our scruples. We knocked at a cottage door, one Sunday afternoon, Joseph, as an excuse, asking for a light. As we drew near we heard the voice of some one reading aloud. Now it was silenced, and a tall old man in his shirt-sleeves came to the door with an open Bible in his hands. Within, on the left, was the dwelling-room of the household; on the right, the stable, cattle, and family share the only entrance. Into the room through a single pane of glass, one ray of daylight fell across the Rembrandt-like shadows. On the mud floor, at the far end, a fire of peat burned with a dull red glow, and its thick, choking smoke curled in clouds about the rafters and softened the shadows. We could just make out the figures of two women crouching by the fire, the curtained bed in the corner, the spinning-wheel opposite. All other details were lost in gloom and smoke. Until you see it for yourself, you could not believe that in our nineteenth century men still live like this. Miss Gordon Cumming says that to the spinning and weaving of the women 'is due much of such comfort as we may see by a peep into some of their little homes.' But our peep showed us only that women weave and men work in vain, and that to speak of comfort is mockery in a cottage of Harris, or, indeed, in any cottage we saw in any part of the islands, for all those we went into were alike in their poverty and their darkness. As a rule, the fire burned in the centre on a circle of stones, and over it, from the roof, hung chain and hook for the kettle. They have not changed one jot or tittle since, a century ago, they moved Pennant to pity.

As we left the hut on the hill-side, the first we visited, 'I beg pardon,' said the old crofter, who had not understood Joseph's thanks. His words seemed a reproach. We felt that we should be begging his pardon. To force our way in upon him in his degradation was to add one more to the many insults he has had to bear. He stood at the door a minute, and then went back into the gloom of the low room, with its mud floor and smoky rafters, which he calls his home.

All day long, even when the sun shone, as it did at intervals during our stay, Harris was a land of sorrow and desolation, but in the evening it became a land of beauty. The black rock of the mountain-side softened into purple shadows against the gold of sky and sea, and in this glory the hovels and the people and the misery disappeared. And when the sun sank behind the western waters and the gold faded, there fell a great peace over the island, and with it began the twilight, that lingered until it grew into the coming day.

NINE: 1890–1914

OF ALL THE VOYAGES made round the Hebrides in the nineteenth century surely the most spacious and the most enviable were the acceptance trials in August 1890 of RMS *Dunottar Castle*, the twenty-first ship built for Sir Donald Currie's Castle Line.

In addition to the hundred and fifty officers and men on board were Sir Donald himself, owner of the island of Scalpay, Skye, and a small party of his friends including W. Scott Dalgliesh who later published a vignette of the voyage.

The ship had accommodation for three hundred and sixty passengers. There were marble baths, a library of nearly five hundred volumes, and a barber's shop 'with a rotatory hair-brushing machine worked by an electric motor'. The *Dunottar Castle* was one of the first Clyde-built ships to have electric lighting, and as Scott Dalgliesh noted, 'It is bright and cleanly and it is always available. It is an immense advantage to be able to turn on a bright light in your state-room at any moment. The evening hours in the saloon, instead of being dreary, are looked forward to with pleasure.'

Almost unbelievably, the ship had been fitted out in all its elegance and luxury in only fourteen weeks – a record probably never equalled again:

> When the ship was launched at Govan on May 22nd, she was a mere hulk. When the trial trip took place on August 28th she was completely finished, furnished and manned. Everything was in its place, down to the minutest curtain-ring and the smallest carpet-tack; and every man was at his post, from the Captain to the cabin-boy.

Also waiting at its appointed station to take his guests into shallow sea lochs where the 3,069-ton liner could not venture was Sir Donald's luxurious yacht, the *Iolanthe*. The trials were conducted with the comfort of the passengers taking priority: 'We are to steam ahead during daylight, and our nights are to be spent peacefully at anchor in quiet waters.'

At Oban the *Iolanthe* brought off more guests and at Tobermory the evening was given up to recreation including dancing to the ship's band:

> This was carried out in the presence of nearly the whole population of Tobermory which had come out, on Sir Donald's invitation, to see the stately ship. Unfortunately however the festivities were marred by a heavy downpour of rain; but that did not prevent the singing of 'Auld Lang Syne' and 'God Save The Queen' or hearty cheers for our host, before the party broke up. One could not but feel sorry for the poor people who had to find their way to the shore in the dark, and through the pelting, pitiless rain.

In Loch Kishorn they anticipated, on a small scale, the frantic night-time rig-building activities of 1977–8:

> The electric searchlight was got into working order and we astonished the natives of Courthill and other solitary houses by flashing the light of day in upon them at midnight. The ship's pinnace and other small craft on the loch appeared like lime-light pictures thrown on a screen.

The voyage continued round the north of Scotland to Leith where *Dunottar Castle* sailed for London and a maiden record-breaking passage to South Africa. Sir Donald Currie owned a succession of magnificent yachts; in the winter he was frequently afloat in the Mediterranean and his summers were spent in northern waters. In those days there was a freemasonry of super-yachtsmen who talked the same affluent language and competed in the nicest possible way to outdo each other in splendour.

The Bulloughs of Rum owned a yacht, the *Rouma*, so large that the South African government were more than happy to borrow it as a hospital ship during the Boer War. The young laird of Raasay commissioned, at the age of twenty-three, one of the most splendid private vessels ever built. The *Rona* displaced over 1,000 tons, was nearly the length of four cricket pitches, and carried on its decks two racing-class sailing yachts.

In 1902 Sir Donald Currie engaged the Clyde builders W. Beardmore & Co. to construct the 999-ton *Iolaire*, and that too had for a time the cachet of being the most elegant yacht afloat. There were other wealthy owners who cruised the Hebrides, among them the Ismays. Tom Ismay founded the White Star line and his yachts, like Sir Donald's, were often more luxuriously equipped than his liners.

It was the custom for a fleet of glittering yachts to assemble in Hebridean waters in August and they proceeded almost in convoy from one sheltered anchorage to another. Lunch and dinner parties were held, passengers exchanged, visitors entertained. A diary kept by Mrs Ismay on board her husband's yacht *Vanadis* in August 1883 is a simple catalogue of hospitality exchanged and picnics enjoyed. At Loch Torridon the Ismays dined aboard *Cuhona* with Sir Andrew Walker after an expedition to Loch Maree: 'we went on shore and found the people very poor. Gathered some lovely flowers and stayed the night.'

To the yacht owners island travel presented no problems – the steam yacht was the leisurely executive jet of its day. But even if you didn't have a boat of your own, Macbrayne's ran scheduled services which would transport you in due and unhurried course to almost any part of the Hebrides. I'm not a great one for turning clocks back but if I were given an opportunity to restore only one amenity of West Highland life now almost completely vanished, it would be the network of steamers that served the islands winter and summer right up to the outbreak of the First World War.

I have in front of me David Macbrayne's timetable of the

period advertising summer tours through what the company somewhat fancifully called the Royal Route. They reminded readers that 'Alexander II, Hakon, Robert the Bruce, James IV, and James V, Bonnie Prince Charlie, Queen Victoria and King Edward' had all sailed round the islands pursuing their various peaceful or warlike purposes.

They laid out tempting itineraries for the tourist: trips to

> pleasant little towns where the steamer puts in for an hour or two, the clachan piers it touches at, to set a passenger or so ashore, and the island roadsteads where a boat comes out and is towed alongside for a few moments in the clear green seas, while the mails are taken on board. There is the plaintive sound of the Gaelic, the fragrance of the peat-reek drifting from the shore, and the bleat of the sheep far up the mountainside that comes faintly to the ear.

Particularly popular were the round trips which could be as short as two days or as long as a week. For 30s you could sail from Oban to Castlebay, Lochboisdale, Lochmaddy, Dunvegan, Loch Pooltiel and Loch Bracadale. There was a week's cruise from Glasgow to Stornoway and back for £4 including all meals. From a centre like Portree on Skye steamers left on various days of the week for Tarbert, Lochmaddy, Dunvegan, Broadford, Raasay, Staffin, Kilmaluag, Rodel, Stein, Kyleakin, Kyle of Lochalsh, Balmacara, Glenelg, Isle Ornsay, Armadale, Arisaig, Eigg, Tobermory, Salen, Lochaline, Craignure and Oban. Today there is no scheduled sea service from Portree at all!

Although the extension of the Dingwall & Skye Railway from Strome Ferry to Kyle of Lochalsh was not to be opened until November 1897 and the line from Fort William to Mallaig was not completed until the spring of 1901, there was an enviable wealth of tours and round trips to the islands from Glasgow, Edinburgh, Inverness and Oban.

In 1896 the Highland Railway offered ten tours from Inverness alone, 'with liberty to break the journey at any point where Train or Steamer calls on the Route'. Three of them took the tourist out to the isles and back:

> No 8. – Inverness by Rail to Dingwall and Garve, by Coach to Lochbroom and Ullapool, Mr Macbrayne's Steamer to Stornoway, Portree and Strome Ferry, thence by rail to Inverness. Fare – 1st Class, 32s 6d. To holders of Tickets for this Tour, the Fare by Coach from Garve to Ullapool, payable to the Coachman, will be 7s 6d, which includes his fee.

> No 8a. – Inverness by Rail to Dingwall and Strome Ferry, Mr Macbrayne's Steamer to Portree (Skye) by Coach to Dunvegan, Mr Macbrayne's Steamer to Lochmaddy (North Uist), Rodel, Tarbet (Harris), Portree and Strome Ferry, thence by Rail to Achnasheen and Inverness. Fares – 1st Class 44s 7d; 3rd Class 25s 3d.

> No 8b. – Inverness by Rail to Dingwall and Achnasheen, by Coach to Loch-Maree and Gairloch, Mr Macbrayne's Steamer to Portree (Skye), by Coach to Dunvegan, Mr Macbrayne's to Lochmaddy, Rodel, Tarbert (Harris), Portree and Strome Ferry, thence by Rail to Inverness. Fares – 1st Class 48s 6d; 3rd Class 32s.

Highly popular in late Victorian times was the longest excursion of all which, weather permitting, landed you in St Kilda. Two ships, the *Dunara Castle* and the *Hebridean*, made between them six summer journeys a year carrying mail and visitors to the island. Let's put the clock back ninety years and let me take you there on a Monday morning in August. The overnight train from Stirling has arrived at Oban at 5.20 a.m. and on it are Mr D. W. Logie and his friend ex-Bailie Archibald Watt.

Depositing their traps in the left luggage office they take a stroll along the pier. The bay dotted with craft of all kinds is dominated by three magnificent and rakish steam yachts. They meet up with a third member of the party, William Campbell, another former Bailie of Stirling. At about half-past eight the *Hebridean* in a belch of black smoke steams into the bay and ties up alongside the railway pier. On board they meet the other two members of the party, the Rev. George Mure Smith of West Church, Stirling, and the Rev. James Whiteford. They partake of a hearty breakfast in the saloon and spend the rest of the morning waiting for cargo to be unloaded. There is plenty to be seen in Oban in high summer. There are boats leaving for Fort William, Staffa and Iona; a steamer arrives from Stornoway, some of the yachts weigh anchor and sail slowly out towards the open sea. At noon the *Hebridean*, having taken on all her cargo, casts off and moves down the Sound of Mull towards Tobermory. As they stand on deck admiring the peak of Ben Nevis and the mountain ranges of Morvern, Ardgour, Mull and Ardnamurchan, the dinner bell rings and the party descend to the saloon once again. It is to be their only complaint: whenever something worthy of note heaves into view the gong rings either for breakfast, tea or dinner.

On board with them are three St Kildans – a man, a woman and a girl. Only the girl has a smattering of English. She tells them that she has been in Edinburgh Infirmary since June. Her aunt and uncle had left St Kilda three weeks ago to come and collect her.

In mid-afternoon the *Hebridean* noses into Tobermory and moors at the wooden pier. There is a chance to step ashore while she discharges cargo. The passengers stroll down the main street and in another half hour they are on their way again, this time to Croig where more cargo is dropped. There are thirty-one passengers on board; a gardener from Dunoon returning for a holiday to his native Coll after an absence of forty years, and a few sportsmen; but most of the passengers are holidaymakers from England and Scotland.

They anchor in Scarinish Bay in Tiree where some passengers are ferried ashore and others embark. Then on to Coll where three more passengers land including an English clergyman for whom a special boat comes alongside. As they leave

Coll, dusk falls and they feel the Atlantic swell. As the passengers turn in the *Hebridean* sails on for Loch Scresort on Rum where during the night more cargo is discharged.

When morning comes, Skye is in sight, the swell increases and a lot of the passengers begin to feel queasy. There is a welcome respite when the boat turns into Loch Harport to land cargo at Carbost, site of Talisker, the only distillery in Skye.

At Dunvegan they tie up alongside the pier and the passengers go ashore for the first time since Tobermory. Hearing that the Rev. John Mackay, who had ministered to the St Kildans for twenty-four years, has retired to Dunvegan, some of the English passengers walk up to tell him that there are three members of his former flock on board the *Hebridean*. Perhaps he would like to see them?

Mackay, who had ruled as a spiritual despot over the St Kildans until mounting dissension forced his resignation in the previous November, declines to leave his house. 'Such', thought Mr Logie, 'is Christian forbearance and kindness, letting alone old friendship!'

In the evening the *Hebridean* sets sail for Loch Eport on North Uist. Here, when the tide is full, they tie up alongside the pier and go ashore to inspect the kelp works. That night the ship lies offshore waiting for first light before navigating the Sound of Harris. The three St Kildans entertain with Gaelic hymns, some of the English passengers oblige the company with song and recitation, and others retire to play whist in the saloon. 'Never on this quiet Loch has, we are sure, a happier evening been spent. In the midst of all our pleasure the hours of parting came and for the second night we all betook ourselves to our quarters for rest.'

At two thirty in the morning the anchor is weighed and the *Hebridean* slips out into the Minch. When the passengers come on deck they find a misty morning with a drizzle falling. By eleven o'clock the islands of St Kilda are in full view and the sun comes out. Mr Logie is moved to prose: 'Nowhere in the

British Isles can the rocks throw on you the same awful and beautiful effect that is felt here. The rugged promontories and beetling headlands are truly magnificent and fantastic.'

They anchor at 11 a.m. to a long blast on the siren and the islanders gather and launch their boat to take the passengers ashore. The three St Kildans are welcomed home with great rejoicing and the visitors begin to explore the primitive village. They are shown a St Kilda loom and the burying ground. The minister is called upon and the schoolmaster, and Logie manages to secure a couple of live fulmars which he is anxious to take back to Stirling. They leave St Kilda at three in the afternoon and make for Scotvin in Benbecula. Here the *Hebridean* takes on board sheep, cattle, pigs and several passengers. More sheep and passengers are taken on board at Eriskay and Castle Bay in Barra and then course is set once again for Tiree. There is a further stop at Coll and it is nightfall before they once again reach Tobermory.

At supper the passengers make farewell speeches, and a travelling pedlar sings them a Gaelic song. Mr Logie is prevailed upon to make a speech and he proposes the

> health and happiness of the English party, who had in every way done so much to entertain the company on the voyage, coupled with the toast the name of Mr Oldham. Mr Oldham in a cordial speech on behalf of the English party expressed the pleasure they had had in the voyage and thanked the company for their hearty response to the toast. Mr Oldham then recited 'the Dover Express' in a masterly manner quite bringing down the house with thunders of applause.

By this time the *Hebridean* had reached Oban Bay and at 1 a.m. moored at the pier next to the station. The Stirling party spent the rest of the night at the Lorne Hotel and caught the five thirty train for the south. It had been 'the most pleasant week we ever spent on the sea'.

Today there are few chances to spend such a relaxing week

cruising among the islands; the only way to do it would be to charter your own private boat. Sea tours have been replaced by coach tours and they are a poor substitute, a second-best way of seeing the Hebrides. Each day you are driven along often crowded roads past scenery which however grand has a tendency to blur into an impersonal, cinematic background. Each night you unpack your suitcase in a different and frequently indifferent hotel.

But eighty years ago a trip by a Macbrayne steamer involved you in other people's lives. As you moved from pier to pier and island to island your progress was slow but you felt the rain and wind on your cheek and you smelt the sea. Villagers came on board and drammed up in the saloon; you were not insulated from life behind a windscreen but thrown right into the midst of it.

It is easy to sentimentalize the pleasures of so leisurely a schedule, but it was a cheap and comfortable way to travel and you saw seascapes which the modern motorist isn't even aware of. He may be able to get about more quickly but his options are limited. Although you can fly to Barra and Tiree there are scores of places which can only be reached with great difficulty. Even St Kilda had its scheduled summer service. To reach it today you would have to make special arrangements to join one of the summer working parties organized by the National Trust.

Perhaps our greatest loss is the capacity for standing and looking without wanting to move restlessly on to the next item in the guidebook. Leaning on the rail of a Macbrayne steamer watching the Hebrides glide by, waiting for the gong to summon you to broth and roast mutton in the saloon, anticipating your arrival in some lochside village round the next promontory but one – it was a very civilized and comforting way to pass a week or so in August.

But even in those days of unhurried peace the ethos of the St Kildans was considered by most visitors to be eccentric in its lack of urgency. Had one been compiling an Olympic team to

Go Slow for Britain the St Kildans would have sauntered slowly away with all the golds leaving South Sea islanders and other tropical lotus-eaters nowhere in the field. Norman Heathcote, who visited St Kilda in 1898 with a camera, a paint-box and his intrepid sister, found it difficult to make up his mind whether they were lazy or not:

> There is no doubt that they waste a lot of time; but I am inclined to think that this is because they are as ignorant of the value of time as of the value of money.
>
> Sometimes they will take a whole day making up their minds to go fishing on the next, but when once started they are most industrious, and do not seem to mind hard work.

Most of the carrying of goods from the shore and peats from the hills was done by women who were broken into it at an early age: 'I have seen a girl of about eleven with a smaller child on one arm and a bucket of water in the other, or coming over the hill with a sheep on her back.'

From what Heathcote experienced, ten days (which was all they allowed themselves on their first visit) seems a very fleeting time in which to get anything done:

> If they were going to take us out in the boat they would say we must be ready by nine o'clock to get the benefit of the tide round a certain promontory. When we had sat for half-an-hour on the rocks two men would appear. They look at the boat and talk for five minutes, then one of them returns to the village to fetch the others. When all have at length appeared and said all they want to say, they proceed to haul down the boat. Soon after ten we were seated in comparative comfort in the stern and have hopes that we are off. Not a bit of it. They have forgotten an oar. Then it is discovered that one of the rowlocks is broken, and a new one has to be made. This is done by whittling a bit of stick. A long conversation follows, and we find that the question now is, what the lady is to sit on: some

advocate a plank, others an empty box. Eventually the box carries the day and we are off, but of course we have missed the tide.

Like many another visitor Heathcote felt that despite their deprived way of life and their dependence on the outside world for almost every necessity of life, the islanders would be worse off if they were evacuated to the mainland:

My view is that they lead a very happy life, that they are better housed and better fed than any other people in their rank of life, and that it would be a great misfortune to them to be removed from their present home, and of course I find that none of them wish to leave. I do not mean that I would discourage emigration. If any of them wish to push their fortunes in other parts of Scotland or in the colonies, by all means let them do so, and let them have every encouragement and assistance. Probably as they become more educated, many of them will become discontented with their primitive life and wish to take a more active part in the progress of the world. All I say is that I do not believe it will add to their happiness. Theirs is indeed a happy life. They have plenty to do, but can do everything at their own time and in their own way. They have good houses, ample food, and no worries.

But they did always have one worry at the back of their minds. When the *Dunara Castle* made its last scheduled call of the summer and they were left marooned in the Atlantic for the winter, what would happen if they ran out of food, or indeed if any of them fell so critically ill that hospital was the only hope?

Thirty years later, the winter of 1929 was so disastrous, the population now so small – a mere thirty-six compared with seventy at the turn of the century – that the islanders realized evacuation was the only possible answer to their dilemma. On 6 August 1930 the *Dunara Castle* ferried away half the sheep on the island; on 29 August the islanders embarked on HMS

Harebell with their remaining possessions. As Alasdair Alpin MacGregor, who was present at the evacuation, wrote:

> men may return to Hirta with the summer; but the people will have gone. The doors of some of the houses they will find locked: others they will find open. The loneliest of Britain's island-dwellers have resigned their heritage to the ghosts and the sea-birds; and the curtain is rung down on haunted homes and the sagas of the centuries.

It was a search not actually for ghosts but for supernatural manifestations that brought Ada Goodrich Freer to the Hebrides. She was a woman whose hold on reality was sometimes marginal; she suffered from delusions, if not of grandeur, then at least of intimate connection with persons whose birth was more distinguished than her own. In their book *Strange Things*, John Lorne Campbell of Canna and Trevor H. Hall describe how she managed to convince the Society for Psychical Research of her supranormal powers, her telepathic gifts, her expertise with crystal-vision and her ability to receive messages through sea-shells. When the Society, prompted by one of its Vice-Presidents, the Marquis of Bute, decided to investigate Highland Second Sight, it was quite natural that Ada's support should be enlisted. The first enquiry was begun in 1892 and it was the second which was entrusted in 1894 to Ada, publicly known as Miss X. She set off for Tiree in July.

Speaking no Gaelic herself, she based much of her subsequent book on the notebooks of the legendary Fr Allan Macdonald, whose knowledge of folklore and the oral traditions of the Hebrides was unrivalled and, fortunately for Ada, unpublished. Her debt to Father Allan is explicitly acknowledged in her preface to the book, but it is John Lorne Campbell's contention, amply supported by a comparison between Father Allan's notebooks and Ada's interpretation of them, that she did a great disservice to Hebridean folklore. So many errors peppered her pages that perhaps it is best not to quote from them.

But her account of the first stage of a journey which was to yield so much valuable material for subsequent lectures and articles is perhaps worth quoting. In company with her companion, Miss Constance Moore, daughter of the Prebendary of St Paul's, and her Dartmoor terrier Scamp, she embarked early one morning on board the *Fingal* bound for what she referred to as 'Tyree':

We had been warned we were unwise to travel at the time of the Glasgow Fair, and that the boats would be crowded, but we were unable to see the connexion of ideas, and did not know, till later acquaintance with the *Fingal* revealed the fact, that our dozen or so of fellow passengers was such a crowd as we were never likely to see upon her deck again.

The morning was grey and chilly, and the piled-up hills of Mull and Morvern were clothed in mist on either hand, but by degrees the sunlight broke through, and by the time we reached Tobermory the unbroken water-line of the Atlantic stretched blue and clear before us. Away to the south lay the dream-lands of Staffa and Iona, and further still to the north were the dim peaks of Ben More in Uist and the Cuchullin hills in Skye.

The sea was clear and blue, not a sail was within sight, and in the entire selfishness of mere animal enjoyment and anticipation, we were almost thankful to the dancing waves for causing the withdrawal, into private life, of most of our fellow passengers. In Oban we had heard fearful tales of the dangers and horrors of a journey to Tyree, but those nine sun-lit hours still stand out in happy memory although only the first of many of a like kind.

The little boat, with her orange-coloured funnel, seemed to manage all her business for herself, for the crew had nothing to do but look picturesque, the Captain and Purser but to make themselves agreeable. Towards afternoon we peeped into the tiny cabin below, but roast beef and batter-pudding seemed an anti-climax, and we begged for something more ethereal on deck. Little guessed we how long it would be before we should look upon their like again!

Soon we were in sight of Tyree, 'the kingdom just emerging from the summits of the waves,' as one of its old names has it, in terse Gaelic, *Rioghachd-bharrthonn.* Slowly the little *Fingal* wound herself into a long narrow creek. There was no pier, not so much as a 'slip' and so far as we could ever discover, the only high ground on this side of the island, which is nowhere more than 350 feet out of the sea, rises most precipitately at the spot at present selected for a landing-place. How we were to get to shore was not obvious, but we cared little, so absorbed were we in the novelty of the scene. On the rocks above us some fifty people at least were collected, and with much shouting, laughing, gesticulating, two small boats apparently already quite full of people were boarding our little vessel. Later we learnt that there were other reasons besides the desire to meet friends, to get the mails, to fetch the cargo, why some of the islanders greet Mac-brayne with such eagerness . . . The tiny mail boat heaved and tossed in the water below – it seemed to us as if the very letters would upset it, but in went the bags. The parcel post, a great institution in the islands, followed – could she possibly survive? we wondered, and we mod-estly declined when courteously asked if we would care to take our places in her, instead of waiting for the cargo boat. Being Glasgow Fair, we were told, the boats were 'rather' full. The cargo boat certainly was. Large baskets like laundry travelling-baskets, full of Glasgow bread, we learnt, went in first, then sundry crates for the 'Mair-chant,' then some luggage, including ours, then all our fellow passengers, finally half a dozen sheep. We remained modest and retiring. We knew that the handsome young Minister, who after a long disappearance was now again on deck, would have to get on shore somehow, and that another boat would surely appear from somewhere. By-

and-by the cargo boat returned, more cargo went in, but few passengers, and no sheep, only the Minister and the men who had so mysteriously come on board and who now came out of the deck-cabin wiping their mouths and smelling of whisky. The Purser advised us to take our seats, the kindly Captain shook hands with us, obviously perplexed as to our business there, since we were no off-shoot from Glasgow Fair, and we were off. We drew up at a perpendicular rock upon which some scratches were pointed out to us as steps. Many kindly hands were offered to help us to shore. The dog was hauled up, and we found ourselves standing beside our luggage in a wilderness of sand with not the faintest idea what to do next. Most of our companions had already climbed into carts and disappeared, and a group of men shouting in Gaelic over the 'cargo' at a little distance, alone remained.

The Minister had looked at us, paused, looked again, and with true Highland shyness walked rapidly away. It was no time for ceremony. I ran after him, and breathlessly presented a piece of paper on which was the address of the house, where, so we had been told, we might hope for shelter. I had written some days before, I explained – was it likely any one would come to meet us? The polite young Minister smiled at our simplicity. The letter was probably in one of the bags still lying on the rocks, or perhaps, if it arrived last mail, in the post-office waiting to be fetched; the farm in question was nine miles off, there was no road for most of the way, there was no vehicle to be had, and being Glasgow Fair they were 'likely full'. We began to feel anxious, not so much for shelter on so glorious an evening, as for food. Could we telegraph anywhere? we asked, glancing at a single wire overhead. No, that only went to the mainland, but the Minister would send a message for us from the post-office whence it would be taken with the letters, or the bread, and meantime could we not go to the hotel? We looked around at the wilderness of rock and sand and short, scant herbage, at the group of men still shouting in a strange foreign tongue, at the funnel of the little *Fingal* disappearing in the blue distance, at some tiny huts scarcely distinguishable from the rocks among which they seemed to hide, at the 'road' a foot deep in loose white sand, at the bare-legged boy driving a herd of cows which clambered awkwardly among the rocks, and found the notion of an hotel somewhat bewildering. He would go with us, this kind young Highlander, and turning back, soon conducted us to an unenclosed house overlooking the harbour, destitute, like most Highland inns, of sign-board – and being conducted on strictly teetotal principles, destitute also of everything else – open doors, loafers, sound of human life, which one associates with inns. A kindly landlady, a quiet sitting-room, a clean bedroom, and a welcome tea soon made us feel that home life in Tyree had begun.

We have long remembered that tea; after nine hours' feast of the eye only, it was very welcome. It certainly was excellent, but we remember it the better because we sat down to its counterpart every time we called for food during our stay in the island, and after a time it palled. Good tea, good cream, good eggs, Glasgow jam, Glasgow bread (it was long before we convinced our friends that we preferred their own home-made scones), Glasgow cake, and from time to time something of the nature of meat out of a tin. Our sitting-room window opened on to the moor or common, that is on to unenclosed space, and the cows often looked on at our meals, sheep and fowls came in at the door, and presumably fish swam about in the sea which lay almost at our feet; but none of these things found their way to the table except once, when we had an orgie of chops – what became of the rest of that sheep we could not discover – and once when we had a fish of species so perplexing that we tossed up who should first venture upon it. It was finally rejected by the dog, and given, through the window, to a cow, who apparently thought it an interesting experiment.

Ada carried baccy for the old men, sweets for the children and at the end of three weeks she had run to earth six second-sighted men. She wrote enthusiastically to Lord Bute from the Loch Leven Hotel at Ballachulish:

The factor, two ministers, two University students, the Doctor, one enthusiastically interested farmer, and others, will now work the ground we have ploughed, and we have planned some little pleasures for the poor in the winter which may help to keep our memory green.

One of the things that drove Ada away from Tiree was physical not psychical. 'The food difficulty,' as Ada described the monotonous diet at the Temperance hotel, made the two women weak and ill and not until they tucked into 'a wild orgie of cutlets and fresh fruit' at Bunessan on their way back to the mainland was the work of restoration begun.

Ada spent three autumns in the islands searching for con-clusive proof of the existence of Second Sight but the inquiry was a failure. Despite the fact that almost all the seers in the Hebrides at that time were monoglot Gaelic-speakers, Ada assured Lord Bute that her lack of Gaelic was little or no hindrance, there was always some friendly fisherman who could tell her what was being said. Among the English visitors to the Gaelic-speaking islands there was a presumption that if anything was worth hearing it would eventually be brought to their attention in English. It was a convention encouraged by the islanders themselves, who had been brought up to believe that Gaelic was the language of the illiterate, a medium fit only for the telling of stories and the singing of songs. When in 1890 the first Catholic schoolmaster was appointed to a head teacher-ship in South Uist, the local committee chose an Englishman from Birmingham who had never heard a word of Gaelic spoken in his life, who indeed had never set foot in Scotland. During his stay in South Uist, which lasted from 1890–4 and again from 1903–13, he never bothered to learn more than a few simple greetings in Gaelic. As John Lorne Campbell observed dryly in his introduction to F. G. Rea's reminiscences:

> A system of education whereby the head teacher was entirely ignorant of the only language with which his pupils entered school and was dependent upon pupil teachers and monitors to act as his interpreters, cannot possibly be considered satisfactory.

For his entire sojourn on South Uist, Rea was the only resident Englishman and there must have been occasions when, surrounded only by Gaelic-speakers, he missed his native Birmingham. Did he perhaps feel a little like the missionary from St Kilda who had been on board the *Dunara Castle* when it put into Lochboisdale?

> He was quite insane. At the boat's last St Kilda visit, some nine months before, he, a young ecclesiastical student, had landed there as missionary, schoolmaster, registrar and postmaster. As he could not speak Gaelic, imagination only can give any idea of what that young man had been through.

Moving to the Isles meant giving up all thoughts of the theatre, concerts, art galleries; conversation was limited, intellectual pursuits apart from reading had to be abandoned. When Rea at last encountered Fr John Macintosh the two men discovered an interest in common: chess. Father John had not had a game since he arrived in the Isles. On the first day they played until two in the morning; on the second day they sat over the board from breakfast until well after midnight and on the third day once more they began playing first thing in the morning and continued without a break until fatigue drove them both to bed. It was a chess orgy.

Like Ada Goodrich Freer, Rea must for much of the time have fancied himself in a foreign country where the natives spoke a language as incomprehensible as Urdu. Indeed one of the highlights of his stay was to find that a young London

teacher had been appointed to be schoolmaster on the neighbouring island of Eriskay. It was as if Stanley had set off to
relieve Livingstone! And the journey was almost as tantalizing:

The thought of soon having a young colleague from
England aroused in me feelings of great pleasure, and when
I heard that he was expected to arrive at Lochboisdale by
the afternoon's boat on the following Monday, I was full
of joyful anticipation. Monday came and we kept a good
look-out in the afternoon for any stranger on the road.
Night came and the postman; I asked for news of the new
schoolmaster and was told definitely that he had not come
by the boat. Feeling very disappointed, I nevertheless
determined to be patient and to expect him by the next
boat, as his train might have been late for the first. All
Tuesday and Wednesday I had someone on the look-out
but could gain no news of him – the postman told me on
Wednesday night that no one had heard anything of him
since he left London six days before. When Thursday came
with no news of him I was anxious. Early on Friday
morning I had been scanning the main road to the north
when I saw a solitary figure appear on the skyline about a
mile and a half away. With the aid of a field-glass I made
out the figure of a stranger carrying a large package or
portmanteau, and I hoped it would turn out to be my new
colleague. At intervals I went out again to see if he were
still approaching my school on the hill: his progress was
slow but undoubtedly he was approaching. When he was
nearer, my doubts as to his identity disappeared – a London
man! Smartly cut and well-fitting clothes, white starched
shirt and collar, stylish homburg hat! Running out of my
gate and across the brae I jumped from the high bank
on to the road before him, extended my hand and said:
'Welcome!' He dropped his heavy portmanteau on the
road and shook hands. 'I have been looking out for you
all the week!' exclaimed I. 'Where have you been?' 'All
round the map!' said he.

It had taken him five days on board the ubiquitous *Dunara Castle* to thread his way among the islands to South Uist. That remarkable ship, whose name has recurred again and again in this book, made her maiden voyage on 21 June 1875 and then for seventy-three years, until her last journey in January 1948, she sailed back and forth from Glasgow to the islands. It was a record only rivalled by the paddle steamer *Glencoe*, which sailed almost continuously in Hebridean waters from 1846 to 1931, a working life of eighty-five years!

Boats like *Lochiel, Lochearn, Lochdunvegan, Clydesdale, Lochbroom, Hebrides* and *Clansman* became an almost permanent part of island life. Their arrival and departure was often the focal point of the week in a remote community. In the summer months they brought visitors and relatives but all year round they were carrying cargo, cattle and sheep, often in weather which would have daunted a skipper unused to such wild seas. D. T. Holmes, who travelled round the Hebrides in all weathers at the turn of the century, has left an evocative picture of what it was like to go from Mallaig to Portree on the old *Lochiel* in the dark days of December, along the chilly Sound of Sleat to Kyle and then through the narrows of Raasay:

> At such a time there is something fearsome and weird in the aspect of the coast, as seen from the cabin window of the brave little boat as she battles and plunges along in the teeth of the north-eastern gale. Her progress is slow, for when passengers are few, Macbrayne wisely economises his coal. The long-stretching hills of Raasay are white from head to foot, and gleam through the darkness of the afternoon vivid and ghostly. As Raasay House, with its lamp-lit windows shining in a snowy recess, is approached the engines slow down, and through the howl of the wind can be heard the plashing of oars. The broad waves swirl and seethe cruelly around the ferryboat and toss it about at all angles, up and down, on crest and in trough, till you fear it will end its struggles keel upwards, and send the mailbags down among the mackerel. But the boatmen

know their trade, and so do the dripping top-booted seamen of the *Lochiel*.

Amid much running and shuffling and casting of ropes and animated bandying of (I fear) strong expressions in Gaelic sung out upon the night, the ship's ladder is cast down and the boat tied thereto. In a few minutes the transfer of mails is over, the ladder up, and the small boat leaping back to land. A new passenger has come on board and is seen to descend the cabin stairs to unfreeze his fingers over the tiny stove. Half-an-hour's heaving still remains before Portree.

Without the boats many a community would never have survived, but as the St Kildans had found, contact with the outside world meant that an epidemic in Glasgow could be transmitted to the islands in a few days. On South Uist, Rea had to close his school for ten weeks in 1898 while scarlet fever raged; nine weeks were lost in the winter through measles; eleven weeks in 1901 through whooping-cough; seven weeks in 1904 through smallpox; a month that spring for mumps; another month in 1907 for influenza. In the days before vaccines and antibiotics these visitations were endured without any effective medical treatment; the fit survived but many were weakened for the rest of their lives. Tuberculosis remained endemic in the islands well into the 1930s. In Rea's time there were many, on the remoter islands, who were never seen by, nor ever saw a doctor. Dentists came so infrequently that when they did arrive they left a trail of aching jaws and extracted teeth behind them.

Isobel Macdonald was brought up in the comparatively well-doctored Isle of Skye in Edwardian times but her memories of illness are traumatic. A young doctor aged twenty-three arrived in Portree straight from medical school eager to try anything once. Isobel Macdonald playing in the garden suddenly heard anguished screams coming from the nursery window; her sister Flora was having a small operation:

a tonsillectomy performed in barbarous fashion by the young doctor without any anaesthetic. The child, sitting on mother's knee, was told to show the doctor her throat; when she opened her trusting little mouth he attacked. She was only five years old, but all her life she remembered the shock and blood and pain.

Stoic in ill-health, hardy in all weathers; these were the qualities demanded of those who lived in the islands all the year round. Travelling, almost inevitably, meant walking on foot. Isobel Macdonald's mother, describing how she engaged a girl from Raasay as a maid, added: 'She came over to see me on Monday night, walking nine miles in drenching rain and crossing in a wild storm so I think she deserves the place.'

Even weddings and funerals involved those who attended them in walks which sometimes assumed marathon proportions. Isobel's mother lost her Raasay girl for a week when she was invited to be best maid at a wedding:

Tuesday, the day Annie went off, was one of unceasing pitiless relentless rain. The sky seemed to rest on top of the trees and houses and empty its contents without mercy. Annie went over with the minister in the morning boat, and was going to get breakfast in Lexy's mother's house and then proceed to the church where she was to meet the rest of the bridal party. They meanwhile had to walk seven miles of a footpath. Annie had three miles to go to the church, and then after the ceremony they all had to trudge the seven miles back again through the rain. It seems that in Raasay old customs still prevail, and however young a bride is she must be married in a bonnet and black cape. The bridesmaid is also supposed to wear a bonnet, but Annie struck at that and bought a new hat with a feather in it. I wonder what the bonnet and the feather were like at the end of a fourteen mile tramp!

After they got home there would be a feast, I suppose, and then dancing till five or six next morning in the bride's house. Wednesday was also to be spent there with more festivities. On Thursday the bride and bridegroom, Annie and the best man were to proceed to Rona where his parents lived and where the young couple were to take up house. So again in the pouring rain they would have to walk three miles to the north end of Raasay, cross to Rona in a boat and walk another three miles to their destination where there would be another feast of welcome home from the Rona folk. Next day they were to cross the island to the lighthouse where there were to be more festivities. Then today came the kirking, also in pouring rain, and tomorrow Annie must be up early, walk three miles in Rona, then cross over to Raasay and walk another thirteen miles to the steamer to get home by tomorrow night. After that I think she will want a day in bed before she is fit for much work. If the bride and bridegroom get through all that without losing their tempers they will surely have a chance of living happily ever after!

Hebridean women were frequently as tough and often more determined than their menfolk. When the men were away fishing on the east coast the running of the house and the croft was left to the wives. Clifton Johnson, an American who visited the islands in 1901, noted that a great deal of the farm labour fell to the women:

> I saw them helping in the peat-bogs and the hay-fields, and constantly met them on the roads carrying heavy burdens on their backs. The crofts were most of them far from the highways and distant from the market. Horses and carts were rare, and the women took the places of beasts of burden to a considerable extent. At the time of year that I was in Skye they were most apt to be loaded with peat, which they carried in creels strapped to their shoulders. The creels were deep, heavy baskets of willow woven by the peasants themselves, and they had a capacity of between one and two bushels. Sometimes it was no less than three miles from the peat moss to the croft village. In such a case

a woman would stop at intervals to sit and rest, and she would relieve her shoulders of the loaded creel by letting it slip back on a convenient bank or dyke. Many of the women had their knitting along, and when they stopped to rest would set their needles flying.

Johnson felt that the crofting life at best was a bleak affair relieved only by the occasional wedding, funeral or communion:

> Weddings are too few and far between to furnish any very material brightness, and, as a whole, the crofters find life hardly less somber-hued than their native bogs. They are not a merry people, yet in their way they find an element of holiday recreation in the most solemn occasion, if it brings a company of them together. For this reason even a funeral is not without its modicum of welcome. It makes a break in the monotony, and it never fails to be largely attended. The people as they arrive are provided with a sup of whisky and with oatcakes and cheese or other light refreshments. After a short service at the house the men form in procession to go to the grave, while the women remain behind. There is no hearse in the island, and the coffin, covered with a black cloth, is carried on the shoulders of six bearers. The distance is often long – sometimes as much as seven or eight miles – and the rule is for the men bearing the bier to give place to others about three times to a mile.

The story of the last two visitors in this book spans two centuries and begins in the week of Christmas 1799 when Godfrey Macdonald, the brother of the eighteenth chief of Clan Donald, eloped with a pretty girl he fell in love with while riding near Hampton Court. She was the offspring of a morganatic relationship between the Duke of Gloucester and the illegitimate daughter of Sir Edward Walpole and a Durham milliner's apprentice. And that's just the opening scenario.

Godfrey Macdonald became the nineteenth chief and when he died both the chiefship and the peerage devolved on his second son. The first-born – illegitimate according to English law – inherited the family estates at Thorpe in the East Riding of Yorkshire.

It was not until 1886, when a very determined woman called Alice Middleton married a descendant of the nineteenth chief, Alexander Wentworth Macdonald Bosville of Thorpe and Gunthwaite, that the legal niceties were once more brought under scrutiny. With great pertinacity she managed to have the stigma of illegitimacy removed, her husband was able to prove his grandfather's legitimacy and in 1910 he was officially reinstated as the twenty-first chief of Sleat.

Skye, long used to the autocratic rule of Lady Edith Macdonald of Armadale, now found itself presented with yet another Lady Macdonald – the newly legitimized Lady Macdonald of the Isles, who decided that she and her husband would assume their rightful place on the island where the usurpers had held sway for so long. They leased four thousand acres of northern Skye including a house, now Duntulm Hotel, which overlooked Duntulm Castle, the ancestral seat of the Clan Donald. They tried to buy the castle but the Secretary of State, Lord Pentland, told them that it was a place of national importance and must remain in the possession of the nation. This rather annoyed Lady Macdonald, 'as we felt sure that in effect it meant that sheep would be allowed to wander all over the ruins and knock them down.'

Although they didn't own the castle they had an unrivalled view of it from the house where Lady Alice busied herself adding new servants' rooms and a big kitchen. She and her husband came to Duntulm each summer until the outbreak of the First World War. The natives were, according to the new Lady Macdonald, full of dignity and a gratifying deference. She recorded in her autobiography how old Donald Macdonald, Parish Councillor, put her politely back on her pedestal when she attempted to demean herself socially:

After a long visit from him tea was ready in the dining-room, so I naturally bid him come in with us and have some. He steadfastly resisted: 'No, I am not worthy.' I tried to insist. Unluckily Alex was out or he would have speedily 'chiefed' Donald. But all the answer I got was, 'It is very nice of Lady Macdonald to be so humble, BUT SHE SHOULD KNOW HER PLACE.' The words sounded in capital letters! So the old boy went off to the kitchen, while a chastened Chief's wife and her guests were left in the dining-room.

There were 'sweeties' for the children in the local school and loyal and wonderful servants:

Old Angus Mackenzie, our boatman, was a constant delight, both to look at and to listen to and he so enjoyed all the stories I told him. I think he had spent a drab-coloured life up to then, and when I found how eager he was to hear old tales, I drew upon the Greek myths for his benefit. He was full of imagination and poetry and they simply enchanted him. 'There will be no one,' he chanted, 'knowing so many stories as Lady Macdonald.'

Lady Alice took her duties as chief's wife with great seriousness during her summer visits and she must have been a commanding and regal figure. Compared with their big estab-lishment at Thorpe, where there were twenty-seven staff and fifteen gardeners, Duntulm was simple, but even in so wild a place Lady Alice liked to keep up her English customs:

I used to have a flower table in our little sitting-room, like I have in the library at Thorpe. The people used rather to wonder that I cared to take so much trouble, but they liked the look of the flowery bank and used to bring me offerings for it. As at Thorpe too, I kept at Duntulm a 'medicine cupboard' and would mix potions for sufferers. With such success, too – that people would come 'fa-ar over the hills for a bottle from Lady Macdonald.'

What the doctor in Uig thought about Lady Alice's role as amateur *locum tenens* is not recorded. What is recorded frequently by Lady Macdonald is the way in which the people took their newly reborn chief to their loyal hearts:

> We were constantly told of the extraordinary resemblance between Alex and the Chiefs of old, and our very dog was a marvel to the people, for never, they said, had such a dog been seen in Skye *since the right people left*.

The Wrong People, the usurping Macdonalds of Armadale, are never mentioned, which is strange, for at this very time Lady Macdonald had moved up from Armadale to Portree to her lodge at Scorrybreck, now the Coolin Hills Hotel. When her yacht, the *Lady of the Isles*, steamed into the bay, the proprietor of the Royal Hotel would rush sycophantically through his revolving doors and let off a cannon to announce to the villagers that their patroness had arrived.

Isobel Macdonald's mother was very much at the beck and call of Lady Macdonald.

> Her Ladyship reminds me [she wrote] of a certain noble-man in the Bible who gathered his servants together and said 'occupy yourselves till I come' and then straightway took his departure. She has given us all our work to do, and then on Tuesday off she goes to London for the winter, and woe betide that wicked and slothful servant who has not made good use of his talents when she returns. But she is a wonderful woman, so clever and so kind and good too.

These were obviously not qualities appreciated by the Lady Macdonald of Thorpe Hall, summer chatelaine of Duntulm only sixteen miles up the road from Portree. It must have been an embarrassment for the members of the Macdonald clan to find they suddenly had *two* chiefs. To whom should fealty be due? The resident but usurping Armadale baron or the summer migrant baronet from Yorkshire? It was all a bit like one of those Victorian melodramas where the long-missing eldest son suddenly turns up to claim his rightful inheritance.

The dilemma, if such it was, was resolved by the outbreak of war. Lady Alice and Sir Alexander hastened back to their Yorkshire estates leaving Skye regretfully to Lady Macdonald. The glittering steam yachts sailed south to become fleet auxiliaries, the shooting lodges were shuttered and the crofters went to die at Festubert and Neuve Chapelle.

After that things were never quite the same again.

Appendix

Researching this book has provided a pleasurable period of therapy: opening often uncut and slightly foxed pages, thumbing through volumes unread for decades and then the intense pleasure of stumbling upon a paragraph which illustrated a moment in the past. But my labours had their longeurs; the nineteenth century was a period of enpurpled prose and many of the books I reached down from the shelves were as lifeless as stuffed rabbits; lots of artistry and no guts. And you could seldom tell from the title what might (or usually might not) lie inside. *Reminiscences of a Four Weeks' Tour in Scotland* by J. C. Rogers, a work privately printed in 1895, struck me as being a potentially valuable source of material, but it turned out to have been written if not by the brothers Grossmith then surely by a close relative. It is pure Pooter even down to the minor trials and tribulations of dealing with the printers:

> I regret to add that several original drawings made by myself many years ago, that cannot be replaced, with which I intended to illustrate the present brochure, by some unaccountable carelessness of the persons employed to reproduce them in the form of printing blocks, have been lost, or destroyed.

Mr Rogers never reached the Hebrides, which is a pity because he was a great believer in recording the trivia of travel however prosaic. Let me give you a taste of what we all missed:

> *Thursday May 30th, 1895* – Left London accompanied by my wife by the corridor train from King's Cross, at 2.20 p.m. Dined in the train, and arrived at the Cockburn Hotel, Edinburgh, at 11 p.m.

Friday May 31st – Called at the National Bank of Scotland, St Andrew's Square, and in the afternoon paid a visit to Northumberland Street. Called upon the widow of Mr George Hastie, formerly deputy keeper of the Museum of National Antiquities, who told me of his illness and death, and that on the previous Saturday he had been interred in the Dean Cemetery.

Saturday June 1st – Called upon Mrs Henderson, 20, Charlotte Square, thence to the Grange Cemetery to visit the tomb of my late relative, Dr Roger.

Sunday June 2nd – There was a sea-fog in the evening which prevented us from getting out.

Wednesday June 5th – Went to the Western Necropolis to visit the grave of a near relative.

And so the holiday continued, rich in religious and funerary experiences. They attended worship in Rothesay ('the minister omitted to pray for the Queen') and spent some time in Oban ('found the Crown hotel very comfortable') before the final return lap of the journey:

Wednesday June 26th – Left Edinburgh for King's Cross Station by the early train in which we made the acquaintance of the Rev. A. Pollok Sym, Parish Minister of Lilliesleaf. It transpired incidentally, in the course of conversation, that the sister of this gentleman's mother was the wife of the late David Playfair, Minister of Abercorn, who, as it so happens was the grandson of my father's sister. We reached London about 7 o'clock p.m. and taking leave of our friend, proceeded to our home of Friar's Watch in the suburb of Walthamstow.

Books Referred To

ONE: 1770–1790

Abram, 'Journal', *Inverness Courier*, 1854.
Boswell, James, *Journal of a Tour to the Hebrides*, 1785.
Faujus de Saint Fond, Barthélémy, *A Journey Through England and Wales to the Hebrides in 1784*, edited by Sir Archibald Geikie, 1907.
Johnson, Samuel, *A Journey to the Western Islands of Scotland*, 1775.
Knox, John, *A Tour Through the Highlands of Scotland and the Hebride Isles in 1776*, 1787.
Martin, Martin, *A Description of the Western Highlands of Scotland*, 1695.
Pennant, Thomas, *A Tour in Scotland and Voyage To The Hebrides*, 1774-5.
Walker, John, DD, *An Economical History of the Hebrides and Highlands of Scotland*, 1808.

TWO: 1790–1810

Brougham, Lord, *Tour in Western Isles, Including St Kilda in 1799; The Life and Times of Henry, Lord Brougham*, 1871.
Garnett, Dr Thomas, *Tour Through the Highlands and Western Islands*, 1811.
Hall, Rev. James, *Travels in Scotland*, 1807.
Hogg, James, *A Tour in the Highlands in 1803; A Journey Through the Highlands and Western Isles in the Summer of 1804; The Highlands in 1803. A series of letters addressed to Sir Walter Scott, Bart, Reprinted from the* Scottish Review, 1888.

Leyden, Dr John, *Journal of a Tour in the Western Highlands and Islands of Scotland in 1800.*

Martin, Martin, *A Voyage to St Kilda 1697* (reprinted by James Thin, Edinburgh, 1970).

Stoddart, John, *Remarks on Local Scenery & Manners in Scotland during the years 1799 and 1800,* 1801.

THREE: 1810–1830

Ayton, Richards, *See* Daniell, William.

Botfield, Beriah, *Journal of a Tour Through the Highlands of Scotland,* 1830.

Daniell, William, *A Voyage Round Great Britain,* 1813–23.

Keats, John, *The Letters of John Keats,* edited by M. B. Forman, Oxford University Press, 1947.

Lumsden, Lumsden & Son's *Steam-Boat Companion; or Stranger's Guide to the Western Isles and Highlands of Scotland,* 1820.

Macculloch, John, *A Description of the Western Islands,* 1819; *The Highlands and Western Isles of Scotland,* 1824.

Necker de Saussure, L.A., *Travels in Scotland,* 1821; *A Voyage To the Hebrides,* 1822.

Scott, Sir Walter, Diary kept on board the Lighthouse Yacht 1814, reprinted in *Memoirs of the Life of Sir Walter Scott, Bart.* by J.G. Lockhart, 1836.

Scottish Tourist, The, 1825.

Teignmouth, Lord, *Sketches of the Coasts and Islands,* 1836.

FOUR: 1830–1840

Abraham, Ashley P., *Rock-Climbing in Skye,* 1908.

Anderson, George and Peter, *Guide To the Highlands and Islands,* 1834.

Finberg, A.J., *The Life of J.M.W. Turner R.A.,* Oxford University Press, 1961.

Fullarton, Allan and Baird, Charles R., *Remarks on the Evils at Present Affecting the Highlands and Islands of Scotland*, 1838.

Geikie, Sir Archibald, *Scottish Reminiscences*, 1904.

Johnson, Dr James, *The Recess of Autumnal Relaxation in the Highlands and Lowlands*, 1834.

Maclean, Lachlan, *Sketches of the Island of St Kilda*, 1838.

Mitchell, Joseph, *Reminiscences of My Life in the Highlands*, 1883–4.

Seldon-Goth, G. (ed.), *Mendelssohn Letters*, Elek, 1947.

Sinclair, Catherine, *Scotland and the Scotch or The Western Circuit*, 1840.

Smith, Rev. Charles Lesingham, *Excursions Through The Highlands and Isles of Scotland*, 1837.

FIVE: 1840–1850

Brown, Rev. Thomas, *Annals of the Disruption*, 1893.

Carruthers, Dr Robert, *The Highland Notebook or Sketches and Anecdotes*, 1843.

Cockburn, Lord, *Circuit Journeys*, 1842.

Grierson, Rev. Thomas, *Autumnal Rambles Among The Scottish Mountains*, 1850.

Miller, Hugh, *The Cruise of the* Betsey, 1858.

Somers, Robert, *Letters from the Highlands*, 1848.

Victoria, R., *Leaves from The Journal of Our Life in the Highlands*, 1848–61.

Wilson, James, *A Voyage Round the Coasts of Scotland And The Isles*, 1842.

SIX: 1850–1870

Bond, Charles, *The Hebrides & West Highlands in 1852*, 1852.

Brassey, Thomas Jr, *Journal of a Voyage Through the Western Isles of*

Scotland and along the Coast of Norway in the Yacht 'Cymba' in the summer of 1856, 1857.

Colquhoun, John, *Sporting Days*, 1866.

Dendy, Walter Cooper, *The Wild Hebrides*, 1859.

Macaskill, Lady, *Twelve Days in Skye*, 1852.

Mackenzie, Osgood Hanbury, *A Hundred Years in the Highlands*, 1921.

Roberts, Sir Randal, *Glenmâhra or the Western Highlands*, 1870.

'Sixty One' (Rev. George Hely Hutchinson), *Reminiscences of the Lews or Twenty Years' Wild Sport in the Hebrides*, 1873.

Smith, Alexander, 'Rambling In the Hebrides', *Temple Bar*, 1862; *A Summer in Skye*, 1865.

SEVEN: 1870–1880

Brooke, Tina and Munro, Bell, *A Trip to Skye*, 1873.

Buchanan, Robert, *The Hebrid Isles*, 1872.

Cooper, T. Sidney, RA, *My Life*, 1890.

'Governor, The' (John Inglis), *A Yachtsman's Holidays or Cruising in the West Highlands*, 1879.

Liddell, Alice, 'Skye Diary', unpublished MS in the possession of Mary Jean St Clair.

Reid, John T., *Art Rambles in the Highlands*, 1878.

Ritchie, J. Ewing, *The Cruise of the* Elena *or Yachting in the Hebrides*, 1877.

Smith, R. Angus, *A Visit to St Kilda in 'The Nyanza'*, 1879.

Smith, W. Anderson, *Lewsiana or Life in the Outer Hebrides*, 1874.

EIGHT: 1880–1890

Bromley-Davenport, W., *Sport*, 1888.

Connell, Robert, *St Kilda and the St Kildans*, 1887.

Cumming, Constance F. Gordon, *From the Hebrides to the Himalayas*, 1876.

Ferguson, Malcolm, *Rambles in Skye*, 1885.

Mackenzie, Hector Rose, *Yachting and Electioneering in the Hebrides*, 1886.

Murray, Frances, *Summer in the Hebrides, 1887; Yachting in the Hebrides* (privately printed extract from *Helensburgh and Gareloch Times*).

Napier Commission, *Report on the Highlands and Islands and Evidence taken by HM Commissioners of Inquiry into the condition of Crofters in the Highlands and Islands, 1883, 1884.*

'Nauticus', *Nauticus in Scotland*, 1884.

Newall, Captain J. T., *Scottish Moors and Indian Jungles*, 1889.

Peel, C.V.A., *Wild Sport in the Outer Hebrides*, 1901.

Pennell, Joseph and Elizabeth Robins, *Our Journey To The Hebrides*, 1890.

Shand, A. J., *Letters from the Highlands*, 1883.

NINE: 1890–1914

Campbell, John L. and Hall, Trevor H., *Strange Things*, Routledge & Kegan Paul, 1968.

Chambers's Journal, 'Cliff and Shore in the Inner Hebrides', 1898.

Dalgliesh, W. Scott, *The Cruise of the Dunottar Castle*, 1891.

Heathcote, Norman, *St Kilda*, 1900.

Holmes, D.T., *Literary Tours in the Highlands and Islands of Scotland*, Alexander Gardner, 1909.

Johnston, Clifton, 'The Crofters of Skye', *Outlook*, New York, 1901.

Logie, D.W., *An Account of a Trip from Stirling to St Kilda*, 1889.

Macdonald, Lady of the Isles, *All The Days of My Life*, John Murray, 1929.

Macdonald, Isobel, 'A Family in Skye 1908–1916', unpublished MS.

MacGregor, Alasdair Alpin, *A Last Voyage To St Kilda*, Cassell, 1931.

Index